"THIS GOOD WORK"

A HISTORY OF EDUCATION
in
BRIDPORT

1238 – 2000

by
Fiona Taplin

"The expense of building such rooms will not be under £400 and we cannot command more than £200..... which is not much more than half of what will be wanted for the completion of this good work."

(Letter, dated August 10th 1822, from the Rev. David Williams, Rector of St Mary's, Bridport, to the National Society requesting help in building a schoolroom for the children of the parish.)

Cover design showing a detail of a class photograph
of St Mary's School Infants
© Mike Taplin 2005

ISBN 0-9551052-0-X
Published by
Pub   Fiona and Mike Taplin   aplin
9 Hemlets Close
Bridport
Dorset DT6 3FB

Printed by
Creeds the Printers
Broadoak, Bridport DT6 5NL

Pupils and staff of Pymore School in 1909. Harold Edward Walbridge is seated immediately behind the slate board. The teacher shown on the right of the picture is probably Mrs Jane Davey.
[Photograph courtesy C Walbridge]

CONTENTS

FOREWORD

I first came to Bridport in the early summer of 1966 having applied for a temporary post teaching English at the Alfred Colfox School. The advertisement in the Times Educational Supplement had described the school as a "Comprehensive", which was what attracted me. I had started my teaching career in a grammar school, but having just spent a year teaching in Sweden, where comprehensive education was the norm, I had grown to like the concept. I was to replace Bruce Critchinson, while he spent a year's sabbatical in Kuwait. My "interview" consisted of a pleasant chat with Major Urwin Thornburn in his office at the school, and another pleasant chat with Andy Chapman-Andrews in the upper lounge of the Bull Hotel where I was staying. By the end of the day I knew I had the job. It was an introduction to Major Thornburn's distinctive style of recruiting and managing his staff. People who worked with him used to refer to belonging to "the Colfox family", and that is how it felt.

After Bruce returned, I spent a year teaching the Junior Special Needs Class under the direction of the redoubtable Joan Ballard, who ran that department with what has since come to be called "tough love". I left the school to concentrate on bringing up my two sons, and had no plans to return quickly to teaching, when another staffing crisis at the school resulted in my being called back by Major Thornburn, "just for a fortnight" to replace Mr William Bayne-Cole who was ill. Sadly Billy Bayne-Cole was much more seriously ill than anyone realised. The fortnight became a term, and in the autumn of 1974 I was invited to rejoin the staff of the school. I finally retired in 2001. As I watch the hoops today's young teachers have to jump through to get a teaching post, I recall those "pleasant chats", and the fact that I never had what anyone would call a proper interview during my entire Colfox career. Far from feeling cheated, I feel rather privileged.

I began work on this history in 2003, after Sophie Hunt, then Curator of Bridport Museum, suggested that I put together a leaflet on the schools in the area and their history. It soon became apparent that the subject was much vaster than any leaflet would be able to comprehend. The research and writing has occupied the last two years in sometimes fascinating, sometimes frustrating ferreting through archives in order to put together a narrative for Bridport, of the many ways and means it has found over the centuries to educate its children. It is of necessity selective. There are many teachers who worked tirelessly and with dedication who get no mention. It would be impossible to name everyone. Oddly enough the most difficult part to write has been the most recent history, and particularly of Colfox School, where my own involvement with the school over so many years has threatened to tip history into memoir. Also the written records for the recent past are much less accessible that those for the earlier period. I hope my former colleagues will forgive me if they feel I have not done them or the school justice, but I have done my best to give an impression of the school.

No book of this nature is a solo effort and in researching and writing it, I am indebted to many people and organisations for their help. I would like to thank, first and foremost the staff of Bridport Museum, Paul Willis and Margaret Milree, for putting the archive material in the Museum at my disposal, and for pointing me in the right direction, and also for supplying me with the majority of the photographs in this book and giving me permission to reproduce them. I also owe thanks to the Dorset History Centre (formerly the Dorset Record Office), whose files on the various schools have proved invaluable. They were also kind enough to give me permission to reproduce a section from the earliest extant map of Bridport. Sarah Duffield of the Church of England Record Centre in London made available to me the files of correspondence between the National Society and the various rectors and vicars of the local parishes. Thanks are also due to Pauline Price who allowed me to borrow the logbooks for St Mary's CE VC School. These have since been deposited at the Dorset History Centre.

For permission to use material on the Weymouth history of Thorneloe School, I would like to thank John Crocker. I also owe a debt of gratitude to the staff at the Worcester Record Office who provided me with information about Thorneloe House in the 1880's. M K Smith kindly gave me permission to use the information on the Infed web-site to flesh out my knowledge of Charlotte Mason and the PNEU schools. To Don England, my thanks for letting me see the original deeds for the Gundry Lane school buildings, and for giving me permission to quote from them. I owe thanks to Rev Michael Currah for allowing me to quote from the copy of the Henry Nobbs Cox papers. The original is in his possession, and to Elizabeth Buckler Gale who was a mine of information on the subject of the Grove School. She also supplied me with several photographs of the school.

I would also like to thank Sir John Colfox, who gave up a morning to assist me in my researches into his family history, particularly for talking about his father, Sir Philip, and grandfather, Thomas Alfred, as well as giving me a brief outline of his own career and involvement with education in the town. He also allowed me to see some watercolours by Louisa Wansey recently acquired by his family. I am particularly indebted to Pam Puley who gave up a morning to take me round the various sites used by Mrs Telford for St Ronan's School, and for sharing her memories of the Bridport Grammar School and St James's College with me. She also helped me identify the people in the photograph of St Ronan's School

5

reproduced in this book. I am grateful to Mr Tony Tiltman, former Mayor of Bridport and ex-pupil of the Bridport General School, who also gave up time to share his memories of the General School with me. Thanks are also due to Elizabeth Wild and Jennifer Jennings for giving me permission to quote from notes on their schooldays; also to Jennifer Ackerman for information about the Convent School. Betty Starkey helped me with her recollections of the first few years of Colfox School, and Ronnie Coatsworth was also kind enough to check over the sections on Colfox and St Catherine's.

I must thank the various past pupils of St Mary's School whom I met in the course of my research for this book, and who were a great help in resolving some of my questions about the school in the inter-war years. I was privileged to share their memories and look at their old photographs. I am particularly grateful to June Arthurs for her permission to use photographs of her father, George Flack, at St Mary's School, and to Robert Stoodley for the photograph of the victorious St Mary's Football Team. Anthony Broad supplied me with a photograph of his class at the Grove School.

I would like to thank Jane Read and the staff of Bridport Library for their forbearance as I monopolised the microfilm newspaper-reader for many hours, in order to trawl through back copies of the Bridport News. To Jane, particularly, for her help in pointing me in the direction of items in the local history files which the library holds. I am also indebted to the Editor of the Bridport News, Holly Robinson, for permission to quote from back issues of the paper. And finally thanks are due to my husband, Mike, for putting up with the hours I have spent researching and writing this history, for proof-reading the manuscript, and for undertaking to design the cover of the book and edit the photographs.

This is not an exhaustive history, and there is still much more to find out and write. Where possible I have gone back to the original sources. In other places I have relied on the testimony of people who were pupils or teachers at the schools, and to them I am most grateful. I have mentioned all the private schools I have found evidence for, but there are probably others still to be discovered. There is more material in the various logbooks, and then there are all the neighbouring village schools whose stories will be equally fascinating.

Fiona Taplin
2005

ILLUSTRATIONS

ACKNOWLEDMENT OF ILLUSTRATIONS

Fig 1 is reproduced by kind permission of Dorset History Centre. Figs: 2, 3, 4, 7, 11, 12, 13, 14, 15, 17, 21, 24, 25, 28, 29, 30, 34, 35, 36, 37, 38, 39, 40 are reproduced by kind permission of Bridport Museum.
I am grateful to the following people for the loan of photographs and for permission to reproduce them: Elizabeth Buckler Gale: Figs 8, 9; Anthony Broad: Fig 10; June Arthurs: Figs 18, 19, 20, 22; Robert Stoodley: Fig 23; Ronald Coatsworth: Figs 26, 27, and N Gale: Fig 31.

I

THE EARLY YEARS

In 1238, a misunderstanding between a group of Oxford University students and the entourage of the Papal Legate who was on a visit to the city, led to a violent confrontation, a death, and the imprisonment and excommunication of a Bridport scholar who had left the town to study at the University. It would seem somewhat far-fetched to claim that this event in far away Oxford could give us the earliest clues to educational activity in Bridport – but such is the case, according to Bridport historian, Basil Short.[1]

Oxford in the thirteenth century was a far cry from Matthew Arnold's nineteenth century city of "dreaming spires". It was a turbulent place, with many outbreaks of violence between the students of the embryonic university and the town. The events of 1238, however, took on national importance as the Papal Legate's own brother had been killed in the brawl, and the legate had had to flee for his life. The culprits, including John de Bridport, were rounded up on the orders of the King and taken to London, chained and *"in tumbrels, like robbers"*.[2] One result of the violence and upheaval, was that many of the clerks [3] and masters fled the University. A number migrated to Salisbury, but Basil Short believes that some came as far south as Bridport. The evidence for this is fragmentary, but it is possible that a small group from the University spent some years in the town continuing their studies.

A further piece of the jigsaw is provided by Giles de Bridport, a rising churchman, who was born in Bridport sometime around 1200. At the time of the exodus from Oxford, he was Archdeacon of Berkshire. By 1253 he was Dean of Wells Cathedral and in 1257 he was consecrated Bishop of Salisbury. Just before his death in 1262, he established a college, dedicated to St Nicholas de Vaux. The site of the college buildings was a meadow, just south of the cathedral precinct near Harnham Bridge, on the north bank of the River Avon. The foundation was to provide for the free education of twenty poor scholars. No doubt it was his intention to accommodate some of the scholars who had fled Oxford. It was known as "The House of the Valley of Scholars of the Blessed Nicholas".

---

[1] "Bridport History and Topography" : Text of a series of lectures given by Basil Short. Local History Collection, Bridport Library.
[2] The account of these events appears in the "Great Chronicle and Maps of Britain 1235 - 1257" by Mathew Paris, the historian of Henry III's reign.
[3] The term "clerk" refers to university students, who had to be in Holy Orders to study at the University. The modern word "cleric" comes from the same root.

A further connection with Bridport is the fact that Giles arranged, as part of the College's constitution *"that the scholars should celebrate annually for ever in the parish church of Bridport the commemorative anniversary of their founder."*[4] In addition to maintaining this connection with his home parish, it is likely that Giles owned land in and around the town, for among the endowments of De Vaux College were two acres of land in Allington, and the advowson of that parish and one acre in Walditch and the advowson[5] also of that parish.

So what evidence is there that some of the masters and students who fled Oxford in 1238 came to Bridport? Basil Short, in his lecture notes, cites a deed of 1240 conveying rights of pasturage to the Hospital of St John, which is witnessed by, among others, a man called Vincent, described as "Rector of Schools (or Scholars) of Bridport". This is only two years after the exodus from Oxford. At the same time there were a number of men residing in the town with the title "Master", suggesting that they were university educated and held Master of Arts degrees. There was Master John Ruffus, Master Bartholomew, Master Henry, Master Hamund, Master Gervase, and another Master John de Bridport who was an apothecary. Though the numbers were probably too small to constitute a college, it is possible that these scholars continued their studies in the town and only left once De Vaux College had been established. Certainly the apothecary, John de Bridport, was the only one to remain in Bridport after about 1260, which suggests that the rest may have joined the staff of the college.

Another connection between the town and De Vaux College is Sir John Holteby of Allington. Sir John, who was a Canon of Salisbury Cathedral, and one of the founders of the leper hospital of St Mary Magdalen at Allington, was the first Warden of De Vaux College. The second Warden was Thomas de Bridport. The fact that Giles, John and Thomas all have de Bridport after their name does not imply a relationship, but literally that they came from Bridport. [6]

No doubt over the years other clever young men destined for the church also travelled from the town to the universities of Oxford and Cambridge, and perhaps, if they were destined for the law rather than the church, to the Inns of Court in London, as they did from other towns throughout the country. Boys' early education consisted almost entirely of

---

[4] "Bridport History and Topography" : Text of a series of lectures given by Basil Short. Local History Collection, Bridport Library.
[5] "Advowson" - in English Ecclesiastical Law refers to the patronage of an ecclesiastical office. To acquire the advowson confers on the beneficiary the right to grant a benefice or living to a person of that patron's choice
[6] "The Book of Bridport" by Basil Short and John Sales 1973 pp 89, 90

instruction in speaking and writing Latin, and they were drilled in Latin grammar. The main aim was to prepare young men to serve in the hierarchies of the church. As the usual age of entry to the Universities of Oxford and Cambridge was 14-years-of-age, boys would have started their instruction young. The "school" would probably be no more than an association between a master and a small number of students taught by the master in his own house. Did Bridport have such a school? Probably, but all we have is some circumstantial evidence from the late fifteenth century in the form of an inventory of items in the possession of St Mary's Church dated 21st April 1476 that is quoted by J Hutchins in his "History and Topography of the County of Dorset", 1774:

"Indenture of ye churchys godys" made in the church *"of the Blessed St Mary of Brideport the 21st day of April in the year of Our Lord MCCCCLXXVI, witnesseth that we, the wardens of the aforesaid church, viz John Bremell and William Rakereyne, on the day of the month and year of Our Lord above said, for the Bailiffs, John Sterre and John Dunne, by the same have received all the ornaments and impliments belonging to the said church, as follows:"* Listed are missals, psalters and sundry other goods, then the indenture goes on to list *"one book called Hugucio; Item, the treatise of Thomas de Hanneia. An alphabet of Latin words, one old missal, one book of logic, one medicinal book."*[7]

According to Nicholas Orme,[8] "Hugutio" is probably that author's etymological Latin dictionary; the treatise of Thomas Hanneia (Hanney) is his "Memoriale Juniorum", which is a general survey of grammar completed in 1313. Together with the alphabet, which would probably be a word list or vocabulary of Latin words, and the book of logic, this library in the keeping of St Mary's churchwardens points to the possibility of there having been a schoolmaster teaching in the town at this time. Though the identity of the teacher who made use of these books is unrecorded, the Rector of St Mary's at the time of this inventory, according to J Hutchins, was John Hyall MA. He served St Mary's from 1468 till his death in 1481. As the initials after his name clearly indicate, he was university educated, a Master of Arts, and it is tempting to consider that it might have been he who was teaching the young men of the town in addition to his other parish duties.

Perhaps that is one guess too far, but before I move on to firmer ground in the sixteenth century, there is one other interesting detail unearthed by Nicholas Orme in his study. A grammatical miscellany of the fifteenth century held in Lincoln Cathedral includes a short tract of a single page on prosody (the science of versification formerly considered part of grammar) called "Flores Accentus", with the note that *"Master John*

---

[7] "History and Antiquities of the County of Dorset", 1774 by J Hutchins: Vol. 2 p29
[8] "Education in the West of England, 1066 - 1548" by Nicholas Orme

Chalurys composed this, who dwells in Bridport",[9] so if we cannot identify a specific school, we can be sure that Bridport was not lacking in education or educated men. Bridport did not, however, have an endowed grammar school until late in the reign of Queen Elizabeth I, and then the endowment was so imperfect that there was no money allocated to pay a schoolmaster for some years after the provision of a schoolroom.

The Bridport Free (Grammar) School

Throughout England, between 1550 and 1640 there was a massive expansion of educational provision, funded by benefaction, often in the form of grants of land that provided an annual rent sufficient to fund the schoolmaster's salary, and in some cases also to provide a schoolroom and possibly also a schoolmaster's house. In various parts of the country schools were established, both petty schools for the education of the poor and grammar schools for the education of the sons of the better off. In West Dorset, Netherbury Free School was probably the first to be established. It was certainly in existence by the early years of Queen Elizabeth's reign, for in 1565/6 when a dispute erupted over the use of the profits from land endowed for the use of the school, it had already been in existence for some years. Beaminster Free School was much later, established in or about 1684. Between the two comes the Bridport Free School, established in 1593. The location was originally part of the Market House ("Markett House and Scole House"), and was very much a matter of the burgesses killing two birds with one stone. Public subscription raised the funds for the Market House and the school came with it.

The Market House stood at the intersection of East and West Street, It is shown on what is believed to be the earliest map of Bridport dating from about 1770,[10] (Fig 1) more or less opposite where the present Town Hall stands. According to the map it was a narrow rectangular structure, but precisely what it looked like is impossible to say. It certainly consisted of a row of butcher's shambles possibly with a room adjoining or above, which would have housed the school.

What was the impetus for such a building at this particular time? In the years just after the defeat of the Armada, Bridport was experiencing economic difficulties. In desperation the Burgesses approached the Crown for help. The result was a charter granted by Queen Elizabeth I. This extended the rights to hold markets and fairs. It allowed the selling of cattle and livestock at the "Satterdaies Markett". Also permitted was an extra

---

[9] Lincoln Cathedral MS88 (A.3.15) fo. 119v . "Cat of the Mss of Lincoln Cathedral Library" ed. R.M.Woolley (Oxford 1927) P49 quoted in "Education in the West of England, 1066 - 1548" by Nicholas Orme
[10] Map of Bridport: DHC/BTB/R2: Copy in BMLHC.

12

Wednesday market for part of the year, as well as three annual fairs: the first in April on the Feast of the Annunciation, the second, three-day fair round the feast of the Ascension and the third on the Feast of St Michael (Michaelmas). No doubt it was this raising of the prestige of the market, not to mention its frequency, that made the provision of a Market House necessary.

The Tudor Market House, more often referred to as the "Shambles" as it housed butchers' premises, was built in a matter of weeks in the middle of 1593, at a cost of about £21. Materials and money came both from the town and surrounding districts, including Beaminster and Lyme Regis. About sixty Bridport citizens contributed gifts of between 1d and 2s-6d. It is interesting to note, in light of the Colfox family's major involvement in education in Bridport in later years, that members of the Colfox family appear among the list of subscribers to the Market House and "Scole". Symond Colfox, shoemaker, and Richard Colfox both subscribed 2d, while John Colfox contributed 1 bushel of malt. "The Widow Colfox" gave 1 peck of malt and the "Widow Colfox of Chideock" gave ½ a peck of malt. The fact that some gave malt or wheat as their contributions and that two of the Bailiffs responsible for fund-raising were described as "Stewards for the Ale" indicates that the town used the time-honoured method of fund-raising, that is holding an "Ale", (brewing a special beer and holding a town celebration, feast and festivity) which was no doubt what the 2lbs of bacon and 3lbs of candles were also for. The "Ale" was held at Whitsuntide.[11]

How long the school remained in the Market House is not clear. Rooms above, or even alongside, a butchers' shambles cannot have been ideal, and it is possible that before long the school moved to occupy part of St Andrew's Chapel, as there is a reference in the Cofferers' account of 1613 to a payment for *"making a seate in St Andrews Schoole"*. And J Hutchins says that in his time, about 1770, a Free School occupied part of the old church of St Andrews, which stood more-or-less where the present Town Hall stands.[12]

How the schoolmaster was paid in the early years is not recorded. There was clearly a problem however, and when, in 1619, the attempt to raise money for repairing the harbour only realised £61, permission was sought to divert the money to pay for a schoolmaster *"which in that town we find to be something defective"*.[13] According to the Charity Commissioners'

---

[11] "A Respectable Society: 1593 - 1835" by Basil Short. Moonraker 1976 pp4-6
[12] "History and Antiquities of the County of Dorset", 1774 by J Hutchins Vol. 2
[13] The petitioners to the Crown regarding the use of money raised for the repair of the harbour for a schoolmaster, quoted in "A Respectable Society: 1593 - 1835" by Basil Short. Moonraker 1976 p7

Reports of 1834[14] a petition was presented to the King by the bailiffs and burgesses of the Borough of Bridport asking for leave to retain money, which had been collected for the repair of the harbour. The petition was, by the King's order, referred to Sir George Trenchard and one John Strode, Esq., two of His Majesty's Justices of the Peace for the County of Dorset, who reported that, as the money which had been collected would not be enough for the original purpose of the harbour, it might better be used in procuring some maintenance for a schoolmaster, and by an order dated the 4th May, 1620, the King directed that the amount of money which had been collected, namely £61, be used for the *"particular maintenance of a schoolmaster"* within the town of Bridport.

To the original sum of £61 was added £20, and the gross sum was laid out in March, 1621 for the purchase of three closes of pasture ground known as Broad Oak in the Parish of Symondsbury (then described as Symondsborough). These were conveyed by one William Crocker to the Bailiffs and Burgesses of the Borough of Bridport in trust for the maintenance of the school and schoolmaster. Three-quarters of the profits arising out of the land were to be employed for the maintenance of the schoolmaster; the remaining fourth part was to be employed for the benefit and maintenance of the poor of Bridport.

A further Charity known as the Malthouse and Brewhouse Charity was set up in 1650 when, as the result of a bequest, the Corporation of Bridport laid out £180 to purchase two houses known respectively as the Malthouse and Brewhouse with "other appurtenances" on the north side of West Street adjoining the river, to be held in trust so that the rents and benefits of the premises might be employed by the bailiffs and burgesses of the Borough of Bridport for the perpetual relief of *"poor and needy persons dwelling in the Borough of Bridport"*. An entry in the old Record Book of the Bridport Corporation dated March 9th 1651 fills in the details:

"Memorandum – That, on the 29th April 1640, Mrs Jane Naper, daughter of Sir Nathaniel Naper, knight bart., by her will bearing date as aforesaid, did give and bequeath unto Bridport the sum of £100 to be employed in a stock or by way of trade for the benefit of the poor there; which sum with the increase thereof was at sundry times, and on 9th march 1651, fully paid in by Robert Naper, of Puncknowl (sic) esquire, by direction of Nathaniel Naper, gentleman, executor of the said will and that the said sum is laid out in the brewhouse lately purchased of Thomas Bartlett and

---

[14] In 1834 Commissioners who were appointed to enquire into charities in England and Wales published their reports. Volume 29 of these reports deals, in pages 46-55, with the charities under the management of the Bridport Corporation. BMLHC

14

Francis his son, amongst other money for the benefit of the poor of the same borough". [15]

The bailiffs and burgesses were to employ part of the rents at their discretion in binding or putting forth poor children in Bridport as apprentices to artificers or tradesmen *"that they might be piously educated, and might also in their calling be fit to serve the Commonwealth".* Although in 1623 the corporation accounts show a payment to a schoolmaster, funding was not really secured until the Charities outlined above were set up.

The first named schoolmaster of the Free School was William Hallett, a dissenter. It is important to remember that this was the period of Cromwell's Commonwealth, when the dissenting clergy had the upper hand, and many Church of England clergy had lost their livings in favour of dissenters. William Hallett died in 1655, leaving a widow Ann who subsequently married a Stephen Colfox in 1661. The second recorded master of the school was Henry Parsons, also a dissenting minister who was ejected from the living of Burstock in 1662, two years after the Restoration of King Charles II to the throne of England. He was offered the living of Uplyme but refused, and became minister of a dissenting congregation at Stoke-sub-Hamdon. It is not clear precisely which years he acted as schoolmaster to the Bridport scholars.

Records speak for certain of only one scholar of the school, and he was the Irish-born writer, Richard Head, who attended the *"grammar school of Bridport, Dorsetshire"* probably in 1650, before going up to Oxford. He found notoriety during the Restoration period as a writer of lewd plays and the author of an equally salacious early novel called "The English Rogue", in which is described in *"The Life of Meriton Latroon, a witty extravagant, being a compleat history of the most Eminent Cheats of both Sexes",* which was so obscene that the first version was turned down by the censor, and it only *"passed stamp"* in a revised version. Head, who made his most settled living as a bookseller in London, was born in Ireland, in Carrickfergus, in about 1637, the son of an English clergyman. His father was killed in the Irish rebellion of 1641. How Richard ended up in Bridport is not entirely clear, though a number of refugees from the massacres in Ireland found their way to Dorset, and it is possible that his mother had some connection with the town. An inveterate gambler who according to John Aubrey *"Brake (was bankrupted) 2 or 3 times",* Head died, according the account of his life in Winstanley's "Lives of the Most Famous English Poets", in 1686, drowning on a crossing to the Isle of Wight, though Aubrey has him dying ten years earlier on a sea voyage to Plymouth.

---

[15] Quoted in "History and Antiquities of the County of Dorset", 1774 by J Hutchins: Vol. 2 pp 33 and 34

As the only verifiable former scholar of the Bridport school, he was sadly disreputable. In his "Brief Lives" John Aubrey describes him as having *"been amongst the gypsies. He looked like a knave with his gogling eies*(sic)." His low-life connections and knowledge of thieves' slang are celebrated in another of his works published in 1673: the "Canting Academy, or the Devil's Cabinet Opened" which details the villainous practices of *"Hectors, Trapanners, Gilts etc. to which is added a compleat Canting Dictionary with several new Catches and Songs etc."*[16] Despite his later disreputable career, Richard Head must have gained a good grounding in Latin and in Bridport, for he left the school to go up to Oxford University, possibly attending his father's former college: New Inn Hall.

No description of the curriculum offered at Bridport's Free School exists, as far as I have been able to ascertain, but a description of that offered at nearby Netherbury gives a clear idea of what it must have been. The churchwarden's records of a visitation in the reign of Charles II state that *"they had a school for teaching the principles of grammar, writing, reading and arithmetic."* [17] The "grammar" referred to would of course be Latin grammar. No doubt the Bridport scholars followed much the same curriculum.

The history of the Free School after the mid-seventeenth century is vague. Some commentators believe it had ceased to exist by the mid-eighteenth century, but there is the reference in J Hutchins, of a Free School in St Andrew's Chapel in 1770: *"The remains of it (St Andrew's Chapel) stand at the meeting of the three principal streets near the middle of the town. Part is a dwelling house; part converted into the sessions house over which is a free school; part made a gaol for criminals; and part is in ruins."*[18] Perhaps, as location for the education of the young, this was an improvement on the butchers' shambles, but not much. The fact that after the Market House burnt down in 1782, there was an initial proposal that there should be a schoolroom provided in the New Market House (the present Town Hall) suggests the school was still in existence right up to the rebuilding. According to a note by Basil Short lodged in the BMLHC,[19] a dissenting parson, the Rev. Matthew Anstis, described as a man *"of too radical opinions"* was apparently invited by the Bridport Corporation to run its school, but either he declined the offer or his *"too radical opinions"* frightened off the bailiffs.

Matthew Anstis was a prominent member of the Religious Society, known later as the Unitarians, in Bridport, and was active in the proposals

---

[16] Dictionary of National Biography Vol IX: Ed. Sir Leslie Stephen and Sir Sidney Lee: OUP 1917 (1950 Edition) p 326 - 328
[17] "History and Topography of the County of Dorset", 1774 by J Hutchins : Vol. 2 p109 1774
[18] Ibid
[19] "Bridport – some historical sites and buildings" notes by Basil Short: BMLHC.

16

for the building of the New Chapel in East Street in 1791. Originally from St Germains in Cornwall, Matthew Anstis came to Bridport around 1767. He had briefly served as minister to the Dissenting Meeting in Falmouth, and later in Colyton, but in both places it would appear his views were too radical for the congregations. In Bridport, though initially he did minister to *"a small society of dissenters,"*[17] it was as an educator, rather than as a pastor that he made his mark. In 1780 he opened a school in premises in West Street.

The location of his school is remembered in the name Education Place, which the 1888 Ordnance Survey Map of the town shows to have been a court running north from West Street. The building that housed Rev Anstis' school is no longer there, it stood on the site of the present Hardy's Restaurant. According to the Universal British Directory of Trade, Commerce, and Manufacture published somewhere between 1790 and 1793, Rev Matthew Anstis: *"Schoolmaster and Dissenting Minister"* was running a *"Boarding-school for Young Gentlemen"*. Though it is generally believed that the charitable funds were also used to send students to various other private schools, the Universal Directory only mentions two schools in the early 1790's. *"Here are two schools, one of them is maintained out of the salary arising from the Bull Inn; the other is from different persons"*. The first is clearly the Daniel Taylor School, and the second is likely to be Matthew Anstis' School. Charity income declined however and by 1823 the Matthew Anstis school had only two pupils.[18]

The plan to locate the Free School in the new Town Hall failed as adding a school room proved to be too expensive and the school facility was omitted from the final plans for the new building (1785-7). To make way for the new building the remains of the old chapel of St Andrew were demolished. It is likely that it was at this juncture that the original "Free Scole" finally closed. Bridport was not to have another "Free Grammar School" until the early twentieth century, though, even then, "free" meant in practice subsidised, as most students had to find some fee or other, and only a very few were supported entirely out of charitable funds.

The other major educational venture of the seventeenth century was brought about by the philanthropy of one man, Daniel Taylor, an influential member of the relatively new Quaker community in Bridport. The persecution of the Quakers was intense in mid-seventeenth century England, resulting in many emigrating to set up communities in America. In Bridport a strong and enduring Quaker community was set up around the

---

[17] Quoted from Matthew Anstis' obituary in the Monthly Repository by Basil Short in his lecture "Thomas Howe (1788-1820) & The Building of the Chapel": Chapter One in Unitarian Matters; an unpublished MS: BMLHC.
[18] "A Respectable Society: 1593 - 1835" by Basil Short. Moonraker 1976 p 50

Meeting House in South Street. They too were subject to violent attacks and this reference to a member of the Colfox family is less creditable than others in this book. *"On one occasion, together with a constable, William Colfox 'a very rude man' came to the Meeting House, getting in, broke all the benches and forms and other conveniences with the glass windows, so that they left not any part whole."*[19]

This building in South Street, that was the subject of the officially sanctioned attack by the authorities in the above description, was itself the gift of Daniel Taylor, who was then a merchant living in West Street. It was originally a barn, which Taylor gave for a permanent Meeting House for the local Quakers in 1697. In addition to donating a house with tenements to be converted to almshouses (still to be seen today next to the Friends Meeting House in South Street), he endowed the Daniel Taylor Educational Trust, and as part of this set up a free school for the scholars of Bridport. The scholars were taught in the schoolmaster's home, but sadly, to date, I have not been able to find out precisely where this was, or the identity of any of the schoolmasters.

During Taylor's own lifetime he also looked to the education of Quaker children in the whole county of Dorset. Accommodation for these scholars was provided at Corfe by one Joan Howard, so it is likely that the school was also in or near Corfe. Clearly this was a more ambitious establishment than the Bridport school, as many of the children attending must have had to board.

The Bridport school however was a day school, and was originally endowed in 1708 for 12 scholars. Eventually it educated between 30 and 40. In this school there was no stipulation that the children must be Quakers. It was for the education of the poor. The description of the schoolmaster to be employed by the Bridport trustees was very specific. He was to be *"honest and discreet, skillful and experienced in the arts of reading, writing and arithmetic and in such other useful arts and sciences as such schoolmaster shall think fit and convenient"*. He was to receive 20s a year for each of 12 poor children: *"sons of the poor inhabitants of the Borough of Bridport"*. The following were among his conditions of employment: *"if the schoolmaster shall at any time be an ill-liver, or guilty of any notorious immorality or misbehaviour, or ignorance, or should be unskilful in the arts of reading, writing and arithmetic, or should refuse or neglect to instruct …. it should be lawful"* for the Trustees to remove him.[20]

---

[19] "Daniel Taylor of Bridport 1642-1714 and the Trusts he Founded" by Frances M Reynolds 1980

[20] " 'A Fine Meeting There was There.' 300 Years of Bridport's Quaker History" by Suzanne Finch pp40 and 41. Publ. by Bridport Quaker Meeting Friends Meeting House. Printed By Creeds the Printers, Broadoak.

The school was funded by rent from the Bull Hotel. If the "clear rent" (after repairs etc) was more than £12, then more boys were to be taken by the schoolmaster, as long as the master received £1 for each child. At Daniel Taylor's death there were 37 children in the school, but in 1778 the Bull Inn premises needed major repair. So extensive were the works required that the Trustees had to borrow £650 to put the place in order. Until this loan was repaid (not finally until 1824) the numbers in the school were kept at 12. In 1827 the number of pupils is recorded as 32 and the master's stipend is cited as £45. The Bull Inn was sold in 1859 for £2,450 and the money raised was invested to continue providing the funds for the various charities.

The Daniel Taylor Educational Trust was by 1861 giving considerable financial support to Bridport General Boys', and Infant Schools: recorded in 1866 as £40 annually to the Boys' School and £20 to the Infants' Schools. At some point, probably in the 1870's, the Taylor School closed and the pupils joined the General School. According to the terms of the trust the Daniel Taylor School was *"open to children of all denominations regardless of religious belief,"*[21] which was also the principle on which the General Schools were founded. The Infants' School reports losing the Daniel Taylor grant in the Annual Report of 1878, at which point a new scheme approved by the Charity Commissioners came into force to provide scholarships and prizes. Even today, the Trust gives assistance to local students, particularly offering travel bursaries.

One other charity was set up to help the schooling of the poor children of Bridport in the early eighteenth century and this was the Bulls' Charity, which was endowed by a Bridport citizen, Robert Bull, who, in his will in 1726, gave £200, *"which sum was laid out in the three per cent Consols, and yielded £250, vested on the rector of Bridport and his successors for ever".* Out of this endowment, £4 per annum was to be used for teaching twelve young children to read, £3 per annum given to twelve poor men at Christmas, *"and if any overplus, to be laid out in books called 'The Duty of Man' ".*[22] The Bull Charity and the Broad Oak (Eight Acre) Charity assisted the Bridport National Schools in the nineteenth century, and provided much needed, if small, extra sums of money at a time when the funding of schools was often very limited.

---

[21] "Daniel Taylor of Bridport 1642-1714 and the Trusts he Founded" by Frances M Reynolds
[22] History and Topography of the County of Dorset", 1774 by J Hutchins Vol. 2 pp 33-36

II

PRIVATE ACADEMIES, COLLEGES AND SEMINARIES: PART ONE

In the late eighteenth and early nineteenth centuries, a number of small private "Academies" were set up in Bridport by enterprising teachers, most of whom came from outside the area. Some of these would probably be better described as "Dame Schools". Some were boarding establishments that also took day pupils and charged quite substantial fees. All were very small by today's standards, or even by the standards of the later elementary schools, and most operated from the houses where the teachers lived. Often they were of quite short duration, and in some cases the same premises housed a succession of schools. It is difficult to be absolutely sure of the precise location of many of these small schools as the various trade directories only give a street name, and the various census returns are often difficult to interpret in the time before houses were numbered.

Nineteenth century Bridport was a much smaller place than today. Three bridges, one at each end of the main thoroughfare, and one on the Harbour Road to the south, marked the boundaries of the parish and town. So it is not surprising that the many small schools were packed into relatively small areas. Early in the century most schools were located at the eastern end of the town, in East Street and Barrack Street; also in Irish or King of Prussia Lane, and in the fine terrace of early Georgian houses known as Prospect Place. This narrow lane leading south from East Street almost forming a crossroads with Barrack Street, is now known in its entirety as King Street. Printed records take us back to around 1823 and that is where I shall start this account.

On the corner of East Street and Barrack Street, occupied today by an antique shop, stood the house and business premises of Joseph Hounsell. Hounsell was a merchant and a prominent member of the Unitarian congregation. Next-door to Joseph Hounsell's house were two substantial three-storey houses (Fig 3) which were used over the century by a succession of schools. One was subsequently demolished and has since been rebuilt, the second is known as Dorset House, of which much more later. In 1841 these two premises were being run, possibly as joint boarding and day schools by husband and wife, Samuel and Henrietta Taylor, and next-door, by Susan and Elizabeth Taylor.[1] Boarding with

---

[1] Samuel Taylor is mentioned in a directory of 1830 and again in Pigot and Co's Dorsetshire Directory of 1842 as running a small private academy in East Street, and the census and rate returns of 1841 record Samuel and Henrietta Taylor, forty and thirty years old respectively as school principals. The Census seems to imply Susan and Elizabeth Taylor were in a the next door premises but this cannot be relied upon.

Henrietta and Samuel was schoolmaster, William Carter aged twenty, but the 1841 census records no pupils. Next door to Samuel and Henrietta, the same census records thirty-five-year-old Susan and thirty-year-old Elizabeth Taylor running a boarding school for girls. Were Susan and Elizabeth Samuel's sisters? Were the two schools linked? Probably, though there is no way of knowing for certain, but a relationship and possibly a link does seem likely. The house Susan and Elizabeth occupied was probably Dorset House. This imposing house, still today looking much as it must have done in the early 19th century, was used as premises for a succession of schools through to the late 1870's, and thereafter by a succession of GP's surgeries.

There were seven female pupils[2] at Taylor's School, and a resident schoolmistress, Catherine Hussey aged twenty. The pupils were Martha Roper (15), Mary Haydon (14); Anna Hussey and Harriet Bartlett (both aged 11); Ann Edmonds and Susan Payne (both 9) and Lavinia Squire (7). Ten years later. in 1851[3] the Taylors have gone and their boarding school, next-door to Joseph Hounsell is being run by Martha Rendell. Martha Rendell was a local women, and as such is quite a rarity among Bridport private-school principals at this time as most came from outside the town. However her one assistant teacher, Eliza Bowman, came from London, and the three boarders: Alice Manson (17), Emily Foss (12) and a boy of ten, Richard H Witherell came from Sheffield, Lyme Regis and Plymouth respectively. The presence of a boy of ten is a little puzzling, though possibly, like many of the later girls' schools, Martha Rendell was running a department for "little boys", though most preparatory departments in girls' schools later in the century did not keep boys much beyond seven years-of-age.

Ten years later in 1861,[4] Elizabeth East has taken over the school, which she describes as a "Ladies' School". Elizabeth G East was thirty-nine in 1861. She came from Chesham in Buckinghamshire and living with her is a resident assistant teacher, and two boarders: Eliza Ann Street, nineteen from Clapham and Sophia Richardson, eleven-years-old from Lyme Regis.

By 1871 Dorset House was again in use as a school.[5] By this time it was the home of George F Brown, curate, and his wife Rosalind Brown. She ran the school and in an advertisement in The Bridport News in January 1871 is seeking pupils for a school at *"Dorset House, Bridport, conducted by a clergyman's wife"*. She offers *"French taught with a pure accent, music and singing. Italian and German if desired; and a sound*

---

[2] Bridport Census 1841
[3] Bridport Census 1851
[4] Bridport Census 1861
[5] Bridport Census 1871

English Education". A *"resident governess"* is also advertised.[6] This was thirty-year-old Elizabeth A Jones. Also resident at the school was seventeen-year-old pupil-teacher Ellen Jefford. Together with the Brown's own five young children, George (9), John (7), Harold (4), Rose (2) and Lionel (1), were two scholars Annie Bankes from Devon and Emma Parker from Crewkerne. Mrs Brown was still in the process of developing her school as the advert states that she has *"Vacancies for a few young ladies as boarders".* Her school seems to have operated until 1872, or possibly the early months of 1873, but by June 1873 the house had been taken over by Mrs Elizabeth Reader for the first of her schools, of which much more in Chapter IV.

On the opposite side of East Street lies the inn known at the time as The King of Prussia Hotel (now The Lord Nelson). The Inn borders the lane that runs south connecting East Street with Folly Mill Lane. Now known as simply as King Street, this was another area of the town where a number of small schools were located and a number of teachers lived. The first I will deal with is John Fursey's Academy[7] in King of Prussia Lane. Not a great deal is known about this school, but in 1841 schoolmaster, John Fursey, by then aged sixty-five, was living in "Irish Lane" with his wife Elizabeth (50) and Jane Fursey, probably his daughter, who was twenty-five and a dressmaker. If Fursey was still teaching in 1848, as the directory entry implies, he would by then have been over seventy, however it is quite likely that his school had existed for some time before 1841, though as records before this date are patchy, it is difficult to know for certain. By 1861 he was dead and Elizabeth, described as a schoolmistress and a widow, was still living in Irish Lane though it is unlikely she was still running the school.

Also listed in the 1841 census living four doors away from John and Elizabeth Fursey was fifty-year-old Mary Roberts, schoolmistress and, in what the 1841 census calls "St Mary's Row, Irish Lane", lived twenty-seven-year-old Susan Locke. Whether there was any connection between these three teachers it is impossible to say. Did John Fursey's Academy educate both boys and girls? There are more questions than answers when the record is so patchy. It seems likely that John Fursey's Academy was a day school as nowhere is there any mention of pupils. It may well have closed when the General Schools opened on the opposite side of the lane, as the census of 1851 makes no mention of Fursey's establishment.

George Philip Mouats (Boarding) School is even more difficult to track down. His name appears, variously spelt, in a number of records, but there is little consistency to any of them. The 1851 census lists a Geo P

---

[6] The Bridport News Jan 13th 1871
[7] Kelly's Directory of Dorsetshire 1848 mentions John Fursey's Academy. Also Bridport Census 1841

Meriat (sic), schoolmaster, living on the north side of East Street, but his Academy is listed in Pigots Directory of 1842 as being in Barrack Street. His name obviously gave the compilers of directories problems as here it is spelt "Moats". Hunt's Directory of 1851 mentions a school in East Street run by George Philip Mouat, but, by this time his school (this time his name is given as Mr Philip Moatt) was already being run by Henry Nobbs Cox who took over the school in 1849.[8] The connection with Henry Nobbs Cox adds a little flesh to the bare bones of directory and census records. Henry Cox had left a post at Yeovil Grammar School to take over Moatt's Academy so the school must have been quite academic. It is also mentioned by Francis (Fra) Newbery in an article entitled "Reminiscences".[9] He is writing about William Edward Forster MP, the originator of the 1870 Education Act who spent his early years in Bradpole. (Appendix B.) He recalls Forster attending school in Bridport and goes on: *"This School was a private establishment for day and term boarders, and in my own day was kept by a successor of Forster's Schoolmaster, Mr Nobbs Cox, a well-known Bridport character."* (For more information on Cox's School see Chapter III.)

At the extreme end of East Street was William Salter Gillard's Academy.[10] The location of this school was probably on the south side of the street next to the East Bridge and opposite Bridge House. Yet again the school operated from the schoolmaster's house. Living with William was his wife Mary and two pupils: fourteen-year-old Jacob Pratt and a ten-year-old boy called George whose surname is indecipherable. Though the census does not record them as scholars, that is most likely what they were. This establishment must have been quite short-lived as Gillard is not mentioned in the 1851 census returns. He would, by then, only have been thirty-eight, so it is possible he left the area.

On the south side of East Street, somewhere between The Three Mariners Inn and Swain's Court, two sisters, Mary and Sarah Wilmshurst, were running quite a substantial girls' school in the 1840's.[11] They employed one assistant teacher Sarah Shickell (20), and three apprentices, Emma Aldridge (18), Elizabeth Wakeford (15) and Sophia Horsey (14). There were seventeen pupils, obviously boarders, ranging in age from nine to seventeen. These were Sarah Barrett, (12), Julianea Barrett (9), Amelia Cartwright and Sarah Conway, both thirteen, Mary Conquest (15) Ellen Coles (14) Elizabeth, Albina and Sophia Elworthy (16, 15 and 8 respectively), Annette George (15), Clara Gill (15), Caroline Eddaile? (17), Marianne and Maria Hargreaves (14 and 11), Martha Perry (16), Mary ?

---

[8] Bridport News, Friday June 29th 1894
[9] Dorset Year Book 1928
[10] Bridport Census 1841; Pigot's Directory 1842
[11] The 1841 census lists them both as thirty-five years-of-age, either they were twins, or the entry contains an error.

(14) and Jane Searle (16) Two female servants made up the household.[12] Such a large establishment would have needed quite a large house, but so far I have been quite unable to identify precisely where this building was.

As is still the case today, the western end of East Street was much more commercial than the eastern end, but there was at least one school near the town centre, located in a house next door to the old Red Lion Inn. Thomas Wainwright was a Yorkshireman from Leeds. What brought him to Bridport is not recorded, but in 1861 he was running a boarding school for boys.[13] He was a relatively young man of thirty-six, married with three children. There are two pupils listed as boarding at the school: brothers Charles and Frederick Lord from Horden in Yorkshire, (11 and 10 respectively). It seems fair to conjecture that the pupils came to the town with their schoolmaster. How many local boys he recruited is not recorded. Also somewhere in East Street was a "Boarding and Day School", presumably for girls, run by Mrs Mary Cannon,[14] who describes herself as *"widow of the late Rev. C. Cannon"*, but I can find no other information about this school, nor make any guess as to where it was.

Rax Lane is the narrow lane that runs parallel to East Street and just north of that thoroughfare. This was another location where private educational establishments came and went. The enduring presence there was, of course, the Unitarian Sunday School and later in the century the Unitarian Grammar School, (See Chapter VI) but in the 1820's there was also a "Gentleman's Boarding School" run by the Rev J.S. Cope in Rax Cottage.[15] There was also a "Ladies' Academy" in Box (sic) Lane (Rax Lane?) run by Ann R Hughes,[16] and some years later another school for girls run by Mrs Sarah Seymour was also located in Rax Lane, possibly in the same premises as those used by Anne Hughes. It would appear that the information in Kelly's Directory was already slightly out of date by the time the Directory was published in 1880, for in January 1879 Mrs Seymour relocated to Magdalen House, West Allington, and was already advertising for a *"limited number of weekly boarders and day pupils".*[17]

South Street seems to have had relatively few schools although a number of teachers lived there. In the 1850's however, Henry Coates

---

[12] Bridport Census 1841
[13] Bridport Census 1861; J.G.Harrod and Co's Postal and Commercial Directory of Dorset and Wiltshire 1865
[14] J.G.Harrod and Co's Postal and Commercial Directory of Dorset and Wiltshire 1865
[15] Pigot and Co's Dorsetshire Directory of 1823
[16] Ibid
[17] The Bridport News Jan 10th 1879

Boarding School was operating from a house just to the north of St Mary's Church on the western side of the street.[18] The house occupied by the Coates family was five doors away from St Mary's Church and Rectory. His wife Emily, described as the *"schoolmaster's wife"*, and two *"annuitants"*, his mother Julia Coates and a Julia Whittle, also formed part of the household.[19] All or some of these family members may have assisted in the running of his school. Intriguingly next door lived the music teacher and organist, Thomas Avant. Thomas Avant lived and worked in Bridport for most of the second half of the nineteenth century. He was well-known in the area, and though he is variously described as "organ and piano tuner", "music teacher" and "musician",[20] he is probably best remembered as organist of St Mary's Church and there is a photograph of him next to the organ in the north transept of the church. At some point in the 1850's he moved from South Street to Downe Street where he was still living in the 1880's.[21] He was clearly well regarded in the town and gave regular concerts, which are reported from time-to-time in the Bridport News. Did Thomas Avant teach at Henry Coates' school? Possibly, but I have no evidence one way or the other. One house servant completed the Coates' household. The question is, where were the scholars? There is no mention of scholars residing at the same address. Possibly they were lodged close by, or perhaps were simply not present in the house the day the census was taken.

The only other schools I have found that were located in South Street were the Misses Tucker's School and the Chapel House School of which more later. Sarah Tucker was teaching in South Street in the 1840's[22] but by 1851 two middle-aged sisters Anna (50) and Frances or Fanny Tucker (45) have taken over the school.[23] What the relationship was between Sarah, and the sisters, Anna and Fanny, I have no idea, nor precisely where the school was.

The development of schools in West Street largely belongs to the latter half of the nineteenth century, but there were a few establishments there in these earlier years of which little but the names are preserved. William Everett, according to Hunt's Directory of 1851 was running a school in West Street. However, the census of 1841 locates William Everett in Higher Folly Lane, while the 1851 return places William and Mary Everett

---

[18] Hunt's Directory of 1851 mentions Henry Coates' Boarding School; also 1851 Bridport Census.

[19] The term "Annuitant" suggests that they were in receipt of some sort of pension, probably a widow's pension.

[20] J G Harrod & Co's Postal and Commercial Directory of Dorset & Wiltshire 1865

[21] Kelly's Directory of Dorsetshire 1880

[22] Pigot and Co's Dorsetshire Directory 1823

[23] Hunts Directory 1851; Bridport Census 1851

as living in Lee Cottage, East Road, which at that time came under Bradpole. Wherever he was living, the census lists no scholars at either address, so the likelihood is that the school was not located at his home, however the problem remains of establishing precisely where in West Street the school was. A few years earlier a "Gentlemen's Day School" was in existence run by William Williams, also in West Street.[24]

The earliest girls' schools I have found recorded in West Street[25] is "The Ladies School" run by the Misses Hart. It was not there for long, for by 1842, the Misses Hart had moved their school to Bradpole.[26] It must have occupied quite good premises in West Street, for their schoolroom was rented by the Association for Mutual Improvement in the 1830's before the Association's own building, later designated the Literary and Scientific Institute, was built in East Street. (Chapter XII)

There were a number of other schools belonging to this early period of which little is known but their names. Many seem to have been very short-lived. Miss Sarah Chick ran a Ladies' Seminary in West Street;[27] Hannah Rendall had a school in Allington, while Frances Hansford was running a "Ladies' Seminary" in Downe Street.[28] The title "Seminary" indicates its social pretensions rather than any indication of the kind of curriculum on offer. The titles "Academy", "College" and "Seminary" were used fairly indiscriminately at this time, largely to confer prestige on the establishments being advertised. Later in the century in 1879 the Misses Mollets, both certificated teachers set up a Ladies Boarding and Day School with a Preparatory Class for "little boys"[29] at No 1 Downe Street, which may or may not have been in the same premises.

The period starting round about 1870's saw a great expansion in the number of more academically ambitious private schools, particularly for middle-class girls, that were set up in Bridport. Some lasted only a few years, like "The Preparatory"[30] in South Street run by a Miss Finch, which may have been a preparatory school for small boys, and the "Ladies' Seminary" at Ebenezer Cottage in "Queen Street", (later known as Victoria Grove) run by a Mrs Parsons. Others however were more substantial "Colleges", and thanks to the increasing habit of these establishments to advertise themselves in the Bridport News, it has been possible to glean more information about them and the people who ran them.

---

[24] Pigot and Co's Dorsetshire Directory 1823
[25] Ibid
[26] Pigot and Co's Dorsetshire Directory 1842
[27] J.G.Harrod and Co's Postal and Commercial Directory of Dorset and Wiltshire 1865
[28] Bridport Census 1851
[29] The Bridport News Friday January 10th 1979
[30] The Bridport News: Friday January 12th 1872

There were two schools set up in the 1870's, which, because of the similarity in the names of their principals, have been confused. (The census return of 1881 also confuses the spelling of Edmunds and Edmonds which does not help!). In January 1878, at Carlton House, Barrack Street two sisters, Eleanor and Ann Octavia Edmonds, originally from High Wycombe in Buckinghamshire, set up a school for girls. Though they were natives of High Wycombe, they describe themselves as *"lately of Henley-on-Thames"*, where presumably they had also run a school. Their advertisement for the opening of the school, states that they intend to open a *"Day School for Young Ladies"*.[31] It should be possible to pinpoint the site of this school, as the premises in Barrack Street were those *"lately occupied by Mr B Cox"*. The High Wycombe connection is confirmed by the fact that two of their referees were clergymen from the Berkshire town.

Their school sadly did not last long. Although it is listed in Kelly's Directory for 1880, even as the Directory was being issued, some crisis had hit the school. What happened to the two sisters in 1880 is not clear but either something had happened to end their lease of Carlton House, or Eleanor had decided to give up teaching, for, by 1881, Eleanor Edmonds, still only thirty-nine years of age, had moved to live alone, at Vine Cottage in Chideock, and thirty-year-old Ann Octavia was in lodgings with a grocer, Emmanuel Draper, and his family, at a house on the south side of East Street somewhere between the Bull and Greyhound Inns.[32] Had the sisters fallen out? It seems odd that they should be living so far apart. Whatever happened to cause this abrupt end to their school, it clearly caused gossip, for in the Bridport News of June 25th 1880, a slightly agitated announcement from Ann Edmonds is printed stressing that she wishes to *"contradict the rumour now circulated that she is leaving the town"* and informing readers that for the future she will be happy to receive her pupils at *"Mr Draper's, East Street, Bridport"*. How much space she had in the grocer's premises for pupils is unclear, but her attempt to keep the school going seems to have been unsuccessful, as I could find no further reference to it after 1880.

Seven year earlier in the spring of 1871 Mrs Eliza Laura Edmunds, originally from Chelsea, decided to open her school at East Street House. Though she had been living abroad immediately prior to opening her school, she had clearly lived as a private citizen in East Street for some years in the 1860's.[33] The 1861 census records her as a widow of fifty-eight, probably quite a rich one as she is described as the "Proprietor of Houses". The opening of the "College For Young Ladies" was announced in The Bridport News of Friday March 24th 1871. *"In accordance with the*

---

[31] The Bridport News: Friday January 11th 1878
[32] Bridport Census 1881
[33] J.G.Harrod and Co's Postal and Commercial Directory of Dorset and Wiltshire 1865

27

reiterated wish of several ladies (parents) that a collegiate school should be established in this town, more particularly connected with the Dissenting interest, MRS E.L.EDMUNDS (her capitation), *recently returned from the Continent, feels much pleasure in stating that it is her intention, after the midsummer recess, to receive, being aided by well-qualified assistants, a limited number of resident and non-resident pupils, taking herself the entire supervision of the establishment"*.

Where was East Street House? Possibly the handsome double-fronted town house, No 74 East Street, now divided into apartments but occupied until quite recently by the firm of solicitors, Roper and Roper. There is anecdotal evidence that this building formerly housed a school. The College was clearly a success, but Eliza Edmunds, at sixty-eight, was already quite elderly when she opened her school.[34] It is possible that she was already suffering from ill-health for by January 1873 she had taken another teacher, a Miss Gale, into partnership, and the school was being run jointly.[35] Barely two years after she had opened the school, on 5th March 1873, Eliza Edmunds died.[36] The school continued with Miss Gale as Headmistress, but in January 1874 she seems to have decided to move the school from East Street House to *"commodious premises"* in West Street. The only clue to the location of this building is that it was *"formerly in the occupation of Mr F Scott, surgeon".*[37]

By September 1876 Miss Gale has clearly expanded her school. She is now *"assisted by Masters and resident English and Foreign Governesses"* and is offering *"Thorough English, Music, Singing, Languages, Drawing, Painting, Lectures on Scientific Subjects"*, as well as *"sea-bathing during the Summer months."* Pupils are prepared for *"Oxford, Cambridge and South Kensington Examinations."*[38] By 1877 she advised parents via the Bridport News that *"The College is divided into Upper, Middle and Preparatory Schools. For the latter an experienced governess has been engaged"*, so by this time she was clearly taking young boys as well. Miss Gale continued to advertise her school until January 1878, but in September of that year a rather puzzling announcement appears in the Bridport News announcing a sale at *"The College, East Street"... "as Miss Gale is leaving the district."*[39] The sale is obviously the furniture and effects of a boarding school as it includes twenty-seven iron bedsteads, and twenty-seven mattresses among other items. The puzzle is why the address of "The College" is once again East Street. Did Miss Gale move

---

[34] Bridport Census 1861
[35] The Bridport News: Jan 10th 1873
[36] Notice relating to her will in The Bridport News: June 6th 1873
[37] The Bridport News: Jan 9th 1874
[38] The Bridport News: September 1st 1876
[39] The Bridport News: September 13th 1878

28

her school back into East Street House, or did the proposed move to West Street not take place? The failure of school advertisements to give addresses for the schools makes it difficult to be sure where the school was in the latter years of the 1870's.

The sheer number of schools setting up in the late nineteenth century seems to have resulted in a marked degree of competition for the available custom. This may account for the fact that a number of schools begin to offer classes to those not registered as pupils of the school. One such was the "Chapel House School", in South Street run by Mrs Elizabeth James. It was a "Boarding and Day School" which at one point shared a French master, Monsieur Braye, with Henry Nobbs Cox's Boys' School. In 1880 Mrs James adds more detail to her advertisement.[40] She is *"assisted by Masters and a resident certificated governess"* and offers *"classes in connection with Trinity College, both General and Musical"* which are *"open to young ladies not pupils of the school".* Also open to those from outside the school, are *"dancing, callisthenic and singing classes".* In September 1880 Mrs James moved from Chapel House in South Street to Grosvenor House on East Street. On the move she renamed her school "Grosvenor House School".

The name Chapel House School, however, did not end with Mrs James' relocation, for the Bridport News of August 25th 1882 announces that a Mrs Benham has taken over Chapel House School and intends re-opening the school in early September, *"Little boys will be received,"* she adds. It is not clear how successful Mrs Benham was, but the Chapel House School is only advertised for a short time. Where exactly Chapel House was in South Street, I have so far not been able to ascertain, but the only chapel in South Street was the Wesleyan Chapel, now the Bridport Arts Centre, so possibly it was somewhere near that building. More research is needed to place it.

Grosvenor House on the other hand has been easy to identify. It was on the north side of East Street, two premises west of Barrack Street and next door to a grocers shop run by John Hoare. Though the name does not seem to have survived, it was almost certainly the tall three-storey house next-door-but-one to the Literary and Scientific Institute.[41] Contemporary photographs show it with area railings, a balcony across the first floor, and a flight of steps up to the front door. (Fig 3) Certainly it would have been big enough to provide the kind of accommodation that schools of this period were looking for. Grosvenor House School continued to operate from its new premises for fourteen years, until 1894.

---

[40] Bridport News January 2nd 1880
[41] Bridport Census 1881

Mrs James came originally from Lyme Regis.[42] She was married to William James, a Londoner, who by the turn of the century had established quite a large twine and string manufacturing business, but in 1881 and 1891 he is described simply as first a "Hemp" and then a "Flax Manufacturer". In 1881, Mrs James had seven girl boarders under her care. The girls were all quite close in age, from fifteen to thirteen, which suggests that she was operating a secondary school, and not educating junior pupils as so many of the girls' boarding schools did at this time. The boarders were Kate Uphill (15) from Shaftesbury, Kate Rendall from Shipton (Gorge?) and Bessie Stevens of Abbotsbury who were both fourteen, Frances Hebditch from Whitchurch (Canonicorum?), Mary Uperaft (?) from Packenham in Suffolk, Kate Bowring from Cardiff and Lola Lenthall from Broadwey who were all thirteen. In addition she was also educating Emily, Eliza and Thomas Dale, her nieces and nephew from London who were ten, eight and six respectively, and one seven-year-old boy boarder, Alfred Hone or Stone. The establishment included two resident "Governesses": twenty-year-old Florence Stevens from Devizes, and seventeen-year-old Emma Moase from Pulborough in Sussex.

From the outset, Mrs James clearly had high academic ambitions for her students as she made sure the Bridport News reported her examination results regularly. A report of the school's annual prize giving in 1893 gives a picture of what the school offered. It included an exhibition of work, which according to the paper *"was visited by more than 300 parents and friends of the pupils"*. In addition to prizes for "Plain and Fancy Needlework", "Drawing" and "Painting", there are the results of the School Certificate examinations and the examinations of the College of Preceptors. Students also followed the music curriculum set by the London College of Music and studied Pitman's shorthand. According to the report, the pupils *"wore the school badge during the exhibition"*. It would be interesting to find out what design was shown on the school badge. We do however know what the school motto was, for it was emblazoned on a banner hung on the wall of the classroom where the exhibition was staged: *"Do a little well and you do much"*. The girls' physical well-being was not neglected. The school had a cricket and tennis club, both of which were well supported.[43]

Grosvenor House School continued to advertise in the Bridport News until September 1894. Thereafter it would appear that Elizabeth James moved her school once more, this time just round the corner to 7 Barrack Street.[44] What is strange however, given Mrs James' previous emphasis on publicity for her school, is that the school ceases to be

---

[42] Ibid
[43] Bridport News July 28th 1893
[44] Kelly's Directory 1895

advertised from this point. There are not even any advertisements in January 1895. Did she move the school halfway through the academic year, or was she simply winding down, and therefore did not need to advertise for new pupils? The school in Barrack Street is not advertised at all in the paper. The only references to it I can find, are a single entry in Kelly's Directory for 1895, and an end note to a lecture given by Basil Short on the Unitarian Church, and he merely mentions Mrs James' School as a reference point for the location of the Old Meeting House. It would appear that the school did not last long in Barrack Street, for after 1895 there are no further references to it.

It is quite possible that by this time, as William James' twine and net manufacturing business had expanded and become quite a major employer, Mrs James decided to retire from her own career to focus on that of her husband. By 1896 she would have been forty-seven years old and her husband fifty-five. As his works were in West Allington, he and Elizabeth moved to Magdalen Villa, 42 West Allington. His products at this time are listed as *"lawn tennis, cricket and fishing nets, lines twines and shoe threads"*. William died in 1915 but Elizabeth survived him by twelve years, living until 1927. The net firm continued to trade under the name "W. James and Co, Line and Twine Manufacturers" until at least the outbreak of World War II. The company was then merged with Bridport Gundry sometime after the war, and the only connection between the pre-war company and the present William James and Co of North Mills, which is actually a division of Edwards Industrial, is the name.

The number of private schools for middle-class girls does seem to have outnumbered schools for middle-class boys quite markedly, but this probably reflected the tendency of middle-class parents to send their boys away to school. There were, however, two notable establishments offering an education to boys. One was Henry Nobbs Cox's school of which more later. The other was run first by the Rev R Stevens, and then, from September 1872, by the Rev Henry Wall. The Rev Wall made no bones about the social strata he expected his pupils to come from. He informed readers of the Bridport News that he had taken *"the select Young Gentleman's School"* at Granville House, West Street expressly to cater for *"the Upper and Middle classes of Bridport and its vicinity"*. Granville House is the fine double-fronted town house, which now houses the Bridport Post Office. It must have offered spacious accommodation for the boys, as well as having a prominent position right on one of the main streets.

Henry Wall described himself as *"a gentleman who has passed through regular collegiate courses in Classics, Mathematics etc. and taken his BA degree"*. His wife, *"who has had considerable experience in schools of first class repute"* was to deal with *"the boarders domestic arrangements.*"[45] He was still advertising his school in 1874, but thereafter it is not mentioned. Whatever the reasons for closing his school, around 1876 he and his wife Marianne left Bridport and moved to Margate in Kent, where he seems once again to have taken up teaching. His household includes two pupils boarding with his family, as well as a young female music teacher. Dating his move to Margate has been relatively easy, as his two eldest children were both born in Bridport, but his youngest children, twins, were born in Margate.[46]

Most of the schools referred to in this chapter have faded from popular memory, or are recalled only hazily. The various buildings they occupied have long since found new owners and uses. Indeed finding them has been a painstaking process of thumbing through directories, poring over maps, consulting census returns and leafing through past copies of the Bridport News, with varying degrees of success. However, several private schools are still remembered locally, and it is these schools I want to talk about in the next two chapters.

---

[45] The Bridport News: Sept 6th 1872
[46] Margate St John Baptist, Kent: Census 1881

III

PRIVATE SEMINARIES COLLEGES AND ACADEMIES: PART TWO

Before modern developments, two buildings dominated the approach to Bridport from the East: one was the Marquis of Granby Hotel, and the other was Bridge House. (Fig 2) These two building which still stand on either side of the East Bridge, once marked the extreme outer limits of the Borough. The Marquis of Granby is now the Masonic Hall and Bridge House has been developed as a hotel, though for a good deal of its history it was in use as a school.

Bridge House was extensively rebuilt in the mid-eighteenth century by the Rev James Rooker in order to house his "Young Men's Academy", which had been founded to provide for the education of boys destined for the non-conformist ministry. James Rooker came to Bridport as the first Minister of the Independent New Meeting shortly after the split in dissenting ranks (over belief in the Trinity, particularly the Godhead of Jesus), which divided the members of the Presbyterian congregation of the Old Meeting[1] in Barrack Street. Those who stayed with the Rev Thomas Collins went on to form the Unitarian congregation in Bridport, ultimately building the New Unitarian Chapel just round the corner on East Street which opened in 1794. The remaining Presbyterian congregation, increasingly referred to as Congregationalists, built a new Independent Meeting House in Barrack Street, before, some years later, building the imposing church, now the United Church, on the south side of East Street.

The Rev Rooker was already involved in education before his arrival in Bridport, having established his academy for young men in Ottery St Mary. On his move to Bridport he transferred the school to Bridge House on the eastern edge of the town. According to Basil Short, in 1768 the *"Rev James Rooker applied to Bridport Corporation for a renewal of a lease of a decayed house on the north side of East Street where he wished to build his house and his academy for training Independent ministers".*[2] The lease was granted on condition that the house was given a *"good stone front"* and had two rooms on the ground floor on the street frontage and two stories. The house was duly completed in 1769, and the school transferred. It was

---

[1] The Old Meeting was behind No. 3 Barrack Street, and the site of the New Meeting is now the site of Bernard Gale's School of Dance. After the new Congregational Church (now the United Church) was built on the south side of East Street in 1859, with a large schoolroom attached, the New Meeting site was occupied by a Temperance Hall, later it was redeveloped as a cinema, the Lyric. The building than became a Liberal Club before being used for its current purpose. For more information on the founding of the Unitarians see Chapter VI.

[2] "A Respectable Society: 1593 - 1835" by Basil Short, Moonraker, 1976

variously known as "The Young Men's Academy" and "The Independent Academy", also "The Rev James Rooker's Academy".

The students of Rooker's Academy were the sons of poor men who needed help from the Congregational fund. Mr Rooker must have been quite a wealthy man for Bridge House is a substantial property and it was said at the time that he *"made no money out of his students; on the contrary he was probably a poorer man for the work."* [3] The property paid a church rate of 2s-6d compared with 1s for an ordinary house. After his death in 1780 Rooker's widow continued to live in the house. His daughter Martha married the Rev James Small of Axminster in 1787 and together they transferred the Academy to that town. Once at Axminster the Academy was renamed and became "The Western College", according to J Hutchins.

Bridge House was destined to become a school again in 1871, but until then it reverted to being a private house. In the early years of the nineteenth century it became the home of Dr John Hounsell, a surgeon. There is a record of a lease for the property being agreed between him and the Bailiffs and Burgesses of Bridport. It was signed on 30th September 1833. [4] The 1841 census records him, at the age of forty-five, living there with his wife Eliza and his family of three sons and four daughters, but he was certainly living in the house in 1829 when a young man called Edward Cree came to study with him as a surgeon's apprentice.

Edward Cree was the son of the Rev Robert Cree, who for a brief spell, 1828 to 1834, was Minister of the Unitarian Congregation in Bridport. He is of interest to this history because he was involved in the setting up of the Mutual Improvement Association in the 1830's (Chapter XII). The Cree family came to Bridport from Preston in Lancashire, but the Rev Cree's time in Bridport was dogged by personal tragedy. Both his wife and eldest son and daughter died within the space of a few years. It is to be hoped that his son's successful career went some way to assuage the pain of these sad events. After Edward Cree's apprenticeship with John Hounsell, he became a surgeon in the Royal Navy. In his Journal for the years 1837 - 1856, which is superbly illustrated with his own watercolours and sketches, he records a brief visit to John Hounsell, his *"dear old master"*, at Bridge House in 1846. [5] John Hounsell, by then a widower, was still living in Bridge House in 1861. [6] He died aged 77 on May 25th 1869. [7] At this juncture Bridge House once more became an educational establishment.

---

[3] Ibid
[4] Borough of Bridport Survey: BMLHC
[5] ."The Cree Journals -The Voyages of Edward Cree, Surgeon RN as related in his Private Journals 1837 - 1856" Ed. Michael Levein, Publ. Webb and Bower, Exeter 1981.
[6] Bridport Census 1861
[7] Notice of Death in Bridport News and Reporter: June 1869

Cox's Boarding and Day School

The man who took the lease of Bridge House was already running a successful school further up East Street. He was Henry Nobbs Cox from Cattistock. According to the newspaper report of his death in June 1894, Henry Nobbs Cox came to Bridport in 1849 to take over Philip Moatt's School. He had been educated in Chard and London, and, according to the newspaper, had originally intended to follow the trade of iron-founder, which is interesting in light of the ironmongery business he later set up with his son. Instead he chose teaching, and by the time he came to Bridport as a young man of twenty-two, he had already been teaching for several years, as an assistant teacher at Yeovil Grammar School and also at a school in Totton near Southampton.[8] The first official mention of Henry Nobbs Cox is in both the 1851 census and Hunts Directory of 1851. The latter describes him as running an "Academy" in Prospect Place, but this is puzzling as Moatt's Academy was in East Street. The 1851 census does not really shed any light on this confusion as it lists him simply as a young man of twenty-four years of age, lodging in Prospect Place with Levi Vicary, a retired accountant.

By 1859 however the picture is clearer. Henry Nobbs Cox is by now occupying the premises in East Street that his "Boarding and Day School" [9] occupied until he moved to Bridge House and which may well have been the site of the original Moatt's Academy. He incorporated into this school another establishment that had been run by a Mr Webster, and it is from an amalgamation of Moatt's and Webster's schools that Cox's School emerges.

Using the 1861 census to try and pinpoint the whereabouts of his school, it would appear that it was in a house five premises east of Barrack Street and four doors away from Elizabeth East's Ladies' School. The Ordnance Survey Map of 1888 shows the probable site to be a long narrow property, with a good frontage, running back from East Street, with gardens at the rear. It may well have been fairly cramped, for on the move to Bridge House he makes a point of stressing the commodiousness of his new premises. In this census return, Henry describes himself as a *"Classical, Mathematical and Numerical Schoolmaster"*, which seems quite grandiose, but gives an indication of the kind of establishment he was running.

By 1861 Henry had acquired a wife, Elizabeth. At thirty-six she was three years older than he was, and was also a teacher. For some years she

---

[8] Bridport News, Friday June 29th 1894
[9] Kelly's Directory of Dorsetshire 1859

ran a "Ladies Seminary" alongside her husband's school.[10] The 1861 census records five boarders, as well as Henry's seven-year-old son, also called Henry Nobbs, later to become an ironmonger and partner his father in the family firm of Cox and Son, Ironmongers. The boarders at this time comprised two nine-year-olds: William Baker of Bridport and Robert Waldron of Burton Bradstock, two twelve-year-olds: James Bush of Bristol and John Miller of Affpuddle, and William Dyer (15) born in Steeple Ashton in Wiltshire.

It must have been a marked step up for the school when, in 1870, a year after the death of Dr John Hounsell, Henry Cox managed to acquire the lease of the much larger premises of Bridge House for his school. The lease describes the property as a *"Dwelling house and garden, North side of East Street."* The lease is dated 9th August 1870, and was for 99 years on three lives.[11] In 1871 Henry Cox, referring to himself in the third person, announced that *"Being anxious to promote the health and comfort of his pupils, he has removed to the large and commodious house at the east entrance to the town,"* where *"the means for healthful recreation are ample, whilst the situation is quite rural and open to the picturesque scenery of the neighbourhood".* Moreover he can now boast: *"The schoolrooms, dormitories etc. are lofty, commodious and well-ventilated."* He describes his school in this notice as *"The Academy, Bridge House"*[12].

Either the school greatly expanded on this move, or the two boys' and girls' schools are listed together for there are now nine boys and two girls boarding and Henry and Elizabeth have two nieces with them: one, ten-year-old Clara Seare, is a pupil at the school and is listed as having been born in Wisconsin in the USA. The other niece, Elizabeth Vivien (17) is working as Mrs Cox's assistant. The boy boarders are Alfred Miller, Henry Morey, John Coombs, Tom Darke, Charles J Gilbert and Edward B Gilbert, Ernest Cox, and John, William and Thomas Hull. The girls are Ann Goddard and Annie Bodenham. Apart from the Gilbert boys who were both born in the St Pancras district of London, all the rest of the boarders are relatively local: Broadwindsor, Burton Bradstock, Lyme etc, and Annie Bodenham from Wayford in Somerset is the only other boarder born outside the county.[13] As boys and girls beyond infant age were not educated together at this period, it is likely that the main school was for boys, and the girls continued to be taught by Mrs Cox and her assistant in a separate part of the house.

In 1877, Henry Nobbs Cox, made a radical alteration to his school, and while remaining as principal, and with his wife continuing to supervise

---

[10] G Harrod & Co's Postal and Commercial Directory of Dorset & Wiltshire 1865
[11] Borough of Bridport Survey. BMLHC
[12] The Bridport News: January 13th 1871
[13] Bridport Census 1871

the *"domestic arrangements of the boarders"*, he engaged the services of the Rev T Worthington, the Curate-in-Charge of Chideock, as Headmaster of what from now on will be described as *"The Bridport Grammar School"*. The newly constituted Grammar School was divided into the *"Mercantile or Commercial Department"* and the *"Classical or Professional Department"*. He states his aim to recruit the sons of *"Professional Gentlemen, Manufacturers, Merchants, Farmers, and the Higher Class of Tradesmen"* by offering a *"thoroughly sound Classical and Commercial Education..... on economical terms"*.[14] The Professional Department aimed to prepare boys for University entrance and also for Civil Service examinations. The Commercial Department made sure boys were *"carefully instructed and prepared for Commercial, Mercantile, Agricultural and Nautical pursuits"*.[15]

Whether or not as a result of this change in its character, the 1881 Census shows the school drawing boarders from rather further afield. Henry and Elizabeth are still living at Bridge House and as Elizabeth Vivien is still acting as assistant schoolmistress, Mrs Cox must still have been running her school. Another niece, Louisa Whittle (14) from Gillingham has joined the school, and Clara Seare is still studying with her aunt. Her two brothers, William and George Seare, have joined the Grammar School. They are described as having been born in Christchurch where the family must have relocated after their time in America. Another assistant has been acquired: twenty-year-old Lawrence Long, and the boarders are William Gale, Robert Young, George Sprent, who was born in Calcutta, Charles Budden, born in Woolwich and Ernest Williams of Askerswell. The only girl boarders by this time are the two nieces.

There is a rather curious reference in the memoirs of a writer who calls himself Fulbrook Lane to "Cox's School" at around this period. Lane facetiously refers to Cox's scholars acquiring *"a knowledge of the secondary uses of inkwells and cucumber frames."* No doubt the reference to "inkwells" and "cucumber frames" refers to some boys breaking a cucumber frame by throwing inkwells at each other or possibly at the young Fulbrook Lane! He does not elaborate, and the reference has all the hallmarks of a private joke. He does however describe the boys' uniform, which he would see when the pupils attended the parish church on Sundays. It consisted of *"pill-box caps with the spidery monogram of the crocodile"*.[16]

In addition to his school-mastering, Henry Cox senior was very active in the local community. He was for a number of years Registrar of Births and Deaths for the Bridport District and also acted, as an insurance agent, for, among other companies, the Church of England Life and Fire. At

---

[14] The Bridport News: March 3rd 1877
[15] Dorsetshire Towns' Directory of 1874/5
[16] "Bridport in the Nineteenth Seventies and Eighties (sic)" by Fulbrook Lane publ. 1934: p19

Christmas 1884, Henry Cox finally retired from the school and was succeeded by G F Wicker. In addition to his role as the Registrar of Births and Deaths, Henry Cox was by now Vaccination Officer, and Clerk to the Burial Board. He served as a Town Councillor from 1865 to 1880, and was elected an Alderman of the Borough in 1889. He was also a JP, a Churchwarden of St Mary's, and a founder member of the Oddfellows Lodge in the town. He also helped resuscitate the Melplash Show Society.

It is possible that as early as 1885, on his retirement from the school, he may have removed to a house in Bradpole Road because the 1891 census records him as living there, while his son, Henry, with his wife Ada and their three children, has taken over Bridge House as his private residence. Henry Nobbs Cox senior lived for a further ten years after his retirement and died on 29th June 1894, after a short illness.

Once Henry Cox junior took over Bridge House, G F Whicker moved The Bridport Grammar School to No 7 Downe Street and continued to operate there well into the late 1890's, not far from where the firm of H.N.Cox and Sons was trading in East Street. The link between Bridge House and teaching was not quite extinguished however, for according to Kelly's Directory of Dorsetshire of 1911, Mrs Margaret E Cox (LRAM) and Dorothy S Cox were running *"Bridge House Boarding and Day School for Children and Young Ladies"*, in part of the house, possibly the part that Mrs Cox senior had previously used for her girls' school. It would appear that this school was quite short lived, as the Directory does not mention it again. In May 1924 Henry Nobbs Cox Junior bought Bridge House,[17] and continued to live in the house until at least 1939.

The latter years of the nineteenth century saw the establishment of a number of prestigious private boarding schools in the western end of the town. Indeed a number of schools that had their genesis in the eastern end of town chose to move west in the 1870's and 80's. In addition, the whole climate for education was changing in the latter years of the century. The curriculum was expanding and the system of public examinations, that is so much a feature of modern education, was already beginning to dictate the curriculum. The schools that were set up in the last thirty years of the nineteenth century whether for boys or girls were all much more academic in focus.

Two sisters, Hannah Evans Norton and her sister followed this route west in the late 1870's. Their *"Ladies' School with Kindergarten Class"*, established in the early 1870's at Melrose Villa, Bradpole Road, moved, in March 1877, to Chard's Mead to a house called Fairfield, and still later in January 1879, run now by Hannah Norton on her own, the "Ladies'

---

[17] Borough of Bridport Survey: BMLHC

School and Kindergarten" moved to Waterloo House, West Street. An advertisement in the Bridport News for Jan 2nd 1880 gives a rather fuller idea of the curriculum offered by Hannah Norton, who is now *"assisted by Masters".* Like Mrs James, now at Grosvenor House, and Miss Mollett in Downe Street, she had joined the competition for outside pupils and was offering *"private classes in French, dancing and callisthenics, open to a few not attending the school."* There are no further advertisements for this school, which probably suggests that the Waterloo House school closed by 1881.

Where was Waterloo House? The only House bearing that name I have been able to find is one mentioned in later rate returns, and this house appears to have been somewhere in the region of Rope Walks next to a place described as Ewins/Ewens(sic) Court.[18] As this part of Bridport has, to put it mildly, been "knocked about a bit", it is difficult to get any idea where either Ewen's Court or Waterloo House were, and to add to the confusion Miss Norton specifically gave West Street as the address for her school. However as the West Street premises largely backed onto Rope Walks, which originally ran right round the perimeter of what is now the Rope Walks Car Park, perhaps this would explain the anomaly. Wherever it was, it does look as if Waterloo House no longer exists in the modern town.

Neither sadly does another building which housed a prestigious Ladies College, but for the location of this building there is plenty of evidence. The compilers of the 1888 Ordnance Survey Map of Bridport considered a house in West Street, on the opposite side of the road to Joseph Gundry's Court Works, important enough to be marked "The College". (Fig 4) Not many establishments had this distinction. Whatever its past history, and whether or not it was the premises into which Miss Gale moved the East Street College, we can be certain that "The College" marked on the map was the building leased for her "Ladies' College" by Miss Mollett from March 1881[19].

The Ladies College, West Street

Miss Mollett and her sister had run a Ladies' School with a preparatory class for small boys in a house on the corner of Downe Street, for a number of years in the 1870's. Sometime between December 1880 and March 1881, Miss Mollett, now sole principal of the school, decided to move into the large house opposite The Court in West Street. Even before the move, she clearly had major ambitions for her school. She is already

---

[18] Valuation Lists for Bridport 1922 and 1928: BMLHC
[19] The Bridport News: March 18th 1881

running series of outreach activities open to the general public: a course of lectures on Botany conducted by a Miss K Reid, and drill sessions in the Drill Hall conducted by a Sergeant Watts.[20] There was obviously a need for better premises than those she currently occupied at No 1 Downe Street. In March 1881, she announced the start of her new term in the West Street premises, and that she will still be running a preparatory class for "little boys".[21] Her tenure of the premises did not last long however, and by the Michaelmas term of 1882 she had been succeeded at the College by "the Misses Diplock".

Like so many of the college principals in Bridport at this time the Diplock sisters were not from Bridport. Elizabeth Diplock was born in 1843, in the parish of St Mary Newington, a parish on the border between Lambeth and Southwark on the Surrey bank of the Thames. In common with her younger sister Druscilla she was clearly educated to a high enough standard to become a governess. The Diplock sisters both grew up in the London area of Lambeth/Southwark. Druscilla described her birthplace as Lambeth, while Elizabeth's two younger sisters, Adah and Eunice are also described as being born in St Mary Newington.[22]

In 1881, thirty-eight-year-old Elizabeth, was still a governess, living in Walcot in Somerset as part of the household of a Hop Merchant, William Pike. William and Matilda Pike were also Londoners, coming from Peckham, so possibly Elizabeth moved to the West Country with them. They had certainly not been long in Somerset in 1881, for their youngest child, a daughter Anna Pike was born, as were her three older brothers, in South London, variously Blackheath, Forest Hill and Lewisham. At the same date, 1881, Druscilla Diplock, aged thirty and described as an *"unemployed governess"*, was still in London, living with her uncle, William Angwin, a grocer, at 147 Caledonian Road.[23] How Elizabeth and Druscilla managed to end up in Bridport is unclear, or how two governesses, one of them unemployed in 1881, managed, by 1885, to be in a position to take over an independent college in Bridport, and in Druscilla's case to buy property, is also a puzzle.

Whatever it was that brought them to Bridport, in June 1882 they announce in the Bridport News of Friday June 16th that *"The Misses Diplock, (successors to Miss Mollett) beg to inform the Parents, Pupils and others that they will be ready to receive pupils on the re-opening of the school at the Michaelmas term"*. The advert describes the school as a "Ladies College" and sets out the terms for boarders as ranging between twenty-five and thirty guineas. References are to be sought from *"parents*

---

[20] Bridport News September 3rd 1880
[21] Bridport News March 1881
[22] Bridport Census 1891
[23] 1881 Census returns for North London and Somerset

40

of former pupils of the *Misses Diplock"*, though whether they had been running a school before coming to Bridport, or simply working as governesses is not stated. Little boys were still to be received at the school and in addition *"to the above will be added a Kindergarten Branch for children between three and seven"*. The College opened on September 11th 1882. [24]

Kelly's Directory of Dorsetshire of 1885 seems to suggest that by then Elizabeth Diplock was the sole principal of the College, but in fact the sisters' partnership was not formerly dissolved until August 1st 1889. An announcement in the Bridport News of Friday August 2nd 1889 states that *"Miss D Diplock* (is) *retiring from the school"* and adds her thanks to the inhabitants of Bridport for their *"kind support during the seven years she has been in connection with the College."*

The building occupied by the college was a fine three-storey house, number 46 West Street, the premises later taken over by Frederick and Ernest Best for their outfitting firm. Sadly the building is now no longer in existence, the site having been redeveloped as part of a supermarket. Fulbrook Lane recalls the *"affixing of a brass plate at the entrance"* which marked the opening of the school, and with rather nauseating archness, describes gazing on *"the charming train of youth which, from time to time, left its portals to seek further bloom for blushing cheeks".*[25] The College was obviously successful and well known in the area. As schools of the period went it was also quite long established, not closing until the summer of 1897. Elizabeth would by then have been in her mid-fifties.

The auction of the contents of the school was announced in the Bridport News of July 30th 1897 by the firm of Wm Morey and Sons who had received *"the favour of an instruction from Miss E Diplock (who is leaving the neighbourhood)"* to sell the contents of the school. Although Elizabeth thus announced her intention to leave the area, the Diplock sisters did retain their connection with Bridport, and continued to own property in the town. Rate returns from 1922 and 1928 connect the two sisters to the ownership of a property variously described as "Meeting House" and "Schoolroom" at No 42a West Street, which was either in, or adjoining the former College premises, and Druscilla is described as owning a house in the row of late Victorian terrace houses formerly called Belgrave Terrace in St Andrew's Road. In the 1920's the house was let to an Edith Stephens, but in 1891 Drusilla was living in Belgrave Terrace with her 7-year-old niece, Emma.

I have said that the school was a substantial one. The details of the items to be auctioned on the closure of the school detail the interior of the

---

[24] Bridport News: August 25th 1882
[25] "Bridport in the Nineteenth Seventies and Eighties (sic)" by Fulbrook Lane publ. 1934 : p20.

building which comprised hall and stairs, a dining room, presumably private judging by the furniture, and an area called "School House" which was furnished with tables, desks, stools and blackboards. The Kindergarten contained wall-pictures, maps and a piano, and in the various bedrooms were *"iron and wood single and double bedsteads",* cots, dressing tables, chests-of-drawers, washstands and toilet sets. There was also a large kitchen, a wash-house and gardens to the rear of the property.[26]

For a picture of the school itself it is necessary to go back to 1891 and the census return of that year. Elizabeth Diplock, by then forty-eight, was sole Principal. Her two unmarried sisters, Eunice (33) and Adah (30), both *"living on their own means"* were living with her. Druscilla, as indicated above, had moved to her own house in St Andrew's Road. The strong emphasis on modern language teaching in the school is evident from the fact that the two teachers were native speakers. Anna Treglar, who taught German, came from Stuttgart. She also taught Music, and Berthe Merric from Brussels, taught French. Mary Hall, who was the Kindergarten Teacher completed the list of resident teachers. There were eighteen boarders, ranging in ages from eighteen to six. A surprising number of the girls (seven out of the total of eighteen) came from Ireland, and the rest from all over the country, from as far north as Lancashire and Cheshire, as far east as Kent and as far west as Barnstaple in Devon. The only "local" students were Edith Pearce from Burton (Bradstock?) in Dorset, Agnes Park who came from Bowood, Lillie Paul from Wraxall in Dorset, and the Green sisters Florence and Adelaide who came from Bournemouth.

There were no Bridport girls boarding, though some may well have attended as day pupils. Two of the pupils were Elizabeth Diplock's nieces: Gertrude Turtle from Lewisham in Kent, and Alice Diplock from St Mary Newington in Surrey. Fashionably, the infant department is described as a "Kindergarten" but how far the influence of F. W. A. Froebel, whose kindergarten movement gained strength and popularity from the 1850's, and encouraged a child-centred style of early-years learning was evident in the organisation is unclear. The Irish connection is puzzling, but one possible explanation lies in the Pike family who employed Elizabeth as a governess Their eldest daughter, Edith was born in Newcastle, County Down in 1872, so it is possible that through the Pike family Elizabeth had kept a connection with Ireland, but as I have no evidence, this is pure conjecture on my part.

The last two decades of the nineteenth century saw a reduction in the number of private schools operating in Bridport, but those that

---

[26] The Bridport News: Friday August 13th 1897

remained were bigger in scale, and increasingly ambitious in scope, and all continued into the twentieth century. Three particularly are still remembered in Bridport, and they deserve a chapter all to themselves.

IV

THORNELOE, CONISTON AND ST HILDA'S

Most people who remember Thorneloe School will tell you that it was established in Victoria Grove towards the end of the nineteenth century, and that later the building was used by another school: St Hilda's. But the story of Thorneloe School and its founder, Mrs Elizabeth Reader, is far more intriguing, and goes a good deal further back than her final triumphant building and opening of Thorneloe House, Victoria Grove, in 1889.

Elizabeth Reader came originally from Worcester. How she arrived in Bridport I have not been able to establish. Probably she came as a governess, which was the means by which many reasonably well-educated young women in the nineteenth century moved from home, but by the late 1850's she had married a Bridport man, William J Reader, a seed merchant. His business was conducted from premises on the west side of South Street, seven premises south of the Castle Inn and three premises north of the Balaclava Inn. (At this period the Castle Inn was on the West side of South Street, probably more or less on the site of the present-day Number 44. The "Castle" building on the east side of the street, now the Museum, housed a "Working Men's Institute and Penny Bank".)

William Reader appears, described as grocer and seed factor, in the local directories from 1842.[1] From the census return of 1851 it would appear that Elizabeth was not William Reader's first wife. His wife at this time, confusingly also called Elizabeth, came from Somerset. There appear to be no children of the marriage in 1851, but by 1861 when he has remarried there is a son called Clement, who is nine-years-old, and a daughter of eight, called Hela or Helah.[2] There is also a baby daughter, Amy, who is only one-year-old. By the census return of 1871 Clement is not mentioned, and there are two more daughters, Maud and Georgia, nine and six respectively, and a son Claud, two-years-old.

It is tempting to conjecture that Clement and Helah were the children of William's first wife, who died, possibly in childbirth, which would account for the big age gap between Helah and Amy, but having so far failed to find any reference in the local parish or Presbyterian registers, I have absolutely no evidence for this, other than the fact that after 1871, neither of the elder children seems to have continued as part of the household, while Amy, Maud and Georgia become integral to Mrs Reader's

---

[1] Pigot and Co's Dorsetshire Directory 1842; Dorsetshire Towns Directory 1874
[2] The spelling varies from the 1861 Census to the 1871 Census

later educational ventures. That said, Claude also disappears from the record after 1871, so possibly he died of some childhood illness.

In neither of these census returns is Elizabeth Reader given a profession so it is clear she was not working as a teacher at this stage, though she must have been a teacher or a governess before her marriage, for when, two years later, she advertises the opening of an *"Educational Establishment for Young Ladies"* at Dorset House, she states in the advert that she is *"resuming her former profession"* .

It is difficult to ascertain exactly how old Elizabeth Reader was at this stage, for the age difference with her husband mysteriously lengthens through the various census returns. In 1861 she is listed as thirty to his forty-five. By 1871 she is only thirty seven, and by 1881 she has only managed to reach forty-two, while he has achieved the logical age of sixty-five. It is tempting to conclude that Mrs Reader, intent on concealing her real age, grew progressively younger with the passing years. Whatever her reasons, by 1873, Mrs Reader had embarked on a radical change of career, and from being a grocer's wife and mother of a large family she has decided to resume teaching and *"having engaged an experienced and accomplished lady (who holds high government certificates)"* states her intention of opening her college *"immediately after the Midsummer recess".* She advertises for *"Day Pupils with a limited number of Boarders, to educate with her daughters"* and goes on *"The superior advantage of the Government System of Education will be combined with those usually afforded in establishments for young ladies. Pupils will be prepared for the examinations connected with Oxford, Cambridge and London Universities".* At the end of the advert she lists her referees. They are an impressive bunch. Among them are The Rev E Hartland, President of the Bristol Institute, T Rowley-Hill and R Padmore both of Worcester, the Mayor of Worcester, E Wall, and the Mayor of Bridport, T Beach. At the end of the advert she announces that prospectuses are available from Mrs William Reader.[3]

By August she has settled on a name for her school: *"The Ladies Collegiate School, Dorset House",* and under this name she continues to advertise for pupils, advertisements appearing in the edition of the Bridport News for the second week in January from 1874 to 1877. There is the usual advertisement for Dorset House College in January 1878, but by this time it is likely that she had already left Bridport for Worcester, for the college no longer carries Mrs Reader's name.

Dorset House is easy to locate as it still bears the name. It is the tall double-fronted town house two doors east of the junction of East Street and

---

[3] Bridport News June 6th 1873

Barrack Street. (Fig 3) Under Mrs Reader the Dorset House College quickly became a highly regarded school. She appears to have established a tradition of holding an annual exhibition of work not long after the college was opened, for a report in the Christmas edition of the Bridport News, December 24th 1875 describes a visit to the college by a News reporter, in order to inspect the work of the pupils. While the report concerns itself mostly with needlework of varying kinds, including *"crochet, braiding and bead work"; "penmanship"* and artwork are admired, as well as *"mapping"*. The reporter states: *"A map of Europe by a young lady of 14 years of age is very commendable and a number of those of England, Scotland and Ireland, by younger scholars, have been very creditably executed, exhibiting well-nigh as accurate a knowledge of geography as those which have been done by elder scholars"*. It is clear from the report that in addition to physical geography the girls also learned French, history and botany.

The report describes the *"spacious college and recreation ground"*. As the day of the visit was *"breaking-up day"* the report ends with a description of an evening party at which the boarders presented Mrs Reader *"with a pretty little time-piece as a token of their affection"*. A list of the Prizes awarded for the term is added to the report and among the prize winners are: Miss G Reader, who is awarded an English prize, Miss M Reader who receives a certificate for English and French and a music prize, Miss A Reader gains a prize for music, specifically for theory, and Miss G Reader is awarded a medal, though it is not quite clear what this is for. Clearly, Georgia, Maud and Amy were doing well at their mother's college.

In December 1876 Mrs Reader again holds what she describes as *"the Half-Yearly exhibition of work accomplished by the young ladies of the … College"*. This time the exhibition is held in the Good Templer Hall in Barrack Street on the 12th and 13th of December and a *"variety of articles (were) offered for sale on behalf of Dr Barnado's Home for the Destitute Children of London."*[4] This is a charity that Mrs Reader went on supporting throughout the life of her school. Once again the newspaper carries an extensive report of the exhibition.

In January and March of 1877 Mrs Reader is still advertising her college, but thereafter the advertisements for the Dorset House College do not carry her name, and through the autumn of 1877 they are much more frequent, indicating an urgency about recruiting pupils. A brief advertisement appeared in the Bridport News of September 28[th,] and even one on October 5th announcing that term will commence on Oct 1st. Not at all like the efficient Mrs Reader. There is another brief advert on October

---

[4] The Bridport News: December 8th 1876

23rd, and a more detailed announcement on November 9^{lh} seems to indicate a very different Dorset House Ladies College for it goes on "*Lectures in Physiography by Mr Beard* [5] *are about to be commenced. French, German and Latin classes are also being formed. Ladies wishing to apply*" were invited to contact the principal, but there is no name, which is not Mrs Reader's style at all. It is likely that, after Mrs Reader's departure, a Miss Marston, who was possibly one of her assistant teachers, tried to carry on the school, for it is on the instruction of Miss Marston that the contents of the school are finally put up for sale in January 1881. The house is offered to let in June of the same year and full particulars of "*this commodious building, now to let, airy passages and lofty rooms 12ft high; suitable for a school or private residence*" were available from J Hoare, Grocer. (At this period, J Hoare's shops occupied premises in East Street on the corner of Barrack Street, and in West Allington, presently the location for the Allington Dental Clinic.)

It seems likely that Mrs Reader moved, with her family, to Worcester sometime in early 1877. No doubt she opened her new school, like the original one, "*immediately after the Midsummer recess*". While she may not have taken the furnishings of Dorset House to Worcester, the sewing machines, pianos and contents of eight bedrooms that were offered for sale in 1881, she clearly took some local girls with her to complete their education, for in September 1878, under the heading "Local and District News", the Bridport News announces the Oxford examination results for "*Miss A.H.C.Edwards and Miss L.M.Maund of Worcester Ladies College, Principal Mrs Reader*". Both Miss Edwards and Miss Maund appear among the prizewinners in the report of the visit to the Dorset House College by the News reporter in 1875. Indeed once established in Worcester, she is actively recruiting pupils from Bridport, for on 29th August 1879 the following advertisement appears for "The Ladies' College, Thorneloe House, Worcester".

"*Preparations for Public Examinations. Pupils passed 100 per cent in Oxford University and College of Preceptors; 95 per cent in South Kensington Science Examinations. HIGHEST REFERENCE. Next term commences Sept 10th. Prospectuses on application to the Principal, MRS READER.*" [6] (Her capitation).

What caused Elizabeth Reader to move her college to Worcester? It is conceivable that she was actually recruited back to her home town to take over an existing college in Worcester, which might account for the Dorset House establishment still trying to function once she had left. Without more research in Worcester, which I have so far not been able to

---

[5] John Beard was headmaster of the Boys' General School, located in King of Prussia Lane
[6]   The Bridport News: August 29th 1879

47

undertake, there is no way to establish this one way or the other. Whatever her reasons, however, by 1881 she was firmly established in Worcester. Living with her at The Ladies' College, Barbourne Road, were Amy, Maud and Georgia, by now twenty-one, nineteen and sixteen years old respectively. Mrs Reader gives her age as forty-two, while her husband was, by that time, a more accurate sixty-five. As he is still described as a seed merchant, it is possible he had also moved his business to Worcester. There is no mention of the older daughter Helah, or of Clement, nor of Claude, who would have been twelve. Maud is now working at the college as a teacher, while Amy and Georgia are not listed with any occupation.[7]

Like the Dorset House Ladies' College, Thorneloe House Ladies' College in Barbourne Road was clearly quite an extensive boarding establishment. It employed five resident teachers in addition to Maud. Two of the teachers, Anna White, and Harriet Edwards are probably two of her former pupils from Bridport.[8] Harriet Edwards is listed as *"Teacher of English and French"*, and the school also employed a Music Teacher, Gertrude Ellis from Essex. Boarding at the college in 1881 were fifteen scholars ranging in age from eleven to eighteen.

If the Dorset House establishment was prestigious, the Worcester College was much more so, for it occupied quite a substantial house in a fashionable part of Worcester. The 1884 Ordnance Survey map of Worcester shows a suburb of large detached houses set in extensive gardens along the Barbourne Road, which is the main road north out of Worcester. Thorneloe House stands at the corner of a square plot, flanked to the front by Barbourne Road and to the north by Thorneloe Walk. To the rear of the property is Thorneloe Road. Opposite, across the Walk is an even larger establishment, Baskerville House, and next door to Thorneloe House to the south is Thorneloe Lodge. It must have been an ideal location for a school, for the area at that time was very rural. According to the map, Thorneloe House had very large gardens, with many walks and full of trees.

The name Thorneloe, according to information kindly supplied by the Worcestershire Record Office, derives from a family, socially prominent in the area in the reign of George II, (1727-1760). There is some confusion as to whether Thorneloe House or Thorneloe Lodge next door was the site of an earlier school run by a Mrs Harris in the mid-eighteenth century. This school's main claim to fame is that the young Sarah Kemble, later famous as the tragedienne, Sarah Siddons, was a pupil in the 1760's.

---

[7] Worcester Census 1881

[8] The prizewinners in 1875 included an A.White and a A.H.C.Edwards. Harriet Edwards is listed on the 1881 census as having the initials C A. As she was born in Yeovil and Anna White in Bridport, it seems likely that these are two of Elizabeth Reader's original Dorset House pupils.

Mrs Reader's stay at Thorneloe House in Worcester was quite brief, for by 1885 she had returned to Bridport, and in January she announced

"To be opened (D.V.) January 20th
BRIDPORT HIGH SCHOOL FOR GIRLS
Principal Mrs Reader
Assisted by a competent staff of Professors.
Headmistress Miss Maund A.A., Oxford Higher Examination for Women; Advanced Science and School of Art Certificates, Continental French and German.
Prospectuses and particulars which are in preparation will be furnished when ready on application to Mrs Reader, Chideock (pro tem)" [9]

Is this the Miss Maund who had been such a successful pupil at Dorset House in 1875? Quite probably. The opening of this school however proved less than smooth, possibly because of delays in securing the premises. In the next edition of the paper, January 9th, she announces that she is to use Dresden House in Chards Mead for the school, but in the very next edition of the newspaper, she is forced to announce that the opening of the High School, scheduled for January 20th, has had to be postponed for six days. The same advertisement announces that her daughter Maude is offering private lessons in singing and painting. Like Dorset House, Dresden House is also easy to locate, for the name is still clearly visible, incised on the stonework that divides the ground and first floors of number 33 Victoria Grove. It is a three-story terrace house, and, while quite large by modern standards, it cannot have offered the same spacious accommodation as either Dorset House or Thorneloe House in Worcester.

Undaunted, however by the shortcomings of the accommodation, Mrs Reader, now assisted by her daughter Maude, gives a remarkably detailed description of what her school will offer in the announcement in the Bridport News, 4th September 1885, of the start of the autumn term:

"The School course includes Instruction in Religious Knowledge, Reading, Writing, English Language and Literature, General History, Geography, French, Latin, Arithmetic, Mathematics, Science, Needlework (Plain and Fancy), and Calisthenics."

This is clearly a grammar school education she is offering, but the moral welfare of the pupils is also a priority. There is one odd stipulation: *"No intercourse is permitted (unless sanctioned by the parents) between the Pupils out of school hours."* What on earth did that mean?

---

[9] The Bridport News: January 2nd 1885

She goes on: *"Pupils who come from a distance can dine at the School at a moderate charge. Resident Pupils will have all the comforts and care of a happy and refined home, and will be trained in such a manner as to fit them for the duties of home and society, while their characters will be moulded on true Christian Principles."* There is clearly no denominational bias at the school for *"The Place of Worship will be at the option of the Parents".* Extras offered included attending the Bridport School of Art. She concludes by stating: *"The town of Bridport is exceedingly healthy, supplied with pure water, and within half-an-hour's walk of West Bay or three minutes by rail. Every facility for bathing. Lessons in Swimming".* It is clear from the wording of this advert that it was not solely intended for the parents of Bridport girls. No doubt she was also advertising in Worcester.

On the face of it the move seems disadvantageous. Mrs Reader was probably, if one takes her age in 1861 as the correct one, in her mid-fifties, and here she is starting all over again. What was the reason for this precipitate return to Bridport barely eight years after she had left? Was it that her husband had died, and she determined to come back to the town where she had spent so much of her life? Certainly his name does not appear in the 1891, census, but then neither does hers. There is no reference either to Amy or Georgia who may well have stayed in Worcester, as it is clear that Mrs Reader still had family outside Bridport whose illnesses required her absence from the school.

Dresden House was obviously regarded as a temporary home for her school. It clearly was not large enough, for, in from the summer term of 1887, she acquired the use of the Forester's Hall to provide extra accommodation. By this time her daughter Maude had become joint principal of the school and the final name, by which the school is remembered had been settled on. It is now described as *"Bridport High School for Girls".* The Forester's Hall, now the British Legion Hall, stands virtually opposite Dresden House on the east side of Victoria Grove and as she asks that *"Pupils will please assemble at 9-30am in the Forester's Hall",* for the start of the Summer term in 1887 it is clear she is using the Hall as overflow accommodation, possibly for lessons, perhaps as an Assembly Hall, while Dresden House would continue to house the boarders and staff. [10]

This was obviously not a situation that could continue for long. Dorset House was no longer available to her. It was probably by this time already a doctor's surgery, as Dr William Clibborn occupied it from at least 1889. [11] The College, West Street, only a stone's throw from Dresden

---

[10] The Bridport News: April 15th 1887
[11] Kelly's Directory of Dorsetshire 1889, 1895, 1898 and 1903

50

House, must have loomed as serious competition. Large houses available for leasing as schools must have been in increasingly short supply, which is probably why she settled on the solution of having a house built expressly to house the school.

Though the Dresden House premises were far from ideal, Mrs Reader once more set about putting her school on the local map, just as she had done with the Dorset House College by putting on high profile events which were extensively reported in the Bridport News. At the end of only her second year of operation, the school staged a *"Matiné Musicale"* in the Drill Hall. It is reported in the Bridport News, Friday August 5th 1887. The entertainment which was to mark the occasion of the annual distribution of prizes was *"decidedly above the average of that usually …produced by schools"* according to the Bridport News reporter. As well as attracting a large audience of parents, Mrs Reader had also gathered together a party of most distinguished guests which included the clergy of all the local parishes, a large party of Colfoxes, including Miss Wansey; Mrs Templer, Mr and Mrs Nantes, Mr and Mrs Stephen Whetham, Mr and Mrs John Stephens as well as Dr Clibborn, from Dorset House, and several guests from Worcester.

The highlight of the musical entertainment performed by the girls was a dramatic presentation of a new "Cantata" entitled *"Britannia and her Daughters"*. The "daughters" in question, who had *"come across the sea to express their love and duty and to show their filial feeling"* were the various subject states of the Empire: Canada, India, Africa, Australia, New Zealand, etc., suitably represented by the girls in appropriate costumes and carrying banners. Britannia was *"seated on her throne, on either side of which floated the St George's Cross, ….with a trident in hand, with an oval shield at the foot of the throne, and surrounded by a brilliant court of nobles, soldiers and sailors &c"* .

After this highly patriotic item came a paper entitled "Domestic Economy" and written by one of the pupils. It was read out on behalf of the pupil by the Rev Edward Henslowe, Rector of St Mary's. The entertainment concluded with maypole dancing and a demonstration of callisthenic exercises *"with poles and rings"*. One interesting fact that emerges from this report is the fact that Mrs Reader was not present, as illness in the family had called her away, possibly, as I conjectured earlier, to Worcester. She sent a letter expressing her apologies and congratulating her assistants, Miss Bussell and Miss Florence Reid, on the success of their pupils in the recent examinations. It is worth quoting some of her letter at length as it gives a flavour of the period as well as an insight into Mrs Reader's motivations.

"With regard to the boarders, they have given me that love which both lends a charm, and lightens the burden of school-keeping; t'is true

some of the young ladies have not naturally that love of order, neatness, and punctuality which is necessary, but they have maintained a cheerful desire to learn and keep the rules of the house." Stating that the Cantata was *"hurriedly got up"* after the June examinations were completed she goes on to direct some advice to the parents. *"I wish to say a word with respect to holiday times. Recreation is needful for all, but let us beware of false pleasures; I refer especially to novel reading, and would caution our girls against those dreadful yellow books, which are so greedily devoured by some. The influence of most of these must decidedly be injurious to intellect and heart; for after all that can be said in favour of the higher education, it is the life-power and character we want. The education of the heart above the head, and it is the privilege of the teacher to assist the parents in so training their girls, that they may become England's true noblewomen, ever carrying with them the gracious influence of a truly cultured and christian life."* [12]

The continuity between Mrs Reader's two Bridport schools is very evident reading the report of the Matiné Musicale. As at the Dorset House Christmas exhibitions, the pupils' work was exhibited for the parents to inspect, and there was also a sale of the work specially produced by the girls in order, once more, to raise money for Dr Barnado's Homes. It is quite clear from the detail of the event, the guest list and the extensive nature of the report which takes up the best part of two columns in the Bridport News, that Mrs Reader had no intention of letting her college be outshone by the Misses Diplock, at their College in West Street.

It is quite possible that the project to build a school was already in the planning stage by 1887, and possibly the building had started on the opposite side of the road, and just to the north of the Forester's Hall. The 1888 Ordnance Survey Map, which was actually surveyed in 1887, shows an empty plot, but by 1889 the house was ready for Mrs Reader to move in, and in the course of that year she transferred the school once more to what she probably hoped would be its permanent home. That this must be regarded as a direct successor to the college that she had run in Worcester is clear from the fact that she gave the same name, Thorneloe House, to the house she built in Victoria Grove.

By the time the school moved into Thorneloe House, with its *"increased accommodation for boarders",* Katherine Charlotte Bussell had been appointed Headmistress of the school. The staff included Mr Albert Stone, Miss Champ and Miss Austen who taught music and singing, and Miss Reid LLA who taught science. Albert Stone had his own music teaching practice nearby, and must have come into the school as a visiting teacher to augment the music education. In the advert for the opening of

[12] The Bridport News: Aug5[th] 1887

the school, now in Thorneloe House, in September 1889, Mrs Reader stresses that Miss Bussell was *"formerly connected with the North London Collegiate School for Girls"*, but it is not clear whether this means that she was a pupil there, or started her teaching career there as a pupil teacher.[13]

Now known as St Hilda's after the later school, 52 Victoria Grove is a distinctive tall neo-Tudor half-timbered house that towers over its neighbours and can be seen from many points in the town. "Mates Illustrated Bridport" written by fellow college principal and close neighbour, Arthur Champ describes the premises as *"lofty, well-lighted and thoroughly ventilated"*. (Fig 6) When the school moved into Thorneloe House, Mrs Reader would have been nearly sixty. By 1895 according to Kelly's Directory, she was still resident at Thorneloe, but while her name is still mentioned alongside that of Katherine Bussell throughout the academic year 1893/4, by September of that year parents were being invited to contact Katherine Bussell to discuss their daughters' admission to the school, and by September 1895 it would appear that Mrs Reader had finally retired and transferred the school to the younger woman, for in the advertisement of the opening of the school in September 1895 Miss Bussell's name appears just under the school name, as well as at the bottom as the person to be applied to for prospectuses. By 1901, Mrs Reader, by then fully admitting to her correct age of seventy, had moved to live in South Kensington, with her daughter Maud, who had married newspaper proprietor Charles Corkran. Thus her long association with Bridport came to an end. [14]

As we have seen from the reference to her in the report of the Matiné Musical, Katherine Bussell was already teaching at the school in 1887. She must have been very young when she came to Bridport for, by 1891, she was only twenty-three. Like Miss Maund, Katherine Bussell was well-qualified, having a Teacher's Diploma validated by Cambridge University. The 1891 census lists several teachers in addition to Miss Bussell: Agnes Ann Deeley (or Deckley – the handwriting is difficult to read) was also teaching English, while Ernestine Sequard was teaching French, and Annie Thornbury was a pupil teacher. There is only one boarder listed: Marie le Conteur who was fifteen-years-old. Despite the fact that by that time she was already headmistress of the school, the census simply records Katherine Bussell as "English teacher". Her ambitions for the school are made clear in a report of the annual prizegiving in July 1893, when she states that she intends to make the school one of the most prestigious high schools in the area. This is reflected in the school's Latin

---

[13] The Bridport News: Aug 9th 1889
[14] South Kensington Census 1901

motto: *"Quanti est sapere"*, which roughly translates as "How much above price is wise discernment". [15]

She continued to run "Thorneloe School", as it was increasingly known, along the same lines as Mrs Reader. It continued to be principally a boarding school though, like Mrs Reader, Miss Bussell did take *"some outside students"*. A contemporary advert from the Bridport News of January 3rd 1896 describes the curriculum, though it principally concentrates on the extras offered in addition to the core subjects. Arthur Champ in his description of the school in Mates Guide states that *"the curriculum can be greatly varied to suit the needs of elder pupils who may desire to pay attention to such subjects as painting, languages and music."* Students at Thorneloe were entered for Oxford Local Examinations, the London Matriculation, Cambridge Higher Locals, and in Music the students sat for the examinations of the Royal Academy and Royal College Joint Board. Indeed music, under a later music teacher, Miss Bullock, seems to have been a major feature of the curriculum and the school boasted a Ladies String Orchestra, which was conducted by a Professor Beaumont.

The girls were taught drawing using a scheme called the "Ablett system of tuition". All I have been able to find out about the Ablett System is that it was a course structured in six grades, each of which was taken in succeeding years throughout the pupil's school career. At the end of the course the pupils were entered for the examinations of the Royal Society. Languages featured prominently, and conversational French and German were both offered. Miss Bussell also conducted an advanced English Literature class. Physical training, tennis and hockey were *"under the direction of a resident health mistress who also* (held) *classes for Swedish gymnastics, dancing etc."* Like Miss Diplock's College, the school also had a kindergarten. The boarding arrangements were under the supervision of Miss Esther Whetham, and given that Austen Whetham acted as Miss Bussell's lawyer, it is quite possible that there was a family connection here, though I have not been able to establish this for certain.

Katherine Bussell ran the High School successfully in Victoria Grove until early 1912/13 when she sold the "Day School Connection" to Ethel May Linstead for £59-6s, to be paid in two equal instalments, the first on January 1st 1913 and the second on 11th May of the same year. [16] In 1912 Miss Bussell transferred Thorneloe School to Connaught Road in Weymouth, but the distinctive building that still towers over all the other houses in Victoria Grove continued as a school for, as already mentioned,

---

[15] The Bridport News: July 28th 1893
[16] Deed of transfer: Austen Whetham: BMLHC.

the day school connection was transferred to Ethel Linstead who set up St Hilda's School at the same address.

Thorneloe's School continued in Weymouth under Miss Bussell until the 1920's when she was briefly succeeded by Miss Annie James, who had been her deputy from the Bridport days. On her retirement Katherine Bussell returned to Bridport and was invited by Alice Lee Colfox to live as her companion at West Mead House.[17] Alice Colfox's previous companion and friend, Phillipa Harcourt had recently died, and as, on retirement, Katherine Bussell probably had no settled home, she no doubt accepted the offer to become Miss Colfox's companion at West Mead with much gratitude. Given Alice Lee Colfox's continued interest in education right up to the time of her death, no doubt Katherine Bussell supported her in many of her activities.

The next principal of Thorneloe's, in Weymouth, was a Mrs Angell, who continued to build the school's academic reputation throughout the 1930's. Sadly, the girls' school did not survive the war being closed in 1940 *"by the military"*. However in 1947 the Connaught Road premises were re-opened, this time as a boys' school, under new owners and with a new spelling for its name; Thornlow School. The prospectus to Thornlow School acknowledges the Midlands *"origin"* of the school, stating, slightly inaccurately, that the original Thorneloc School was founded in Worcestershire in the early 1870's.[18] While the connection between The Ladies' College in Barbourne Road and a Boys' Preparatory School in Weymouth may seem a little tenuous, Mrs Reader would doubtless be pleased to have the continuity of her endeavours thus acknowledged.

Although the name Thorneloe House could no longer be used once the name had been transferred to the Weymouth establishment, the Victoria Grove house continued as a girls' school. By today's standards, it seems a highly unsuitable building for use as a school. It occupies a fairly small site on a precipitous slope, and the house itself is very tall. But then many apparently unsuitable buildings were quite successfully occupied as schools in the period up to the Second World War, and St Hilda's is remembered with affection by the girls who attended the school in the inter-war years.

St Hilda's School

St Hilda's School, as the new school was called, was established in 1913 by Miss Ethel May Linstead, who remained principal until at least

---

[17] The Colfox Papers: BMLHC: BRPMG55
[18] My thanks to John Crocker for permission to quote the above information from an e-mail sent to Bridport Museum(BMLHC). John Crocker has written and published a history of the modern school: "Oh! To Be at Thornlow".

1939.[19] Another long-serving member of staff was Miss Constance Mary Friend, the kindergarten mistress. She witnessed the document transferring the day school connection in 1913, and gave as her address Holmcroft, Chelmsford Road, Woodford NE. It is quite likely that she accompanied Miss Linstead to Bridport, but I have not been able to establish that.

She was still at the school in the late 1930's. A former pupil, recalling the kindergarten at St Hilda's between 1937 and 1940 in a short memoir, remembered that *"Miss Friend had a fluffy ginger cat called Mickey"*. Other teachers mentioned in the memoir are Miss Perkins and Miss Biles. The memoir paints a vivid picture of the kindergarten. There were *"wooden benches in the cloakroom as you entered with large black coat-hangers around the wall."* The room was furnished with wooden tables and small chairs. There were *"Orange wooden boxes with sliding lids which had mosaic shapes inside."* The children did *"finger exercises on the tables (taps etc.)"* and *"saved silver paper – folded it up and pasted it in a tall silver cardboard home-made silver-coloured box."* They also *"marched in (a) circle to Miss Friend playing the piano – 'The Soldier's March'"*. Dinner, cooked by *"Winnie"* the dinner lady, will make many a school child of that era wince with recognition. The menu was *"fish and beetroot, tapioca pudding made with water, jam and custard."* After dinner the small children lay on their backs on the school tables, presumably for an after-dinner rest.[20] By 1933 the school had about forty pupils.

Another pupil, Elizabeth Wild, who attended the school in the 1930's, described the impression the school made on her when she arrived there as a kindergarten pupil. She recalled the Kindergarten Room as being very large, with the Dining Room adjoining. On the floor above were classrooms for the older children, with a small room kept specifically for French lessons, and on the floor above that the boarders' bedrooms were situated. Pupils were not allowed to use the front door of the house, but entered through the rear door that opened onto North Street. The garden was also out-of-bounds, used only for school photographs. Discipline was reasonably strict and Elizabeth Wild recalled one form of punishment used with the small girls in the Kindergarten. Apparently the offending pupil had to stand on a box in a corner of the room until the Mistress *"felt you had repented sufficiently"*.[21]

As the garden was out-of-bounds and school grounds were non-existent, most of the physical education took place indoors, and consisted largely of gymnastics, cartwheels, handstands, and other activities using some formal apparatus. The girls also learnt country dancing with Molly

---

[19] Kelly's Directory of Dorsetshire: 1939
[20] Handwritten notes by Sally Trevett: BMLHC
[21] Taped interview with Elizabeth Wild for the Dorset Schooldays Project: BMLHC (BMS/Sch/01)

Perkins. In the summer they were "crocodiled" up Victoria Grove to the tennis courts in Pymore Road, but Elizabeth Wild does not recall any other outdoor games being played. The uniform was a brown beret with the school badge, a brown gymslip and white blouse, and in the summer the girls wore panama hats. At age eleven the girls could sit the scholarship exam for the Grammar School. Like Thorneloe School in Weymouth, it seems that St Hilda's did not survive the Second World War. The school closed round about 1943.

Coniston School

The development of Coniston School so exactly mirrors that of Thorneloe that it is difficult not to conclude that Arthur Champ and Mrs Reader offered one another some assistance in developing their two schools. Coniston House is on the opposite side of Victoria Grove and a little to the north of Thorneloe House. (Fig 5) It, too, is an impressively large house, and was built expressly to accommodate Arthur Champ's school. Moreover both houses were completed and opened in the same year: 1889.

The coincidence doesn't end there. Like Mrs Reader, Arthur Champ had started his school in temporary quarters, and once again in the same year, opening just six months earlier than the Dresden House school, on 20th January 1885, in East Street.[22] In his announcement in the Bridport News, he states that he intends opening *"a Junior School for boys at which the usual branches of English Education will be taught, with Music, Drawing and other extra subjects if desired. Terms (moderate)"* were available on application. Four years later he moved his school to Coniston House, and the school continued on the same site until 1909 when, on the opening of the new Bridport Secondary School in St Andrew's Road, he joined the staff of that school as Art and Woodwork Master. Coniston House then became, for a time, the recognised boys' boarding house for the new school. Arthur Champ continued to live at Coniston House into the 1920's.

In the 1891 census, two years after the new school opened, the occupants of Coniston House are listed as Arthur Champ and Ada Louise, his wife, also boarding at the house was an assistant master, Hubert Davies, and one seven-year-old boarder William Ernest Hannam, born in Liverpool, as well as two servants. The Champs' two daughters are not mentioned in the census.

In a school prospectus Arthur Champ describes his school as being *"planned with a view to the health and comfort of the boarders. The rooms*

---

[22] The Bridport News:16th Jan. 1885

are lofty and well-ventilated and the boarders are provided with single beds" [23] The fact that he felt this worthy of mention leads to some speculation as to the sort of sleeping arrangements boarders usually had to endure!

The playground, in a contemporary photograph described as the "drill ground", was in the garden behind the house sloping down to the fields that border the river Brit. It is a pleasant spot, and today little changed. The ground drops away quite steeply from the back of the house. A long sloping garden gives way to two small fields divided by a stone wall. The River Brit runs through the lower of the two fields, and on the opposite bank the students would have been able to see the long winding-sheds of North Mills, and dominating the whole view, the wooded slopes of Allington Hill. Pleasant though it is, the garden at Coniston seems singularly limited as school grounds. Once again it is on a slope, though not so extreme a slope as Thorneloe/St Hilda's had to contend with. The school aimed to give "a sound commercial education"[24] and the curriculum included "French, book-keeping, shorthand, and commercial arithmetic". Mr Champ went on to add that a "satisfactory feature in an agricultural district like West Dorset is the instruction in land surveying".

Arthur Champ was an accomplished artist. He describes himself as having had "considerable experience under the Government Science and Art Department". A number of his paintings are in the possession of Bridport Museum, including two views of the town in oils, as well as a number of watercolour sketches of local rural scenes. It is therefore no surprise that he put a considerable emphasis on instructing his pupils in drawing and painting, covering oil painting and water-colour, as well as perspective. He asserts that a number of his pupils were successful in the South Kensington examinations. Pupils were also entered for the usual range of examinations, Cambridge "locals", Royal College and Royal Academy Associated Board music exams, College of Preceptors examinations as well as Pitman Shorthand.

Like Thorneloe's, music seems to have been a feature of the school and, according to the prospectus, Coniston had a "string band". The pupils had the opportunity to learn piano, violin, clarinet and cello as well as taking singing lessons and learning music theory. In addition to resident teachers there were also those who came in to teach various specialist subjects. There was an emphasis on physical drill, Indian club exercises etc., and the pupils also played football and cricket, and "sea-bathing (was) under the direct superintendence" of Mr Champ himself. In addition to teaching his boys, Mr Champ also held a Ladies' Painting and Drawing Class on

---

[23] Prospectus for Coniston School : BMLHC
[24] The Bridport News: Friday January 3rd 1896

58

Wednesday afternoons. As a practising artist he was a worthy predecessor at the Secondary, later Grammar School to that other well-known local artist and teacher, Francis Tighe.

Coniston schoolboys had to wear a uniform cap displaying the school badge. Fees were from twenty-seven guineas per annum for full boarders to four guineas for day students. The usual tally of extras added to the cost, with Drawing and Painting, Piano and Violin lessons, German and Latin, as well as Drilling, Football and Cricket featuring as extras. The variation in the cost of these various subjects probably reflected the fees charged by the visiting teachers: German for example cost three guineas per annum while Latin only cost £1 11s 6d. Drilling, Cricket and Football at 7s 6d, and Drawing and Painting at one guinea were relatively cheap, probably because Mr Champ taught these himself. But like the German tutor, the music teacher must have been quite expensive as the boys had to pay three guineas per annum for his services.

The prospectus requested parents that each boarder must be provided with *"a knife, spoon, two forks, serviette and ring, and towels"*, as well as *"money for Sunday offertory"*. Mrs Champ supervised the *"household arrangements for the boarders."* In addition to his paintings, Arthur Champ has also left to posterity a small but very useful guide to the town: "Mates Illustrated Bridport" of 1903 which he wrote and designed, and which has been invaluable for providing some of the information used on these pages.

It does seem that Victoria Grove was a positive hive of educational activity in the years before and after the turn of the twentieth century. In addition to Coniston and Thorneloe, there was Miss Brown's School, Highfield. Described as being at 53 Victoria Street[25] it not entirely clear where it was located. Today No 53 is on the opposite side of the road to Thorneloe House but census returns for 1881 and 1891 place Miss Brown as living two premises to the north of the Catholic presbytery. This would put Highfield almost next-door to Thorneloe House, and on the same side of the road.

The first mention of Emma Frances Brown's school I could find is in G Harrod & Co's Postal and Commercial Directory of Dorset & Wiltshire of 1865. It is described as a Ladies Seminary and located in Chards Mead.[26] In the 1881 census, aged fifty-five, she is described as *"Schoolmistress for Preparatory School For Boys and Girls"*, while the 1891 census simply describes her as a *"private schoolmistress"* and adds the fact that her niece Hannah Brown was living with her at this time. No pupils

---

[25]The Bridport News: Friday January 3rd 1896
[26] Chards Mead was the original name used for the street sometimes called Queen Street, or Victoria Street and occasionally Victoria Road, which ultimately became Victoria Grove.

are recorded in either census return, and it is likely that her school was a day school, not a boarding establishment.

She advertised for pupils fairly regularly in the Bridport News through the 1870's, 80's and 90's; an advert appearing in the same edition of the paper in which Mrs Reader announced the opening of her High School in 1885. But the Directories are actually misleading, as the Dorsetshire Directory of 1874/5 only lists her as a private resident in Queen Street and the Kelly's Directories of 1880 -1895 also list her solely as a private resident living at 53 Victoria Grove. Why she chose not to advertise her school in these editions of the Directory is not clear. Kelly's Directories of 1898 and 1903 do list her school, but by this time she would have been in her late seventies, so it is not exactly surprising that by 1911 all reference to her school has disappeared. I have so far been unable to find out any details about her school, but it must have been successful to have lasted as long as it did. Indeed, if the references are to be relied on she was running her private school for close on forty years.

To add to the ferment of intellectual activity in this part of town, the Rev John P Wills, of Holmleigh, Victoria Road, advertised himself as taking *"pupils for General Education"*.[27] Indeed Victoria Grove, for a few years at the end of the nineteenth century and the beginning of the twentieth must have seemed like an extended campus, as in addition to all the private schools, there were also music teachers as well as the Roman Catholic elementary school and the Sisters of the Visitation boarding school. These last will be dealt with in a later chapter.

---

[27] Bridport News: Friday January 3rd 1896

V

SOUTHAYES, THE GROVE SCHOOL AND ST RONAN'S

In detailing the history of schools, it is difficult to find a neat dividing point between the late nineteenth century and the early years of the twentieth, as many of the schools that educated the middle-class boys and girls of Bridport had their genesis in the later nineteenth, but developed well into the twentieth. Of most of these later schools we know quite a lot, but the first school I will mention in this chapter is a bit of a puzzle.

In the Bridport News, January 4th 1895 a school, describing itself as *"The Grove, Bridport, Ladies School"* suddenly appears on the scene, advertising for pupils. The advert states that it is being run by *"The Misses Carey"*, and offers boarding places and places for a limited number of day pupils. It seems to have been quite an academic establishment offering London Matriculation exams, and Oxford Senior exams as well as qualifications validated by South Kensington College (Arts and Science) and "Trin. Coll. French, Paris,. Brussells, Vevey". By September 1896 only one Miss Carey is listed as the Principal, but this seems to have been the school's last year as by September 1897 the school has ceased to advertise itself. Unfortunately the advert gives no address and I can find no reference in any of the Directories to this Grove School, or to the Misses Carey.

The Grove, still so named, is a large square Georgian house on the north side of Rax Lane, near the junction with Downe Street. It currently houses the Bridport offices of Social Services. According to the census return of 1891, Grove House in Rax Lane was occupied as a private residence by the widow, seventy-four-year-old Harriet Templer, who was a member of the rope and net making Hounsell family. Part of the house was occupied by her brother, William Hounsell. By the 1901 census the Grove is unoccupied, and Harriet Templer and her brother, William Hounsell, now in their eighties, have moved into the larger Mountfield House close by. Was the house used for a short while as a school in the mid-1890's? If so? where did the school go? More research is needed to answer this mystery. There is also the possibility that this Grove School had nothing to do with Grove House in Rax Lane. There was also a Grove Ironworks on the western perimeter of the town, and on the 1888 Ordnance Survey map of the town, the street adjoining Rope Walks is also named as The Grove, so it is possible that the school was located elsewhere.

Whatever the nature and duration, and even the location of the earlier school, a completely different Grove School occupied the Rax Lane building many years later from 1938. There is no connection other than the name between these two "Grove" Schools. The second "Grove School"

61

was originally called Southayes School, and was renamed on the move into the larger premises.

Southayes School was established in West Bay Road, probably in 1932, by Miss F Violet Thwaites who was the daughter of a former vicar of Bothenhampton. Dating the school is a process of deduction. The 1931 Kelly's Directory does not mentions it, but there is a photograph taken in 1932 showing the children with Miss Thwaites grouped on the front lawn of the house. Kelly's Directory of 1935, misleadingly, describes the school, as being at No 51 West Bay Road, but this address does not exist and details in the photograph suggests it was in fact number 50. This house had already been used as a school by Miss Evelyn W Brown. Her Boys' and Girls' Day School occupied 50 West Bay Road in 1923,[1] according to Kelly's Directory of Dorsetshire, but that school seems to have been of quite short duration as so far I have found no other mention of it. However it seems likely that Southayes was set up a few years later in the same house.

The West Bay Road premises, now a private house, is one of a group of late Georgian Houses, originally known as Portville, built on the southern approach to Bridport by the Galpin brothers around about 1837.[2] It is a large detached house. There are gardens front and rear, and at that time there would have been relatively little traffic on the narrow road to the coast. There would also have been fields on the opposite side of the road and orchards and fields to the rear of the house. It must have seemed a pleasantly rural site for a school.

Southayes School offered an impressive curriculum for such a small school, and seems to have employed three other teachers in addition to Miss Thwaites. There was a kindergarten for the youngest students. The subjects taught in the school included Scripture, English, which comprised reading, writing, grammar, dictation, and recitation, Arithmetic, History, Geography, Nature Study, French, Handwork, Class Singing, Folk Dancing, Drawing and Painting, Drill and Gymnastics, Physiography (Physical Geography), General Knowledge and Science. An impressive list![3]

The photograph already referred to, dated 1932, a copy of which is in the local history collection of Bridport Museum, shows the staff and pupils seated on the lawn at the front of the West Bay Road house. There are twenty-one pupils, boys and girls, in the photograph, though as most of the boys seem very young, probably the school only took boys till a

---

[1] Kelly's Dirctory of Dorsetshire 1923
[2] "Bridport Burgh and Borough 878AD- 1974 AD : A Short History" by Richard Hindson printed by the author 1999, p91
[3] Notes on Southayes School including the photograph referred to on p1 : BMLHC.

maximum of nine years of age before they went on to Preparatory School. Certainly this was the case onoc the school relocated to the Grove.

In January 1938, control of Southayes School was taken over by Miss Ruth E M Crook, who came to Bridport from Shrewsbury. By then the numbers had declined to ten. The previous year, she had purchased The Grove in Rax Lane from Physician and Surgeon, Dr Allan Pimm, and she moved the existing ten pupils there early in 1938. By December, possibly reflecting the attractions of the much larger building, the numbers had grown to twenty-seven.

Re-established in the centre of town The Grove School flourished. A prospectus published during Miss Crook's time as principal describes the aims of the school being *"to provide such education as will give the pupils wide and sensible interests and such training in habits of religion and self-discipline as will fit them to take their places both at home and in a wider sphere as good and useful citizens."* To that end Guides, Brownies and Wolf Cubs were run in connection with the school.

The Grove School was a Parents' National Educational Union School, and as such was part of a progressive movement in education founded by Charlotte Mason, and centred on her College in Ambleside, Cumberland. It was at Ambleside that Ruth Crook had obtained her teaching certificate, and she was clearly trained in the methods developed by Charlotte Mason. It is possible that Southayes School was already a PNEU school when she took it over, but it is more likely that it was Ruth Crook who introduced the methods of teaching and learning which identify such schools.

Charlotte Mason was a pioneer in educational theory and methodology, but is surprisingly little known by comparison with other pioneers such as Pestalozzi, Montessori or Dewey. She founded the Parents' National Educational Union in 1887, and in 1892, with only three or four students, she set up a college in the Lake District which she called the House of Education, in order to train teachers in her methods. At first the course was only of one year's duration, but later it was extended to two years.

Charlotte Mason was born in 1842 at Bangor, near Liverpool, the only child of a Liverpool merchant. She was educated by her parents until her mother's early death when Charlotte was only sixteen. At eighteen she went to the Home and Colonial School Society teacher training college in London. This college was dedicated to advancing the methods of Pestalozzi,[4] the Swiss education reformer. These influences, and her own

---

[4] Johann Heinrich Pestalozzi 1746-1827, follower of Rousseau in believing that education should centre on the individual child, and that the best education was given by parents of exceptional ability and character and therefore schooling should do its best to emulate these conditions

experience as headmistress of an Infant School and later of a High School for Girls, as well as her travels induced by periods of ill-health, helped to form the ideas that she put into practice in her later work at Ambleside. She believed that all children should be treated as individuals. She advocated the widest possible curriculum, taught in a way that made learning exciting, to encourage all children to become self-motivated. She believed children should strive for excellence in every aspect of their lives, both at school and at home, and in games as well as academic pursuits. Kindness to others, tolerance, conscientiousness and good sportsmanship were all encouraged. Above all things, Charlotte Mason believed that learning could and should be fun.

She encouraged parents to be actively involved in the schooling of their children, believing that such co-operation and team-work would benefit the child. She was a pioneer in the use of distance learning to support anyone involved in educating children, be they teachers operating in schools, or governesses, or parents attempting to educate their children at home, through correspondence materials. She also wrote textbooks, which were used in schools following her methods, notably a scheme for teaching geography called "The Ambleside Geography Books".

Some of her ideas sound remarkably modern, and indeed schools using her methods are still in existence today. She believed above all in the importance of narration as the main focus of learning. This consisted of a child reporting back, orally or in written form, what had been learnt, or read in a session. Charlotte Mason demonstrated that children could, by attentive listening, acquire an almost total verbal recall of what they had heard or read. She had no doubt that this discipline had a valuable effect in developing the skills and confidence of young learners. In her method, she stressed that teachers should not talk at children, but with them. She felt that it was for the teacher to offer sympathetic support to learning, occasionally clarifying or enlarging on some point, but the actual work should be done by the scholars. In her view teachers should teach less.

She believed that children should become accustomed to reading good quality books. Even those regarded as adult reading could be enjoyed by children, in her view, and her system encouraged a very broad teaching scheme and included such things as the study of great pictures, a feature often remembered with great affection by those who used her home education materials. Above all, she believed that parents had to be involved in their children's education, for in her view a child cannot have two loyalties, so parents and teachers must be partners in a common task.

Her books: "Home Education", "School Education", "Parents and Children", and "Ourselves" set out her educational ideas and programmes of study.[5]

As in all the other PNEU schools, the pupils at The Grove were tested through papers set by the Ambleside College. The syllabus offered differed little from Southayes School but added Latin, Citizenship, Picture Study and Architecture, in line with Charlotte Mason's ideas. Physical recreations offered included netball, tennis and cricket. Fees ranged from 35 guineas a term for full-time boarders over 12-years-old, to 3 guineas for children under 6-years-old, who attended only in the mornings. Dancing, Music, Elocution, Swimming and Riding were extras.

By 1940 Miss Muriel Lorton had taken over as joint principal with Miss M E Moore, a Cambridge Natural Science Bachelor of Arts graduate, who, according to the school prospectus, had come to the school from teaching Biology at Sherborne College. Miss Lorton, who was originally a kindergarten teacher lists as her qualifications: Arts and Crafts, Physical Culture, Domestic Subjects, Needlework, Dress-making and Millinery. Once again the breadth of curriculum suggested is a feature worthy of remark.

By 1940 the fees for boarders had been reduced to £30 per term, possibly reflecting the difficulties of wartime conditions.[6] The school survived the war but in 1947, Ruth Crook who still owned the building, sold it to Joseph Gundry and Co Ltd, and the school was forced to move once again. Still under its joint principals Miss Lorton and Miss Moore, the school moved, only a matter of a hundred metres or so, to the much larger building of Mountfield, which Miss Lorton rented.[7] An advert for the Grove School dating from the period after the move to Mountfield describes the school's high academic as well as practical aims for their pupils. The advert stresses that *"opportunity is given for girls to specialise in Art and Music, Domestic Science, and to prepare for Entrance and Scholarship Examinations, and Secretarial Careers."*[8] The school still catered for boarding and day pupils, taking girls from five to eighteen, junior boys and nursery pupils from three to five.

A brief memoir of the Grove School by Jennifer Jennings (née Aldridge) who attended the school from 1947 just after the school had moved to Mountfield gives a picture of life at the school.[9] At that time there were about fifty pupils at the school which also provided a nursery school

---

[5] The information comes from "The Work and Aims of the Parents' Union School" by Miss O'Farrell, The Parents' Review, November 1922 (v33 no 11 pps 777-787). Also from "Charlotte Mason" by Aimee R Natal published on the internet by Infed.
[6] School Prospectus for 1940: BMLHC
[7] Mountfield now houses the Town Council Offices. The information about the ownership of the Grove and Mountfield comes from a survey of "Property in Bridport owned by West Dorset District Council": BMLHC
[9] Information drawn from unpublished notes by Jennifer Jennings: BMLHC

for children from three-years-old. As at Southayes, boys were admitted, but only until they were about nine. (Fig 7) The school catered for boarders and day pupils. Jennifer Jennings recalls seven teachers in addition to Miss Lorton. Miss Howe taught science but left the school in 1949. Miss Page taught history and Mrs Kup(p) who had returned to the school from South America after her husband's death, having taught there previously under her maiden-name of Miss Mingis was also on the staff as was Miss Lorton's father, who taught PE. There was also a Miss Dines and Miss Margaret Hine. Interestingly she does not mention Miss Moore, who had perhaps left by the time Mrs Jennings was a senior pupil and is therefore omitted from her memoir.

Mrs Jennings remembers swimming lessons at West Bay when the pupils learned to swim by the tried-and-tested Bridport method of being *"dangled from a belt into the water"*. As the school had no science laboratories, Miss Howe restricted herself to Natural History and Botany, and Mrs Jennings recalls the silk worms she kept in her classroom for the pupils to study. For Games and PE the students had to walk down to St Mary's Playing Fields. Boarders were not exactly waited on hand and foot. They were expected to set the tables and serve the food at mealtimes, and then wash up afterwards!

It was probably in 1953 that Miss Lorton was once again forced to move her school, as Mountfield was about to be sold to the Bridport Rural District Council for use as Council Offices. It would appear that she was offered alternative accommodation at Battlecombe House in East Road, as this was already owned by the Bridport Town Council. Mountfield was sold to the Rural District Council by its then owner in 1954, by which time The Grove School was, yet again, operating from new premises.

Here I must digress for a few paragraphs, for Battlecombe House has a story of its own. It was originally built as the Dower House for The Hyde Estate in Walditch, home of the Gundry family. By 1935 it was being run as a boarding house by a Miss E Light, though by 1939 it is described as a Guest House.[10] During The Second World War, it was taken over by the Evacuation Committee of the Bridport Borough Council, and run as an evacuation nursery. In 1945 Dorset County Council acquired control of the nursery, taking out a twenty-one year lease on the building from the Bridport Town Council. The nursery was run under the aegis of the Public Assistance Committee and was known as Battlecombe Residential Nursery. There was an unsuccessful attempt in 1947 to change the name to "The Cottage" as some members of the Public Assistance Committee felt

---

[10] Kelly's Directory of Dorsetshire: 1935 and 1939

the name "Battlecombe" had unduly belligerent overtones. However no decision was made and the name remained.

The Nursery was supposed to cater for twenty orphan children, boys and girls, up to the age of five, though the number rarely seems to have risen above sixteen or seventeen. It was run by a succession of Matrons, none of whom seem to have stayed very long.[11] While it is recalled locally as a school, any instruction given to the children was probably quite limited. As the years passed and presumably the children grew up, the upper age of the orphans seems to have reached around twelve-years-old. One former pupil of St Mary's School recalls a girl of about twelve, from Battlecombe, joining her Guide Troop, and certainly some of the older children attended the General School. One entry in the General School Log, from the late 1940's, records an incident where one clearly very distressed little girl tried to run away when her class were returning to the school after a PT lesson in the Drill Hall. There is an unconfirmed story that some of the children were sent to Canada when the Home closed, but I have not been able to verify this.

The children clearly elicited the sympathy of the local population, for many local people gave gifts of toys and clothing. The girls of the General School donated soft toys and books, and St Ronan's Brownies knitted a blanket for use by the orphanage. Ruth Hounsell, who was a child in Bridport in the 1940's remembers toys being collected at a special Toy Service at the Chards Mead Baptist Chapel for the children at the orphanage. The building was in a poor state of repair when it was taken over for the nursery, and much money had to be expended in repairs. Dry rot was discovered in four of the wooden floors in 1948, and these had to be replaced.

The County Council must have decided to close the Nursery in 1952/3, taking the option to terminate the lease after only seven years. The building then reverted to the Town Council who no doubt looked for a new use for the building. It is quite likely that Miss Lorton then took over the lease, for the building and grounds seem to have remained in Local Authority possession until they was acquired by the Hanover Housing Association, for retirement accommodation.

Battlecombe House gives the appearance of being two houses attached back to back. The Asker Mead frontage is stone and Tudor in style, while the East Road frontage, which is strictly speaking the back of the house, is painted white and is much plainer. The main entrance is from the narrow lane known as Asker Mead. There were two staircases when the house was used as a school: an elegant main flight in the front of the

---

[11] DCC Public Assistance Committee Minutes 1945-1948: DHC/ DC/A/17/1 /4.

house, and the former servants' stairs to the rear. Miss Lorton and Mrs Kup(p) who was still teaching at the school in the late 1950's, lived in the main house, which also provided pleasant well-lit classrooms on two floors for the pupils. (Fig 9) There were lawns to the front, and the house was surrounded by a walled garden.

Flanking Asker Mead was a large coach house and stable block, now private housing. Miss Lorton "converted" this block to provide a large open space for indoor games and exercise, though the fact that the names of the horses that had once stalled there could still be discerned painted on the walls, suggests a none-too-radical conversion. This room was also used for the performance of the plays the pupils put on from time to time. (Fig 8) The loft above the stables was converted into a flat, which provided some accommodation for teachers. According to Elizabeth Gale (née Buckler) who taught at the school from 1954 to 1958, Miss Lorton was particularly keen on drama, often taking a part in the plays herself, and on one occasion the school put on a full-scale production of "She Stoops to Conquer" which, because of the scale of the production, was performed in the Methodist Chapel in South Street.

Once the school had moved from Mountfield, the age range, particularly of the boarders, narrowed to an upper age of about eleven or twelve though there were still some senior day pupils into the early 1950's. Small boys were still taken until about the age of seven. (Fig 10) The reduction in numbers was inevitable as there was simply not as much accommodation at Battlecombe as there had been at Mountfield. The uniform the children wore was principally grey: grey skirts with white blouses for the girls, and grey shorts for the boys. The tie was grey with a pale blue and yellow stripe. In winter the children wore grey overcoats, and the uniform also included grey blazers with the school badge on the breast pocket, and velour hats for the girls. The school, which continued as a PNEU school throughout the post-war years, finally closed in 1959, when Miss Lorton retired. She continued to live in the house as a private resident. The site was divided when St Ronan's Primary School moved there from St Andrew's Road in 1962, and the stable-block was further converted into classrooms for use by the new school.

It is quite appropriate to follow the story of The Grove School by that of St Ronan's, which followed the Grove into the former stable-block at Asker Mead. A private primary, St Ronan's was founded in 1928/9 by Mrs Edith Telford. The choice of St Ronan as the saint the school was dedicated to may be explained by the fact that both Mrs Telford and her husband, "Tommy" Telford who taught Latin at the Grammar School, were Scots, having been students at Edinburgh University before migrating south.[12] The school was originally based in their house, No 7 Sparacre Gardens. An interesting, if entirely coincidental connection with an earlier era in Bridport education is the fact that the last two mistresses of Miss Gundry's Infant School, Miss Rose Travers and Miss Rose Dade lived, in their retirement, in a property in the close vicinity of Sparacre House.

Number 7 Sparacre Gardens is a relatively small semi-detached house and cannot have provided very spacious accommodation for pupils. The school soon moved to the one-roomed annex alongside St Andrew's Church in the summer of 1931, then, when Mr and Mrs Telford moved to Westlands in Crock Lane in 1933, the school occupied an elevated site in the gardens to the rear of the house. Westlands is a very large semi-detached Victorian house built in 1886. It was already converted into flats by 1933 and Mr and Mrs Telford occupied the lower flat. The gardens to the rear rise steeply up the slope of Bottom Hill, and the school building was in a converted croquet and garden store which was a large wooden building adjoining the croquet lawn perched at the very top of the garden. Extant photographs of the pupils show a line of pine trees, some of which are still there lining the lower edge of the croquet lawn and a bank of rough grass and then a field on the upper side. This whole area has been developed and the site of the school no longer exists.

While the children had the croquet lawn to play on at Westlands, there was no area large enough to accommodate games and so once a week the pupils would walk down to the Bridport Cricket Ground at Brewery Fields, now the site of the Bridport Leisure Centre, for cricket lesson with the club professional. A former pupil of the school, Mrs Pam Puley, seen in the photograph (Fig 11) under her maiden-name, Pamela Briant, recalls: *"We used to walk right down Crock Lane to the gate* (now the Pasture Way turning)*, across the field to the railway line, cross the line, then across more fields to a gate opposite the Brewery, and so to the Cricket Ground. It was quite a long way but we didn't seem to mind. I expect we were glad to be out in the air."*

In 1938, Mrs Telford moved the school to purpose-built premises at the back of the house she and her husband built in St Andrew's Road. St Ronan's House (170 St Andrew's Road) is set a little back from the house line and had, before the present garden wall was built, quite a large parking area outside. The school building was at the back of the premises approached by a drive to the north of the house and was quite secluded. Pupils also had the use of the extensive grounds that led down to the railway line. In the summer, when the field was mown for games, passing trains added to the entertainment. Beyond were fields and ultimately the

---

[12] Probably St Ronan of Iona, a celtic monk of the 8th Century, the patron saint of the Scots' Border town of Innerleithen. Legend has it that he founded the town and brought Christianity to that area. Innerleithen is about twenty miles south of Edinburgh.

River Asker and Happy Island. At the edge of the playing fields Mr Telford kept his goats and hens, and the animal population was completed by the Telford's cats and dogs. A photograph shown to me by Pam Puley, taken in July 1942 of the pupils and teachers lined up outside the building shows a light airy wooden building with a range of doors flung open to the air, many windows, and a steeply pitched roof. There are fifty-eight boys and girls in the picture, and three teachers including Mrs Telford. Here the school continued until Mrs Telford's retirement in 1962. I have been unable to find out whether the name St Ronan's was attached to the school before the move to 170 St Andrew's Road, as most references to it before this time simply refer to "Mrs Telford's School".

In 1962 it looked as if the school would have to close, but a parents' group was formed to ensure its continuity, and in 1963 it transferred to what was to be its final location: the old stable and coach house buildings at Battlecombe House. St Ronan's also acquired a relatively narrow rectangular site, consisting of part of the former gardens of Battlecombe House. Miss Lorton continued to live in the old house for some years after St Ronan's occupied the western half of the site.

Miss Lacey was appointed headmistress of St Ronan's on the school re-opening at Asker Mead, and on her retirement she was succeeded by Mrs Crawley in 1975 and subsequently by Mrs Owen. The school buildings were greatly updated and improved in 1981. The Primary School finally closed in 1997. The Nursery class of the school continues, however, in the relocated St Ronan's Pre-School based in the old Girls' General School building in King Street.

A school prospectus gives an insight into the organisation of the school in its latter years. It catered for children from thirty months to three years old in its Nursery Class, which operated in the mornings from 8-55am to 12pm. The main school took children from five-eleven years old. The fees for the school in 1983 ranged from £130 per term for the Nursery class to between £220 and £230 per term for the main school. School dinners were an extra £2-55p per week. The school uniform was royal blue. The badge was a shield with the emblem of the thistle in blue.

The main school was divided into three classes: Infants, Juniors and Seniors. The curriculum was much as in the state Primary Schools with the Infants concentrating on reading, writing, comprehension and number work, with the addition of creative play and music. To these basics were added project work, art and handwork in the Junior Class, and the Seniors commenced French, elementary science, and their mathematics was extended to include basic geometry. They also started "computer understanding". Seniors were also expected to take on greater

70

responsibility both for supervising younger children at certain times and in assisting the teachers by carrying out "specific organizational tasks"[10]

St Ronan's battled on into the 1990's but eventually declining numbers forced it to close in 1997. With it a chapter in the educational history of the town also came to an end. It was the last of a long and distinguished line of private schools that operated in the town from the late eighteenth century, gaining particular momentum in the 19th and early 20th centuries, but all now gone. The only private establishments in the town today cater for pre-school and nursery education.

Even though relatively little time has elapsed since St Ronan's closed, all trace of the school at the various sites I have described has gone. For a while in the 1980's the old school building behind St Ronan's House in St Andrew's Road was used for Yoga classes. At that time the house belonged to the novelist Tom Sharpe, who lived there with his family. Recently however the whole site to the right and behind the house has been redeveloped for housing. No trace of the old school building remains, and the only clue to its existence is the name of the main house: St Ronan's House, and a few neglected apple trees struggling against the encroaching overgrowth.

Battlecombe House is now part of a development of sheltered retirement flats, renamed Hanover Court, and the old stables that once housed the school have also been converted to private housing. The name Battlecombe is all but forgotten, and the term-time hustle and bustle of the St Ronan's children, dressed in their distinctive royal blue uniforms, arriving and leaving each morning and afternoon, is a rapidly fading memory.

---

[13] Prospectus for St Ronan's School 1983: Local History File: Bridport Reference Library.

VI

THE EDUCATION OF THE POOR LABOURING CLASSES:
SUNDAY AND INFANT SCHOOLS

While educational provision for the middle-classes was well-established by the late eighteenth and early nineteenth centuries, the education of working class children, or the "*children of the poor labouring classes*" as they were generally called at the time, was largely neglected. In 1818 Parliament was sufficiently concerned about the inadequate provision of education for the poorer classes to appoint a Select Committee to enquire into the Education of the Poor. This enquiry, which covered the whole country, listed three charity schools in Bridport at this time: educating respectively twelve boys, five boys and twelve children (which probably meant infants of both sexes). There was also a Boys' School, a Girls' School and a CE and Non-conformist Sunday School.[1] The precise identity of these schools is not given. It is possible that one of the charity schools identified is the Daniel Taylor School. The boys' school could well be the Matthew Anstis' school and possibly the infant school is the one that became Miss Gundry's. However it is significant that in common with many parishes throughout the country Bridport too had already begun to address the education of the poor by setting up Sunday Schools. The two mentioned in the report would be St Mary's and the Unitarian Sunday Schools.

The first organised movements to begin to teach the children of the labouring poor had to take into account the fact that most children worked from a young age. Sunday was the only day when such instruction could reliably take place. In Bridport, between the late eighteenth and the mid-nineteenth century, Sunday-schoolrooms were added to all the churches and chapels in the town. Soon after, the attempt was made to encourage some of these Sunday schools to extend into daily schools, and in many cases night schools were set up to accommodate children who had to work during the day.

The Sunday School movement began nationally in the 1780's with the work of Robert Raikes, an evangelical churchman and editor of the Gloucester Journal who launched the movement. In 1783 he published his experience of Sunday work with street urchins and the movement was quickly taken up by Methodists, evangelicals and later the churches in general. The purpose of Sunday schools was simple: to teach children to read the Bible and "*to train up the lower classes in habits of industry and*

---

[1] Quoted in "Development of Elementary Education in Dorset from the Early Nineteenth Century to 1870" by WFE Gibbs: DHC/D:372(091)

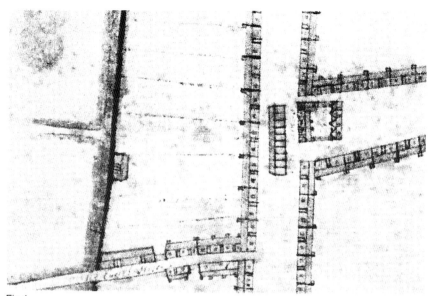

Fig 1
Detail from the earliest surviving map of Bridport, drawn before 1786, rotated east-west, showing the junction of South Street, and East and West Streets. The long narrow rectangular building is the Market House or "Shambles", probable location of the first Bridport Grammar School. St Andrew's Chapel stands on the site of present Town Hall.

Fig 2
Bridport from the East Bridge 1893. Bridge House seen on the right of the picture: originally The Rev Rooker's Young Men's Academy, later Cox's Grammar School

Fig 3
East Street in the 1890's. Grosvenor House is second house on the left of picture. Tall
building also on the left, with chimneys visible is Dorset House. Both housed schools.

Fig 4
West Street looking towards the Town Hall, late 19th century. The tall building on the right of
the picture with the imposing doorway and windows is The Ladies' College run by the Diplock
sisters. It is tempting to conjecture that the young ladies in their pinafores might be some of
the pupils.

Fig 5
Coniston House in Victoria Grove, originally Coniston School run by Arthur Champ.

Fig 6
Thorneloe House, Victoria Grove.
The site of Mrs Reader's
Thorneloe School and later St
Hilda's School.

Fig 7
The Natural Climbing Frame in the grounds of the Grove School at Mountfield. 1945/6.
Third, fourth and fifth from left: Josephine Leaker, Roger Davies and Andrew Payne.

Fig 8
Grove School play, December 8th 1955, in the former stable block at Battlecombe.
Miss Muriel Lorton (Headmistress) is seen at the back dressed as a witch.
(L-R) Front: Paul Coomber (standing soldier) / - / Frances Leaker / - / Gillian Dommett, June
Ward (kneeling centre, white dress) / - / Gillian Baker (kneeling, wearing bonnet) / - / Ann
Burden?, Jenny Fenwick / - / Jenny Coleman. Second row : Susan Palmer, Shirley Cooper/ - /
Alex Marshall, Carole Bush, Elaine Hudson, / - / - / - / - / Tim Coomber (soldier right).
Third row : Sharon? / - / - / - / Anne Palmer. Fourth row: Brian Baker (white knight), David
Perry, Jenny Cox / - /, Patricia Fenwick, Patsy Russell, Louise ?, Roger Legg / - / Ruth
Broomfield, Elizabeth Bruce?, Sharon Bell , Jill Osborne, Wendy Fraser / - /. Back row :
Carol Hayball, / - / Christine Barnes, Susanna Brooks, Beverley Lenthall, Gillian Smith.

Fig 9:
Miss Buckler's Class, The Grove School at Battlecombe House in 1955.
(L to R) Front: Patsy Russell, June Ward, Jenny Fenwick. Centre: Anita Hargreaves, Alex Marshall. By the window: Elaine ? ; Back: Roger Legg, Carole Bush.

Fig 10
The Grove School summer entertainment 1960. Group outside the main door at Battlecombe House. Anthony Broad is back row, fourth from left.

Fig 11
St Ronan's School at Westlands, Crock Lane. (L-R) Back row: Dutch student, Howard Abbott Sheila Hine / - / Geoffrey Hider, Mrs Telford / - / John Fowler, Tony Bishop.
Middle Row: David Hine, Hugh Armstrong, Pamela Briant, Jennifer Ford, Ron Cornick, John Hawkins, Peter Castle, Stanley Hetherington, Roger Moon.
Front Row: Keith Abbott, Edward Briant, Peter Knight, Margaret Crawford, Ivan Coram, Hugh Lambert.

Fig 12
Miss Gundry's School, West Street, showing the mill leat enclosing the small schoolyard.

Fig 13
The fire that destroyed Miss Gundry's School in 1906 has just broken out. Smoke can be seen coming from the roof of the building. The site is now a car park.

Fig 14
Unitarian Church outing showing Miss Rose Travers and Miss Rose Dade in the foreground. Both were headteachers in succession at Miss Gundry's School. Miss Dade was the mistress when the school burnt down.

Fig 15

Miss Harriet Crabbe, photographed in 1906 at
the age of ninety-six, at which time she was still
the lady superintendent of the Bridport Unitarian
Girls' Sunday School. She had been associated
with the School, first as a pupil and then a
teacher for ninety years.
The Unitarian Sunday School was established in
1787

Fig 16
Digitally enhanced sketch of the building in North Allington that housed the Industrial Branch of the General Girls' School. Later it became St Thomas's Cottage Hospital.

Fig 17
The Staff of St Mary's School, Gundry Lane around 1900, showing the Boys' School headmaster, Henry Saloway, seated in the centre. The teacher to his left is Annie Stickland, head of the Infants, the teacher sitting to his right is probably Mary Maud Reed, Girls' School headmistress, and on her right could be Clarissa Rendell.

Fig 18
Infants' class at St Mary's 1918/19. George Flack is second from the left, back row

Fig 19
St Mary's Infants' Department, Class 2, in one of their classrooms, probably in 1921/22.
George Flack is in the front desk on the left, pen poised.

Fig 20
St Mary's Boys' School in about 1926/27. Probably showing Standard Six with senior boys (Standard Seven) outside the Boys' School with their headmaster, Henry Saloway. George Flack is seated in the front row second from left; fourth from left is William John Fowler.

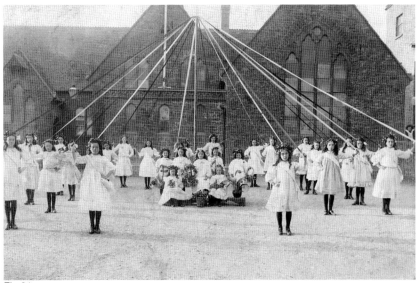

Fig 21
St Mary's Girls' School May Day celebrations, showing the May Queen in the centre with her attendants. Probably around 1906.

Fig 22
St Mary's School May Day celebrations in St Mary's Rectory garden, in about 1937. The May Queen is Sheila Coombs, seen centre with her attendants. Also in the photograph are Wendy Little, and June Flack seen at the back with her head turned.

Fig 23
St Mary's Football Team,1956/7. Winners of the Bridport Primary Schools' Football Competition. (L-R) Back Row: Mr Bond and Mr Roy Pethen (Headmaster).
Middle Row: Michael Hughes, Alan Graham, Desmond Stebbings, Colin Poole, Robert Stoodley, Melvin Scadding Front Row: Brian Thompson, Malcolm West, Stuart Hobbs, David Hunt, Stuart Tattershall.

Fig 24
Alliington School football team 1925/6.
(L-R) Back Row: Mr Theodore Walker (Headmaster), H Corrick, A Gale, ? Hussey, Jack Burt, Fred Record, Mrs Rosa Walker.
Front Row: Albert or Roger Pinket(t), Reg Harp, Albert David Spiller, Frank Roberts, Len Oxenbury, H Haines.

Fig 25
Bothenhampton School Treat 1914 – probably in the Rectory garden.

Fig 26
The Boys' Boarding School of the Visitation Convent in Pymore Road in the 1950's. Reverend Mother Agatha-Christine, is seated centre and standing at the back is Sister Magdalen.

Fig 27
St Catherine's School Netball Team 1976: winners of the Small Schools' League
Back Row: Miss Eleanor Ackroyd, Judith Clapp, Hannah White, Laura Knott, Sarah Light and Mrs Cynthia Coatsworth.
Front Row: Sarah Montague, Elaine Brown, Emma Waring, Teresa Hansford, Maureen Day

piety" (Hannah Moore). Hannah Moore of Somerset was an early champion of education for the poor. With her sister she opened a Sunday School in Cheddar in the face of much local opposition as she believed that the ability to read was essential for a Christian society.[2] Incidentally, while championing the teaching of reading, Hannah nevertheless considered writing an unnecessary accomplishment for the poor: a view widely held at the time. In a time of widespread child labour, Sunday-schools provided a first opportunity of some rudimentary education for the children of the poor, and despite their religious objectives, a comparison with today's Sunday-schools is simply misleading.

In Bridport, the first Sunday School to be set up was the Presbyterian Sunday School attached to the Old Meeting House at the rear of what is now No 3 Barrack Street. Exactly when the Sunday School was set up is not known, but in all probability it was sometime in the mid-eighteenth century. As soon as the "New Meeting" (Unitarians) built their Chapel and the Independent Meeting, now the Congregational Church erected their church in East Street, both made it a priority to install purpose-built schoolrooms. Here it is appropriate to tell the story in more detail of one of those Sunday Schools which grew to include a grammar school, and continued to play a significant part in the education of Bridport children well into the twentieth century.

The Unitarian Sunday School and Grammar School

In 1672 John Golding obtained a licence for a Presbyterian Meeting House probably in premises to the rear of No. 3 Barrack Street according to Hutchins' map of Bridport dated 1770. This was known as "The Meeting", later the "Old Meeting". Despite the general prejudice against non-conformist congregations, The Meeting thrived until the 1740's when a crisis hit the congregation. Some members of the congregation began to suspect that their current minister, the Rev Thomas Collins, held less than orthodox views on the Godhead of Jesus, and the doctrine of the Trinity. On being openly questioned on the matter he admitted his "Unitarian" beliefs and in the resulting controversy the congregation was split between those who agreed with his beliefs and those who did not. After the two congregations went their separate ways in 1742, the "Unitarians" acquired the site of The Crown Inn on the north side of East Street, where they built the New Unitarian Chapel which was opened in March 1794.[3]

---

[2] "A Social History of Education in England" by John Lawson and Harold Silver 1873
[3] Information drawn from "A Respectable Society: 1593 - 1835" by Basil Short. Moonraker 1976 pp34-35 and "Bridport Unitarian: The Chapel in the Garden": a leaflet produced for the Unitarian Chapel written by Alfred G Munden, quoting the historical notes by Rev G. Randall-Jones

Like the "Old Meeting", the new Unitarian Chapel had a Sunday School. The benches where the children and teachers used to sit during service can still be seen today in the Chapel gallery. There is a teacher's pew and, fronted by an iron balustrade, seating for the boys on one side and girls on the other. Given how little the Chapel has changed since its building, it is easy to imagine the children crammed onto the hard wooden benches high above the congregation. According to Alfred Munden, the school met in the gallery of the Chapel. However the Sunday School Minute Books and the Treasurer's Report for the year ending March 1841 which cites an annual rent for the Sunday Schools of £4, suggests that, while the children sat in the gallery of the Chapel to attended service as part of the Sunday School routine, this was not where they were taught their lessons.

In a paper by Thomas Alfred Colfox on the "History of the Bridport Unitarian Congregation" which he read at the celebrations of the Chapel Centenary on March 9th 1894, he asserts that the early Sunday School was *"carried on for some time first in a cottage in King of Prussia Lane and later in a house in Rax Lane."* He goes on: *"I am unable to say when this school first started, but as our respected friend, Miss Crabb(e), tells me that she went to it 76 years ago, and has remained in it* (the Girls' Sunday School) *as a scholar and teacher ever since, that brings it back to the year 1818".*[4] In fact according to Hutchins the Unitarian Sunday School was established in November 1787, and Harriet Crabbe continued to serve as Lady Superintendent of the Girls' Sunday School into her late nineties, and if her memory is to be trusted, probably started as a pupil of the school in 1806. (Fig 15)

Probably the Rax Lane premises only catered for the girls for, in his Annual Report for 1840/41, Rev Samuel Wood describes the Boys' School accommodation as *"lacking a well-aired and convenient room"*[5] and it is also clear from the reports that the Boys' School and the Girls' School operated quite independently. Also in Rev Maclellan's account of the opening ceremony for the new Schoolrooms, he describes the teachers and children as gathering in *"The New Schoolrooms",* while the members of the congregation present as guests *"were entertained.... in that* (room) *appropriated on Sundays to the Girls."*[6] Furthermore, morning school broke for service at 10-25am, which suggests that time had to be allowed for the children to move from their classrooms to the Chapel.

---

[4] History of the Bridport Unitarian Congregation". A paper by TA Colfox, read at the celebrations of the Chapel's centenary, March 9th 1894: DHC/NU.1:Co1/1)
[5] "Unitarian Matters" by Basil Short, an unpublished MS in the BMLHC: Part 3 " Samuel Wood and the Sunday School", quoting from the Sunday School Minute Books.
[6] Ibid

Whatever the exact location of the Sunday School classes in these early years, in 1841, encouraged by the inexhaustible Samuel Wood, the congregation managed to raise enough money to erect new Sunday Schoolrooms at the back of the chapel. These were opened on 18th November 1841.

Samuel Wood served the Unitarian Chapel as minister from July 1840 to June 1841. He came to Bridport fresh from a tour of the major cities of the eastern seaboard of the United States: New York, Philadelphia and Washington. The purpose of his tour was to visit and study Sunday School provision in America across a range of denominations. This tour built on the work he had already undertaken in London. He had long been a strong advocate of a national system of education available to all classes. He did not believe in compulsion, but he did believe in state funding. While he was minister of a Unitarian congregation in Newington Green in London, he played an active part in the Sunday Schools' Association, which was set up in London in 1834. Also in 1834, in his capacity as secretary of a British School in Harp Alley just off Fleet Street, he was called to give evidence before a Select Committee of the House of Commons which was enquiring into "the present state of Education of the People in England, and into the application and effects of the grant made in the last session of Parliament for the creation of school-houses, and to consider the expediency of further grants in aid of Education".[7] This Parliamentary grant had been a mere £20,000. By 1839 the Parliamentary grant, as a result of the enquiry, had been increased to £30,000.[8]

When Samuel Wood arrived in Bridport in June 1840, the Unitarian congregation must have wondered what had hit them. He wasted no time in launching into his programme of reform. He was already presiding over the Quarterly Meeting of Teachers of the Boys' Sunday School on June 7th, at least three weeks before he officially took up his ministry on the first Sunday in July. He set out what he considered to be the defects of the school at that initial meeting, and immediately proposed improvements. One can only guess at the reaction of the teachers and officials. Among other things he asked for and got an agreement that the school be connected to the Sunday Schools Association in London.

The meetings followed thick and fast. On July 12th Samuel Wood held a further meeting of all the teachers to press forward his improvements. By the time of this meeting he had already taken an inventory of the book stock. The list, which covered a total of 534 books across 22 titles, gives us a glimpse of the kind of instruction the children were given. It included the First and Second Lesson Books produced by

---

[7] Christian Reformer 1835 pp 18ff,91ff quoted in "Unitarian Matters" by Basil Short
[8] "Education for a New Society" by Ernest Green quoted in "Education in England" by W.K.Richmond [Penguin 1945] P68

the Sunday School Book Society, copies of Isaac Watts Hymns for Children, as well as a few copies of Johnson's Dictionary, and a copy of Robinson Crusoe by Daniel Defoe. The aim of the stock-take was to upgrade the book stock, and he duly proposed the exchange of some of the books with the Sunday School Union for ones he preferred the school to use. One of the exchanges was Carpenter's Catechism and Watt's Hymns for a set of Bible Stories compiled by Samuel Wood himself. This last was arranged with the publisher and copyright holder of the Bible Stories, a Mr Smallfield. Wood was careful to stress that he would not benefit financially. He was also careful to add that he could purchase the books at a discount.

At this meeting, a sub-committee was appointed and given the task of drawing up a new list of Rules for the school and a plan for a new schoolroom. The sub-committee was to meet on Friday July 17th, but when they got to the meeting they discovered that Wood, impatient as ever, had not only already dispatched 186 books to London for exchange, but had single-handedly produced a rough draft of the new Rules for the schools as well as a plan for the new schoolroom. The reaction of the committee members can well be imagined! Perhaps to mollify the committee Wood proposed that both items should be submitted for discussion at a further meeting the following Sunday.

The speed with which Wood drove through his plans cannot have pleased everyone, particularly perhaps Joseph Hounsell who seems to have been a key figure in the Sunday School at the time of Wood's arrival. He was Secretary of the Boys' School at the time of the first minute in the 1840 Minute Book, but seems to have been rapidly supplanted by Wood. At the meeting of 12th July, Wood acted as secretary in Joseph Hounsell's absence and by September 20[th,] when the New Rules were adopted, he had replaced Joseph Hounsell as secretary of the Boys' School and also of the committees of both schools. Joseph Hounsell was however appointed Treasurer, a role he filled until 1854.[9]

The proposed rules and the plans for a new schoolroom were approved by two Teacher's meetings for final consideration at the General Meeting of the Chapel on Sunday, September 20th, but money was going to be a problem. By September, the total sum raised was only £186 15s 6d with a further £15 promised. This was far short of the £300 or so that was needed. However, instead of moderating his plans, Samuel Wood now proposed a further enlargement of his scheme. He now wished to build the Sunday School, not on the small plot behind the Chapel, but on land on the

---

[9] "Unitarian Matters" by Basil Short, an unpublished MS in the BMLHC: Part 3 " Samuel Wood and the Sunday School", quoting from the Sunday School Minute Books and the Christian Reformer. This Minute Book was started in 1840, probably also due to the influence of Samuel Wood.

other side of Rax Lane behind the Seven Stars Hotel in Barrack Street. He had apparently already made enquiries, and the plot of land measuring 30ft by 57ft could be purchased for £60.

On September 20th the General Meeting of the Chapel was held. This adopted the New Rules, which included one forbidding children from bringing *"any fruits, sweetmeats or playthings"* into school, and laying out a stipulation that any child missing school for three successive Sundays would be deemed to have left the school. The New Rules also dealt with the duties of committees, officers, and teachers as well as scholars. The outline plan for the new school building was also given general approval together with a resolution to solicit further subscriptions to the building fund. At a further meeting only three days later, at which a plan drawn up by Samuel Wood for a building on the land in Rax Lane was submitted, it was agreed to approach *"Mr Wallace, the architect"* to see about specifications and estimates "if the charge be not considerable".

At the time of all these deliberations the superintendent of the Boys' School was a Mr Old and of the Girls' School, a Miss Slade. The Boys' School consisted of five classes, and no doubt the Girls' School had a similar number, though they had fewer teachers. Under the previous system the Sunday School superintendent, the "Master" as he was called, had not necessarily been a teacher, but had often been a cross between a disciplinarian and a caretaker, responsible for the accommodation rented for the school. Under Wood's Rules the Master and Mistress were definitely to be teachers, and as, after the new schoolrooms were opened, Mr Old was given notice, it is possible that he had not indeed been a teacher. In the year to March 1841 the annual stipends were £2 10s for Mr Old and half that amount for Miss Slade.

Negotiations over the new building went on for several months. The estimate for the school on the land behind the Seven Stars was £377, but Wood estimated that the total cost of setting up the school would come to about £450. By January 1841 the subscriptions had only raised just over half this amount: £243 2s 6d. It was therefore decided to revert to the original plan and build instead on land behind the Chapel. A meeting in April 1841 heard that this could be done for £331 10s.

The building of the Schoolrooms proceeded through the spring, summer and autumn of 1841 without any further mention of them appearing in the Minute Book and they were formally opened on November 18th 1841, at a final cost of £360. By this time, however, Samuel Wood was no longer the minister. His term of office had come to an end in June 1841. Reading between the lines, his tenure had not been a happy experience for either party. Either he was not asked to renew his appointment, or he chose not to continue. The fact that he was not present at the opening ceremony, nor was his part in the building of the Schoolrooms mentioned, according to extant accounts of the event, suggests the former.

A letter written by Wood to Joseph Hounsell, who was once again acting as Boys' Sunday School Secretary, contains the following rather puzzling sentence: *"it is my sincere wish that the Congregation may find a Minister who will serve them more faithfully and zealously than I have done."*[10] A lack of zeal does not, on the face of it, appear to have been one of his failings. Perhaps he was being ironic. It is clear that the vestry had already proposed inviting another Minister, the Rev R. E. B. Maclellan to become pastor at their meeting in May 1841, more than a month before the end of Samuel Wood's term of appointment.

The opening ceremony for the new schoolrooms, held on the evening of Tuesday, November 18th 1841, consisted of a Social Tea Meeting. All the children attending the Sunday Schools (over one hundred) their teachers and members of the Unitarian Congregation were invited. The "Tea" was held in the new Schoolrooms, which were decorated for the occasions with flowers and evergreens, and in the former Girls' Schoolroom. Afterwards everyone went into the Chapel to be joined by townspeople of various denominations who swelled the gathering to between four and five hundred. Mr Gollop of Strode Manor took the chair at this gathering, and there were various addresses, given by a number of visiting ministers from neighbouring congregations. The proceedings closed with a prayer and blessing from the new minister, the Rev Maclellan.[11]

So what was the Sunday School like both before and after Samuel Wood's ministry? The following information is taken from Wood's Annual Report for the year of his ministry, presented to the Annual General Meeting of teachers and subscribers on Sunday March 7th 1841. This report makes clear that the Sunday School was more than simply a school to teach children the tenets of their religion, though that clearly took up a good deal of their time. One of the important tasks it had to address was to teach the children to read, though not to write, hence the desire to set up an Evening School to fill that gap. The school operated on Sundays, from 9 o'clock in the morning until probably about 5 o'clock in the afternoon. The morning started with lessons from 9-00am until 10-25am, followed by Chapel service. After lunch, for which the children went home, they reassembled in their classes at 2-30pm. At 4-00pm all assembled for the General Lesson, and the afternoon ended with singing and prayers. A long

---

[10] Letter quoted in "Unitarian Matters" by Basil Short, Part 3 " Samuel Wood and the Sunday School". Unpublished MS: BMLHC
[11] An account of the opening by R.E.B.Maclellan quoted in "Unitarian Matters" by Basil Short, : Part 3 "Samuel Wood and the Sunday School". Unpublished MS: BMLHC. Rev Maclellan incorrectly dates the opening as 16th November.

day, when one considers that for many of the children it might be their only day off work.

One class of older girls were already attending an additional Evening School, probably on Wednesday evenings, but the report indicates that, once the new schoolrooms were opened, the Committee were keen to extend this to more of the scholars so they could learn writing and arithmetic, *"as there is a great want of a good week-day school for the poor in this town".* [12] The only one at this point was the embryo National School in Gundry Lane, but as that was Church of England, it would hardly have suited a Unitarian congregation, and it is not clear from the sparse records of this school whether it had as yet itself become more than a Sunday School.

Homework was set, mostly learning hymns and spellings, and a number of reading books were employed, including "Wood's Bible Stories". The highest class of girls had completed a reading of "Wood's Scripture Geography" and were at the time of the report engaged on Gallaudet's "Youth's Book of Natural Theology", of which more in the next paragraph. Wood had also introduced to the school a lesson called the General Lesson. This he had learned about on his tour of America. It consisted of an illustrated lesson given to the whole school. An account of what this could consist of appears in the report.

"The same lesson (from "Youth's Natural Theology") *is also read by the Secretary* (Wood) *to the greater part of both schools assembled together at the close of the afternoon, and being illustrated by Cheselden's large folio plates of the Bones, it has excited much interest, and will, it is hoped, leave deep and distinct impressions on the minds of the children of the wisdom and greatness of the First Cause."* [13]

This book, which was illustrated with dialogues between a mother and her son Robert, and was further illustrated visually with numerous engravings, was written by Thomas Hopkins Gallaudet, an American clergyman whose work, no doubt, Wood came across while in America. It aimed at explaining God through natural science: anatomy, human and animal, insects, fish, plants, birds. The accompanying engravings included an elephant, bones of the human arm, a Venus fly-trap and also an illustration of the sign language alphabet for the deaf. (Gallaudet went on to make his name in pioneering work with deaf-mutes. His sons continued his work, and today an American University for the deaf carries the family name.)[14]

Also in the General Lessons conducted during the year, Wood had covered Scriptural Geography illustrated by Chambers' large map of the

---

[12] "Unitarian Matters" by Basil Short, Part 3 " Samuel Wood and the Sunday School". BMLHC
[13] Ibid
[14] Information from Edited Appleton's Encyclopedia. http. famousamericans.net

Holy Land. He was a strong advocate of the use of visual stimuli, and to that end had encouraged members of the congregation to subscribe to the purchase of Roake and Varty's series of forty coloured lithographic prints of subjects taken from the New and Old Testaments. *"It has been delightful to witness,"* he wrote, *"the pleasure which these have afforded both to the younger and older children; and it is hoped that they will serve to impress deeply on their tender minds some of the leading events of sacred history."*[15] In many ways, although Wood used pictures rather than objects as stimuli, his General Lesson was not a million miles away from the Object Lessons that would be a staple of the later elementary schools.

Attendance at the Sunday Schools was carefully recorded. As with the later daily schools, punctuality and attendance were always an issue, and not just with the scholars - some of the teachers had also been irregular attenders over the severe winter of 1840/41. Wood admitted in his report that the cold weather, coupled with the fact that a number of the boys lacked suitable winter clothing, was a major cause of the problems. It was suggested that a Clothing and Provident Society for the Boys' School be set up so they could save towards new clothes, to be bought at the end of the academic year, which in those days fell in March. Apparently there was already one operating in the Girls' School. Ultimately a Provident Society was formed to serve both schools, open to all who were in regular attendance and the weekly contributions of not less than one penny were paid into the Bridport Savings Bank on the children's behalf. At the end of each year a bonus of one penny was added to each whole shilling according to the Society records, and the money thus raised was to be spent buying the children suitable clothing.

In the return to the Sunday Schools Association for 1840, activities connected to the Girls' School are listed as: *"Library, General Geography class; Writing and Arithmetic"* (presumably all taught at the Evening School) as well as *"Provident Society and Benevolent Society"*. The roll at the time of this report was forty-eight boy pupils and fourteen male teachers, and fifty-one girls with eleven female teachers. There is a sting at the end of the report, which might also have contributed to the Rev Wood's unpopularity. Due to his expenditure on new books and the printing costs for 500 copies of the New Rules, the combined Sunday Schools were in arrears to the tune of £4 6s 3d. The combined cost of books and stationery, and printing totalled £7 11s 4½d. Rather defiantly Rev Wood writes: *"The Committee have endeavoured to avoid any unnecessary expenditure, but they are decidedly of the opinion, that no school can flourish, unless it be provided with good books and other school apparatus."*[16] Two other reports: the

---

[15] "Unitarian Matters" by Basil Short, Part 3 " Samuel Wood and the Sunday School". BMLHC.
[16] Ibid

Treasurer's for the same period, and the Boys' Superintendent's Report to November 1840 also add information. Somehow despite the deficit caused by expenditure on books and equipment, Joseph Hounsell managed to balance the books, perhaps partly by the proceeds from a fund-raising "Tea" held on January 6th 1841, which raised £3 9s.

The Sunday School continued to thrive and in 1843, Thomas Colfox joined the ranks of Sunday School teachers. The Evening Classes continued to expand. Monday Evening Classes open to both boys and girls were devoted to writing and arithmetic *"and other branches of secular education"*[17]. The hope was still that this venture would be the precursor to a fully-fledged day school. In addition both the teachers of the Boys' and Girls' Schools met separately on several Mondays on the month for *"mutual improvement"*, possibly the first example of in-service training I have come across! It is possible that the boys' attendance at evening school was not good, for in 1845 there is a proposal to introduce writing and arithmetic into the Sunday afternoon curriculum, altering the timing of afternoon school to accommodate this. Another attempt at evening school seems to have been made in 1846 when a class for teaching Geography was proposed, girls being allowed to attend as long as they were accompanied by one of the female teachers!

The Sunday School records for 1851 also give a pleasant glimpse of the annual Sunday School Treat. That year, and probably most years, the destination was Eype. Though it is quite possible that on earlier treats the children walked the mile-and-a-half to Eype across the fields, by 1851 they were being transported by waggon. In all it cost £5 5s 7d mostly to cover the hire of waggons and turnpike costs, as well as food and fuel for the picnic tea. The route was doubtless via West Road through the turnpike gates at the Toll House opposite West Mead. Sunday School treats took place in late July. The Treat tea was quite possibly the only time some of the children had the chance to eat cake, which was supplied for many years by Uriah Allen and Isaac Way.[18]

The "Inquirer" of 2nd August 1845 leaves us an even more detailed account of one special July treat to celebrate the passing of the Dissenters' Chapel Bill through Parliament when the minister with about thirty teachers and one hundred children *"proceeded to that romantic and very attractive spot* (Eype) *early in the afternoon, where they found that a large Marquee had been erected for their convenience, and that many members of the congregation of all ranks, ages and sexes were scattered over the cliffs and hollows in picturesque groups, at their own several gypsy tea parties"*. The children were accompanied by nearly three hundred adult chapel members

---

[17] "Unitarian Matters" by Basil Short: Part 4: quoting the Sunday School Minute Book: BMLHC.
[18] Ibid.

and friends and, as the organist had managed to assemble a brass band by persuading several members of the Bridport Musical Society to join them, there was music for dancing.

"*The music in the open air, among the rocks, and by the sea, was peculiarly attractive*", the account continues. "*Many of the youth present passed pleasant times in dancing Quadrilles and the good old 'Sir Roger de Coverly'. So akin in a Unitarian's heart are cheerfulness and devotion, that it seemed not harsh to the same parties, after sunset, standing up with uncovered heads, to sing together the Evening hymn.*" [19]

The Sunday Schoolrooms built in 1841 went on being used throughout the nineteenth century and into the twentieth. Later in 1890, on a garden area next to the Chapel, a further extension to house a Boys' Day School was built on the east side of the Chapel and alterations were made to the Sunday Schoolrooms. A careful scrutiny of the Rax Lane elevation of the present building shows evidence of two doorways, now partially walled up and housing windows. One clearly gave access to the Sunday Schoolrooms and the other to the Grammar School. At some point the current door, which gives access to, both must have been opened up, and suggests that, at some point after the building of the Grammar School, it absorbed the former Sunday School accommodation. This enlarged facility took Secondary and Grammar School pupils until the establishment of Colfox School in 1956, when the school closed.

The Unitarian Sunday Schoolrooms and later the Unitarian Grammar School premises were much borrowed by other educational establishments: by the General School, for example when they were having a new floor laid; by the Winter School run by the Bridport General Girls' School. A number of former General School pupils recall having domestic science lessons in the Unitarian Grammar School, where I am reliably informed, the sinks used for the purpose can still be seen. The Bridport Secondary School actually started its life in borrowed accommodation in the Unitarian Schoolrooms and they housed the Pupil Teacher Centre until the new Secondary School was built, and during WWII, the rooms were once again used for domestic science lessons by Bridport Grammar School girls, when their own cookery room had been requisitioned as a school canteen.

Sadly now their original purpose is just a distant memory. The various schoolrooms are presently rented by the Bridport Operatic and Dramatic Society as a costume store (the old Grammar Schoolrooms), and Bridport Pantomime Players as a scenery store (Sunday Schoolrooms). The lower classrooms are used by the Unitarian Chapel as a bookstore and

---

[19] DHC/ NU.1:SC1/1

overflow coffee-room. However as little has changed in the actual fabric of the building, it takes very little imagination to see it as it was. The old Sunday Schoolrooms are still divided by the wooden partition. The same high windows let in light, placed just high enough so that the children could not see out and lose concentration. The combined entrance to the various schoolrooms seems little changed, even the pegs for coats and hats are still there, and it is easy to imagine the children's feet clattering up and down the two sets of dusty wooden stairs to the classrooms above.

Few of the other former Sunday Schoolrooms are still in their original form. The Wesleyan Methodist Chapel in South Street (Now the Bridport Arts Centre), which was built in 1838 also added *"commodious school premises"* at the rear of the building in 1858 now in use as part of the Arts Centre. There was also the Church of England Sunday School in Gundry Lane, of which more in the next chapter. The Baptist Church, which was built in 1841 in Victoria Grove, added a schoolroom and classrooms in 1866. After the fire at Miss Gundry's Infant School, the scholars were sent to that school for a time in 1906, and still later evacuees during the Second World War were taught there for a while. The Salvation Army Hall in St Michael's Lane also had a Sunday School in the 1930's, but by this time the role of Sunday Schools in providing a modicum of general education had passed.

The large number of children attending Sunday Schools in the early nineteenth century is indicated by the fact that in the procession through the town for the 1814 "Peace Celebrations", were four hundred Sunday School children. This, as it turned out, premature celebration of "the long wished-for Blessings of Peace" with France after the capture of Napoleon, and his imprisonment on Elba, was held oddly enough on Bastille Day. The town put on a festival and an elaborate procession in which were represented the major trades of the town, wound its way through the main streets to the Town Hall.

However important they were as a first step, Sunday Schools could never really address the task of properly educating the children of the poor. The next move towards a proper national system of education was promoted by a range of societies set up in the closing years of the eighteenth and the early nineteenth centuries to push forward new ideas in education, and much of the initial impetus came from non-conformists. Perhaps it was this, or just a fear that the working classes would be made less easy to control if they were educated, but the move to educate the "labouring classes" beyond the most rudimentary ability to read, and possibly to write, met with strong opposition.

It seems difficult from our perspective at the beginning of the twenty-first century, when universal free education has become one of the rights all people expect for their children, to understand the opposition that there was to this concept two hundred years ago. However it is important to remember that the late eighteenth century and early nineteenth century was a period of almost unprecedented social upheaval. War, revolution in France and the fear of it in Britain, were the backdrop to huge social change. The old rural economy, under attack from widespread enclosures of common land, gave way to the burgeoning industrial towns, and the need for workers drew people in large numbers into these towns often to live in quite wretched conditions. The moral degeneration of these "huddled masses" crowded into the industrial cities horrified the early philanthropists, and made action imperative. Men like Robert Owen, and Joseph Lancaster were among many who saw an increasing need to begin to educate the children of what they called *"the poor labouring classes"* so they could read the Bible and become honest and useful citizens. The scandal of child labour, gave impetus to those who saw education as a way of saving children from the drudgery and danger of the early mills and factories. The emphasis on early years education may have begun in the late eighteenth century, but it found one of it strongest advocates in another of the great nineteenth century philanthropists, Robert Owen.

Robert Owen was one of the pioneers of child-centred education. A Welshman, he conducted his experiments in education, as well as into industrial relations, in the model industrial community of the New Lanark cotton mills just outside of the town of Lanark in South West Scotland. He became director of New Lanark in 1800. The New Lanark schools took children mainly from the age of three to ten. The children were governed *"not by severity, but by kindness"*. There were no rewards or punishment and the learning was to be conveyed to the children in *"as pleasant and agreeable a manner as can be devised."*[20] He believed in giving even small children a wide curriculum, adding to the core of reading, writing and arithmetic, sewing, geography, history, natural history, religious knowledge, and singing and dancing. Half the infants' day was spent in small groups doing simple tasks and the rest amusing themselves *"at perfect freedom"* under supervision. Out of his work at New Lanark came The Infant School Society, which was set up in 1824 to promote his enlightened educational ideas

In his "A New View of Society" Owen wrote that children *"should learn to read well and to understand what they read. To write expeditiously a good legible hand, and to learn correctly so they may comprehend and use with facility the fundamental rules of arithmetic. The girls are also taught to sew, cut out and make up useful family garments, and after*

[20] Robert Owen: "An Outline of the System of Education at New Lanark" (1824) quoted in "A Social History of Education in England" by Lawson and Silver pp246-247

acquiring a sufficient knowledge of these, they are to attend in rotation in the public kitchens and eating rooms to learn to prepare wholesome economical food and to keep a house neat and well-arranged"[21]. The Bridport elementary schools show clearly the influence of this thinking. Robert Owen eventually emigrated with his ideas to America where he set up a community to put his ideas of equality and personal freedom into practice. It was not a success. However his influence on early years education cannot be over-emphasised, as it is still felt today.

The Kindergarten movement of the latter part of the nineteenth century based on the work of Froebel shared many of the child-centred views of Robert Owen and the movement he inspired, and later the work of Maria Montessori also drew on similar views of how small children should learn. Kindergartens, however were mostly taken up by private schools, though how far the distinction was really only in the name applied to the early years teaching, and how far the child-centred approach of Froebel was followed, is not something it is easy to answer without more evidence of the kindergarten curriculum in the individual schools. As we have seen, both Thorneloe School and Miss Diplock's Ladies' College advertised kindergartens.

Miss Gundry's Infant School

While all the Bridport Elementary Schools included Infants' Departments, there was one school however that was set up specifically as an Infants' School. This was the school later known as Miss Gundry's in West Street. This school was established in the old thatched Malthouse and Brewhouse on the north side of West Street next to the West Mill. The building dated back to the sixteenth century and had been used to help fund education in the 17th and 18th centuries, notably the original Free School (Chapter I). By the early 19th century the original use of the building had clearly ceased for in the 1830's it is described as "originally pawn stores, afterwards weaving shops" which was to be "transformed to an infants' school with a residence for a mistress close by"[22]. The school was formally established in 1835, according to a Government report into Voluntary Schools, though some sources say 1838.

Of interest, taking into account the above, is a paragraph in a report on the Bridport Charities produced in 1954 which states that in 1834 the premises were let to a man called George Knight, at a yearly rent of £15, and were at that time used as an auction room, and that adjoining was a plot of ground of about one rood in area then occupied by Joseph Gundry

---

[21] Quoted in "A Social History of Education in England" by Lawson and Silver p247
[22] Kelly's Directory of Dorsetshire 1889

that yielded a rent of £2 15s 6d. This report curiously enough makes absolutely no reference to the building having become a school merely observing that the *"premises were burnt down in a disastrous fire in the year 1906"*, that the *"funds now subject to this charity are represented by a holding of Consolidated Stock"*,[23] and that after the fire the site of the buildings was used as allotments.

Also of interest in this context is an open letter written by Elizabeth Channon Lee (Chapter X) to the *"The Inhabitants of Bridport"*, particularly *"public-spirited individuals"* who might *"unite in adopting some plan for establishing an INFANT SCHOOL"*. She had been saddened by the deaths of two very young children from fire, one of whom *"languished in extreme suffering for twenty-eight days."* She felt that *"The lives of children may frequently be preserved and many serious calamities averted"* if children could be admitted to such schools as she had seen elsewhere in the country.[24] These schools admitted children from eighteen months, or as soon as they could walk, until the age of six. Her letter is undated, but it seems unlikely it would have been written after the establishment of just such a school; and it is tempting to conjecture that her influence might have been as instrumental in the founding of this establishment as it was in founding the Girls' Industrial School some years later.

The first master of the Infant School was a Mr Bishop who had previously run a school in King of Prussia Lane. Pigot and Co's Dorsetshire Directory of 1842 names the next master as John Hopkins. The fact that both the early teachers listed were men, suggests that the school initially aimed to educate boys and not girls. Most infant teachers were women. By 1848 the school is being referred to, in Kelly's Directory, as a *"Wesleyan Infants' School"*, and the name of a schoolmistress, Mrs Dorcas Hardy, is added. In the census return of 1851 John Hopkins is recorded as living in St Michael's Lane with Hannah, his wife who is described as a shopkeeper. It is possible that by this time he had ceased to have any connection with the school for, in the same census, Dorcas Hardy, "Schoolmistress" is already living in the schoolhouse in West Street next door to West Mill with her two daughters Charlotte and Maria, who are both described as dressmakers, and her son, Norton, who was, at that time, still a schoolboy. Dorcas Hardy came to Bridport from Hazelbury in Somerset, and she became one of the longest serving Mistresses of the Infant School. The name *"Miss Gundry's School"* does not appear in the Directories until 1867.

When the decision was taken to convert the old Malthouse into an infant school for 130 children, it was still in the ownership of the Borough. It remained Borough property until 1865, when Joseph Gundry bought it for

---

[23] Paper entitled "Bridport Municipal Charities: Historical Survey" dated May 1954: BMLHC
[24] Colfox Papers: DHC/ D/Col C49

£600, at which point presumably the funds were converted into Stock. Once Joseph Gundry had acquired the building, and in recognition of the fact that it was then endowed by Miss Mary Gundry, it became "Miss Gundry's School". In January 1871, following the 1870 Education Act, the school's trustees placed a notice in the local paper to announce that the school *"is now placed under Government inspection with a certificated mistress"*.[25] The children had to pay one penny per week, and the age range was from 18 months to seven years of age. This really was "early-years" education. The school day started at nine, and broke for lunch between twelve and two o'clock. The day ended, depending on the time of year, either at three o'clock or four.

Throughout the change of ownership, Dorcas Hardy was still the schoolmistress, but by 1871 the census records the Infant School as being occupied by Judith Baker and her daughter described respectively as former twine spinner and twine spinner, and next door, presumably in the schoolmistress's house was Louisa Reeves, the schoolmistress. Photographs do show small windows in the thatch of the schoolroom, so it is possible that there were rooms above the school which were also let to tenants. Perhaps that might account for the fire starting in the roof above the schoolroom, though given that the Boys' General School also suffered a fire in the roof probably caused by the flue from the stove, this may well have been the cause of this fire too.

The 1880 and 1885 Directory entries list a Miss Maria Ayles as schoolmistress (1881 census lists her as living with her sister Alice Ayles, then a pupil teacher). She was followed in the post by Miss Rose Travers who was mistress of the school in 1889. Living with Rose Travers was her sister, Martha and a niece, Miss Rose Dade, though by 1901 they were no longer living at the school but at 46 West Allington.[26] (Fig 14) Miss Dade, described in 1901 as "Assistant Schoolmistress", succeeded her aunt in running the school, and was the mistress when it burned down.

Early photographs of the school show a snug L-shaped building situated between the West Mill, which was a flour mill, and the Court, which was the administrative buildings for Joseph Gundry's net and rope works. (Fig 12) The thatched building faced onto West Street but was separated from both West Street and the Court by the mill leat for West Mill, which still skirts the site today. A bridge across the leat gave access from West Street to the school. Sadly the old thatched building was destroyed by fire in 1906, and now only a gate and a bridge to nowhere mark the place where generations of children once walked. Frederick Treves in his "Highways and Byways in Dorset" of 1906 describes the school as fulfilling *"any*

---

[25] The Bridport News: January 20th 1871
[26] 1891 and 1901 Census returns for Bridport and Allington

conception of what a seat of learning for country infants should be like. It is an ancient thatched cottage with a thatched veranda, where the infants can take the air when resting from their studies. The playground is an old-fashioned garden by the side of a stream. This charming little academy is the village school of a child's idyll." Sadly, by the time his book was published, the school's days were numbered.

A memoir written by E.E.O in the Dorset Year Book 1974/5 recalls Miss Gundry's school just before it was destroyed by fire:

"We sat on forms, and had desks to write on. When reading we had to stand in a half circle which was chalked on the floor. I remember the large lettering on a block, which hung above the back of the gallery. It read "Inasmuch as ye have done it unto one of the least of these my little ones.."

"There was a shelf rather high up on the wall where the Bible was kept". It was "taken down for morning reading".

"On cold and frosty mornings teachers and pupils would join hands and dance round the stove in the middle of the schoolroom singing 'Here we go round the Mulberry Bush.' "

The fire broke out on 12th November in 1906 at about noon. (Fig 13) A former student of the school who was coming in for music lessons with Miss Dade during the lunch hour, recalls the events:

"...as I entered the front door about 12-30pm I noticed smoke coming from the thatched roof, but did not know what this meant. My lesson had started when a woman opened the door and told Miss Dade that the school was on fire. Action had to be taken quickly to save the contents of our school. Willing helpers soon came, and furniture was saved; but the school was beyond help and was soon a mere shell."[27]

After the fire, which completely destroyed the building, the scholars were taught for a while in the Baptist Sunday Schoolrooms in Victoria Grove and then the children were dispersed to the three infant schools in the town. The school was never rebuilt. Ultimately the area was absorbed into the Bridport Gundry site and is now a car park.

How far the conduct of Miss Gundry's School was influenced by the ideas of Robert Owen and the Infant School Society is not clear, but the two educational societies I am going to deal with next did have a major influence on the elementary schools in Bridport, as they had on schools nationally.

---

[27] Quoted in Dorset Evening Echo, Oct 19th 1998

88

"The British and Foreign School Society" and "The National Society for Promoting the Education of the Poor in the Principles of the Established Church".

The British and Foreign School Society grew out of the educational work of Quaker, Joseph Lancaster. He opened a school for poor children in 1798, in which he pioneered his efficient system of education: an *"arrangement for the education of every poor child in the Kingdom at a very trifling expense to the public."* [28] This was the Borough Road School, which ultimately became an establishment for teacher training later in the century. However his finances did not prosper and in 1808 the Royal Lancasterian Society was formed to rescue his work and expand it. Six years later, in 1814, and without Lancaster, it became the British and Foreign School Society.

The National Society turned for its methodology to Dr Andrew Bell, a Church of England clergyman working in Madras, who was also conducting experiments in schooling at the same time. In 1791 he set up his school in Madras, where, with the help of only four masters, he taught two hundred poor boys. Here he pioneered his ideas and, as a result, his system of education was originally known as the "Madras" system. He said of his system: *"Every boy is either a master or a scholar, and generally both. He teaches one boy, while another teaches him."* [29] This system, and that pioneered by Lancaster, became generally known as the "Monitorial System" from the use of older children as monitors to teach their juniors.

Much controversy raged as to which of the two men should be given the accolade of inventing it, a good deal of it conducted by the two men themselves. In 1804, by which time the Rev Dr Bell was Rector of Swanage on the Isle of Purbeck, the two men actually met, by all accounts quite amicably, but by 1805 the controversy had broken out and vituperative comments were flying from both sides. A writer in the calmer waters of 1819 felt that both would be honoured *"with sentiments more elevated and spiritual than those due to the talents of a Watt and an Arkwright."* [30] As the Monitorial System of education, with its rigid procedures and regimentation, did rather mirror the industrial processes of the factories and mills of the industrial revolution, the comparison with Arkwright and Watt is not perhaps quite as odd as it might otherwise seem. By the time Bell took up the benefice of Swanage, he was in his early fifties

[28] Quoted in "A Social History of Education in England" Lawson and Silver p 241.
[29] "Bell v Lancaster - Contribution to Elementary Education of the Rev Andrew Bell, Rector of Swanage" by Allan TP Cooper ACP FRSA in the Dorset Year Book 1971/2.
[30] Henry Gray Macnab: "The New Views of Mr Owen...of the Rev. Dr. Bell and that of the New British and Foreign System of Mutual Instruction" London 1819 P212

and so perhaps no longer had the energy to set up a school in Dorset to carry forward his ideas. Instead he contented himself with re-modelling the Swanage Sunday School.

The Monitorial System was very mechanistic. It used older and notionally more able pupils to supervise the learning of small groups of younger children under the overall supervision of the master or mistress. One teacher could thus supervise the teaching of a large number of children at one time. The British Schools used the Lancasterian system and the National School Bell's "Madras" system, but the differences were slight. In Lancaster's system the central area of the schoolroom was filled with rows of benches and desks for writing drill, and the surrounding space, where children spent most of their time, was for use by groups of children standing for instruction by the monitor, usually, but not always with the aid of cards hung on the wall. In Bell's system, the desks for writing occupied the outer space, facing the wall and the central area was used for group instruction. Both types of school used one large schoolroom, and had all age groups together. The students were rigidly disciplined and their activities ordered by a series of commands issued by the monitors (called *"assistants"* by Bell). Every action throughout the day was governed by these commands, and this format meant, in theory, that order could be maintained over a large and disparate number of children by one adult.

The British Schools were notionally non-denominational, but in reality the Society came to be seen as a largely non-conformist organisation. It was in an attempt to restore the balance between the non-conformist Lancasterians, and the established Church, that The National Society was set up by the Church of England in 1811 to encourage and assist parishes financially in setting up Church of England day schools throughout the country. Above all it was seen as important to begin the process of training teachers, a duty The British and Foreign Society also took very seriously. National Schools, funded and run by the local parishes and the various dioceses, with grant-aid from the National Society, were set up all over the country, and eventually became far more widespread than the non-denominational British Schools. By 1815, the year of the Battle of Waterloo, there were over 560 National Schools throughout the country, whereas only about 150 British Schools had been established.

While he gave support to both Bell and Lancaster, Robert Owen was doubtful about the Monitorial System. He felt that *"it is impossible, in my opinion, for one master to do justice to children, when they attempt to educate a great number without assistance"*.[32] Whatever his views however, the Monitorial System was the system under which generations of

---

[32] Quoted in "A Social History of Education in England": Lawson and Silver p 246

children were educated in elementary schools up and down the country. As noted earlier in this chapter, it had the merits of being cheap.

The National and British and Foreign Societies were powerful lobbies, and though their power diminished towards the end of the nineteenth century, William Forster MP could not ignore them when he was drafting his groundbreaking Elementary Education Act in 1870, (See Appendix B) and was forced to bow to pressure, from them, to exclude their voluntary schools from state control. The School Boards set up by the Act provided public elementary schools to supplement, not replace, the voluntary schools. Government money, however, after 1870, mostly went into building the new Board Schools. The voluntary schools were offered a six-month period of grace to apply for grants for new school buildings. This accounts for the extraordinary number of new schools, including the National Schools in Allington and Bridport, that were built in the 1870's.

VII

THE BRIDPORT (ST MARY'S) NATIONAL SCHOOL

J Hutchins states in his History of Dorset: *"By indenture, dated 21ˢᵗ July 1823,"* it was *"proposed by the inhabitants of Bridport to erect a school-house for the instruction of poor children belonging to the Established Church on Bell's system, to be denominated Bridport Sunday School. Henry Charles Sturt Esq demised to certain trustees a piece of ground measuring 68ft from east to west and 100 ft from north to south, bounded by Gundry Lane on the north, upon trust, to permit the committee of the said Bridport Sunday School to erect a school-house thereon, and to enjoy the same for such purposes as they should think expedient for educating boys and girls in the established religion by persons belonging to the Church of England."* [1]

In fact there was already a Sunday School attached to St Mary's parish operating somewhere in the town, possibly in South Street. This Sunday School, which was set up, according to Hutchins, in January 1788, had been united to the Diocesan Dorset Society in May 1816. It was already catering for about three hundred pupils by 1822, but a note adds that the Rector, the Rev David Williams expected *"that the number will be increased when proper accommodations are afforded."* [2] The original school was supported by an *"annual collection"* which usually raised between £80 and £90 per annum, most of which would have gone to pay a schoolmaster and or mistress.

David Williams was rector of St Mary's from 1801 to 1829, and much of the credit for the establishment of the school in Gundry Lane must go to his energetic pursuit of support and funds. It is clear from much of the correspondence that Bridport was not a wealthy parish, and that there was a nagging and persistent fear, engendered by the growth in wealth and power of the dissenting congregations in the town, that the established church would lose out. In a letter dated August 10ᵗʰ 1822 supporting the grant application Rev Williams stresses the urgent need for proper accommodation for the school: (I copy his capitation).

"Mr Sturt of this County has very handsomely given Ground for erecting School-Rooms in this Parish; and as we are put to the greatest Inconvenience for want of proper Accommodations for our Sunday School children, we think it necessary to commence building immediately. Our

---

[1] "History and Antiquities of the County of Dorset", 1774 by J Hutchins: Vol. 2
[2] Application for grant aid for a new building sent to the National Society and dated 27ᵗʰ August 1822. National Society's School File on Bridport National School held at the Church of England Record Centre.

92

present number of scholars is about 300; but we intend to build two rooms large enough to hold 200 each. The expense of building such rooms will not be under £400, and we cannot command more than about £200. The majority of the opulent Inhabitants of the Town being Dissenters, and the Annual Expense of the School pressing heavily on the members of the established Church, there is no possible mode of raising, in the Parish, more than the above stated sum, which is not much more than half of what will be wanted for the Completion of this good Work." He goes on: *"The great want of School-Rooms in this Parish, and the circumstances of its inhabitants, are well known to Mr Pitt and Mr Archdeacon England."* [3]

Both the Archdeacon and Mr Pitt of Kingston Maurward near Dorchester had written to the National Society supporting the application for aid, and it is worth quoting Mr Pitt's letter in some detail, as it again gives an insight into conditions in Bridport at the time. After outlining a brief description of the town and the parishes he goes on: *"The Corporation and the greater part of the superior class of inhabitants are avowed Unitarians, and Unitarianism is decidedly gaining ground in that place."* He adds: *"Bridport and Allington carry on a considerable trade in hemp and flax and there is a very large number of children in want of education."* After paying tribute to Rev Williams exertions he stresses, *"his means are limited and he can expect but little assistance from the more wealthy part of his parish."*

"Mr Sturt, late member for Bridport has generously given a piece of freehold land with old buildings upon it," Mr Pitt states.[4] On this land it was proposed to build a structure comprising two rooms one above the other of the following dimensions: the boys' school-room to be 50ft long, 22ft wide and 11ft high to the ceiling, and the girls' to be of the same dimensions except in height. As it would be 7ft high *"to the binding beams"*, it is clear that the girls' room was to be under the roof. This building it was deemed would give each child an area of 6 sq ft. The estimated cost of the building was £421, with an additional £14 to fit the rooms up. The annual cost of the master and mistress had been *"for some time"* between £80 and £90, but *"what it may, in future, be cannot as yet be exactly ascertained,"* the Rev Williams states with commendable honesty. The National Society granted aid of £100 and in a letter of thanks, dated Jan 30th 1823, Rev. Williams states that *"the building is now finished"* and *"the Tradesmen's Bills must soon be paid."* [5]

By 1848 William and Mary Cox were master and mistress of the Boys' and Girls' Departments of the School, while three years later in 1851 the school was being run by the Henfrey family. George Henfrey and his

---

[3] National Society's School File on Bridport National School held at the Church of England Record Centre
[4] Ibid
[5] Ibid

son, also George, were master and assistant in the Boys' Department, while Mrs Mary Henfrey was in charge of the girls. The fact that her daughter, another Mary was teaching the infants, indicates that the school had already developed an Infants' Department, though at this period the girls and infants shared the same room. None of these teachers stayed very long at the National School. By 1859 the Henfreys had left and Thomas Biddlecombe and Mrs Annie Bragg were in charge. [6]

Though initially built as a Sunday School, the application to the National Society implied that the intention was to develop a day school as soon as the facilities were in place, and all the evidence points to the fact that a day school was operating soon after the completion of the schoolrooms, and certainly, according to Hutchins, by 1864. Although the school seems to have begun on a reasonably sound financial basis, it does seem to have hit financial difficulties from time to time and by the mid-1860's the school's finances appear to have been in crisis. Contemporary references make no mention of a schoolmaster in either 1865 or 1867. Miss Emma Foot is Girls' Mistress in 1865 and in 1867 Mary Elizabeth Spratt is in post.[7] It would seem that, not for the last time in its career, the Boys' Department had been forced to close.

This closure, coupled with the success of the Boys' General School under John Beard, seems to have given rise to a singularly acrimonious dispute in 1866/7 between the Rector and Churchwardens of St Mary's parish, and the Trustees of the Daniel Taylor Charity. A pamphlet published at the time details the dispute. It was written by John Stephens representing the Daniel Taylor Trustees and reprints three letters. According to the first letter, which comes from the Rector, the Rev. Melville Lee and his two Churchwardens, Thomas Wainwright and James Templeman, *"the National School, in which the Church Catechism and the Doctrines of the Church are taught..... has of late years fallen off so much that no master can be maintained, only a mistress".*[8]

In this emergency the Rector Melville Lee and the Churchwardens clearly regarded the Daniel Taylor Charity as a possible source of funds. The letter expresses their strong feelings that it is unfair that the Boys and Infants General Schools should be assisted annually to the tune of £40 and £20 respectively, and that the National Schools should get nothing. The Vestry clearly felt that *"the Daniel Taylor Charity should be divided between*

---

[6] Bridport Census 1851. Kelly's Directory of Dorsetshire 1848 and 1859
[7] Hunt's Directory: 1865, Kelly's Directory of Dorsetshire 1867
[8] "The Correspondence between the Bridport Churchwardens and the Charity Commissioners of England and Wales and the Trustees of the Daniel Taylor Charity", written in January 1897 by John Stephens representing the Daniel Taylor Trustees , and published by W.C.Frost: Local History Collection, Bridport Reference Library.

the National and General Schools.... There would then be a good school for those people who desire more than a secular education for their children". To that end the April meeting of the Vestry passed a resolution "That the Churchwardens communicate with the Charity Commissioners to ascertain whether the Charity called Daniel Taylor's School Charity, is in their opinion, applied in accordance with the will of the testator." The burning sense of injustice felt by the churchwardens at the failure of the Taylor Charity to allow any money to come to the Church School rings through every line of their letter. It was "a very great hardship on the poor church-people, who form between 65 and 70 per cent of the poorer classes in Bridport; they cannot have their children taught the doctrines and formularies of their church without sacrificing their secular education." [9]

This appeal to the Charity Commissioners was the spark that lit the fuse, and the response from the Trustees of the Daniel Taylor Charity was predictably angry, particularly the statement that the General Schools provided a "secular education". John P Stephens, in his letter on behalf of the trustees writes that the churchwardens "must have known at the time they wrote (to the Charity Commissioners) that the treasurer (of the General Schools) is a Churchman - that the committees are composed of some of the most respectable Churchmen and Dissenters in the town, who work most harmoniously together - that the inhabitants of the town generally support the school, and that while no denominational nor sectarian teaching is allowed, the Bible is read and taught in them daily, that these schools are most efficiently conducted, and at a very small cost, afford a most useful education to large numbers of the children of the working classes in the town."[10]

Mr Stephens also pointed out in his letter, which is addressed to F W Gundry, that the charity which was set up by Daniel Taylor in his lifetime as a Deed of Gift was specifically directed to be used only for non-denominational education. Such had been established in 1861 when the Trustees, through their solicitors: Messrs Gundry and Nicholetts had submitted the terms of the Charity to the Commissioners for a ruling on precisely how the money could be disbursed. "Mr Daniel Taylor," the letter goes on, "belonged to the Society of Friends, and was twice imprisoned by the dominant Church party, on account of his religious beliefs. It is well known that the Society of Friends utterly repudiates the Church Catechism, and very much of what is called Church doctrine. It is absurd therefore, to suppose that Mr Taylor ever contemplated that any portion of his Charity should be appropriated to the teaching of such catechism or doctrine."[11]

---

[9] Ibid
[10] Ibid
[11] Ibid.

The Charity Commission found in favour of the Taylor Trustees, observing *"Under the circumstances, the Commissioners are of the opinion that it is much more in accordance with the spirit of the foundation to apply the funds so as to support a system of education as free as possible from the peculiar teaching of any religious denomination."*[12]

The depth of the animosity between the two religious camps in the town at the time can be gauged vividly from the tone of John Stephens final summing up of the correspondence between the various parties. He states: *"judging from the efforts which the advocates of the same formularies (which Daniel Taylor opposed in the 17th century) are now making to reduce the nation again to priestly rule and spiritual slavery, it is possible, were he now living, he might again be troubled by those who would inevitable regard him as belonging to that body of Christians which present an embodiment of perhaps the extremest protest made against the ceremonial religion sanctioned by the Church of Rome and adopted by a large portion of the Church of England."*[13] He finished his letter by describing the Rev Melville Lee's conduct in the matter as *"unfriendly and unbecoming."*

Ill-feeling from the supporters of the National Schools towards the General Schools and what are perceived as their powerful dissenter supporters, surfaces from time-to-time throughout this period,[14] though nothing quite so nakedly hostile as the feelings expressed in this unique correspondence.

Exactly how the financial problems of the Boys' National School were resolved is not at present clear but money must have come from some source for by 1871 a master was once more employed; Robert Roberts, with his wife, Emily, as mistress of the Girls' School were in post, but by this time plans to build a new and improved school building were well under way. The Rector of St Mary's parish by the time the application for grant aid for the new school was made to the National Society was the same Rev Melville Lee who had sparked off the controversy over the Daniel Taylor Charity. He was Rector from 1851 to 1872. The application is dated 21st December 1870 and is for a school of much greater size than the original Gundry Lane School, to be built on a school site *"given by the Rector"* which was in fact glebe land attached to the Church of St Mary. There were to be three schoolrooms: a boys' 45ft long, 18ft wide and 12ft

---

[12] Ibid

[13] This seems to be a reference to the Oxford Movement which was gaining increasing influence in the Church of England and ultimately resulted in the High Church movement

[14] Bridport was a dissenting town from the seventeenth century, if not before. By 1735 a survey by the Bishop of Bristol, Thomas Secker, found that 92 families in the town were returned as Presbyterians, and it was believed at this time that "the magistracy is pretty much in their hands" from "The Wesleys and the Early Dorset Methodists" by Barry J Briggs. P19

high; a girls' 38ft long, 18ft wide and 12ft high, and an infants' room of the same width and height as the others but 40ft in length.

Early elementary schooling was not free, and the school fees at the new school were to be 4d for boys, 2d for girls and 1d for infants. The estimated cost of this building including architect fees of £80 was £1500. The building was to be of stone under a slate roof with wooden floors. This 1870 application deliberately excludes provision for a teacher's residence attached to the school.[15] None of the church schools in the area seem to have seen the provision of a teacher's residence as important, with the possible exception of Bradpole. This is in marked contrast to both Miss Gundry's School and the three General Schools, all of which had teacher's residences built either attached or adjacent to the school buildings. What happened to this application is not entirely clear, for a letter dated April 1873 seems only to be concerned with *"improving and enlarging the existing school buildings"* at an estimated cost of about £600.[16]

The old schoolhouse in Gundry Lane still stands and the former Girls' and Infants' Department schoolroom, which is now used as a antique shop, is still recognisably a nineteenth century schoolroom. The sliding doors have been removed, but the woodwork that supported them is still intact. The narrow staircase up to the schoolroom is probably little changed, and it is quite possible to imagine the small children clattering up and down the steep stairs at the start and end of each school day.

Gundry Lane is not now, and was not then, a suitable site for a school. There was a large industrial area just yards away, at the bottom of the Lane. In the area between St Michael's Lane, Priory Lane and the river, were three large manufacturing concerns: Whetham's Priory Mill, William Edwards & Sons, and William Gale & Sons, all involved in one aspect or another of the staple trade of hemp and flax; rope, twine and nets. Wagons trundling to and fro, loaded with raw material and manufactured goods, must have been a constant hazard for the small children as they travelled to and from school. There was also a livestock market in St Michael's Lane close to the junction with Gundry Lane which, on market days, must have swelled the traffic still further.

To get a flavour of what life was like in the old school building in Gundry Lane, I will quote from the earliest extant Logbook of the school, that of the Girls' and Infants' School, which dates from 1870. The keeping of school logbooks was a requirement of the Revised Code of 1862, which introduced the system of inspections and grants based on performance that

---

[15] National Society's School File on Bridport National School held at the Church of England Record Centre
[16] Ibid.

characterised nineteenth century elementary education throughout the second half of the nineteenth century.[17]

The first entry reads: *"Emily Frederica Anne Roberts took charge (of) the Bridport National Girls and Infants School on December 26th 1870".* The signature: "Melville Lee, Rector", is appended to this declaration. The Log goes on: *"1871 January 2nd: Opened school, a very poor attendance owing to the extreme cold and snow. The Rev Melville Lee called in the morning, admitted from the General School: Selina Loveridge, Charles Loveridge, Blanche Loveridge, Maria Pomeroy.*

The state in which Mrs Roberts found the school on her arrival is obvious from the next few entries: *January 3rd: Attendance bad. Examined children in the Holy Scriptures, found them very backward. The Rev. M Lee called, asked him for books and pictures to instruct the infants, there being nothing of the kind in school – Opened night school."* (Night School was for children who worked during the day – which many did, as children started work as young as seven or eight.)

"January 4th: Very few in school, the weather so very severe. The Rev M Lee and the Rev G Brown called. Mrs and Miss Lee called in the afternoon and examined work.

January 5th : Examined the school and tried to arrange the children according to Standards. The Rev. M and Mrs and Miss Lee and the Rev G Brown visited the school – Night school.

January 6th : Standard 1 very backward, have no idea of copying from 'Blackboard'. Rev M Lee called in the morning. Night school; only two present.

January 18th: Found that Fanny Stickland had gone back to General School, without giving any reason, made enquiries and found that Mrs Stickland said she did not like the infants being in the same room as the older children besides many other foolish excuses – Informed the Rev. M Lee of this."[18]

Here we can see at first hand the disadvantages to the Old School of only having two school rooms, forcing the girls and infants to share one room. The three General Schools, Boys' built in 1850, Girls' and Infants' in 1855, had separate Boys', Girls' and Infants' Departments housed in separate classrooms.

The Logbook goes on: *"January 20th: Dictation on Paper to first and second class, very badly done. Found that in the previous teacher's time, the girls had never been taught to write from dictation, few of them even knew the meaning of the word. Taught Infants a hymn...."*

---

[17] Appendix C
[18] Bridport National Girls' School Logbook 1870-1902: DHC/S.329

"January 23rd - *Admitted from General School: Tryphena Brett, (later to become a pupil teacher), Matilda Turner, Emma Barber, Ellen Sprake, Mary Anne Strong. The Rev M Lee and Rev G Brown called and much approved of the new curtains. Night school – admitted two new girls."*[19]

In the light of the controversy of 1867 the sense of triumph in attracting pupils from the General School is understandable, but the traffic was not all one way. In the following July: *"Mrs Helyer informed the Mistress that she had taken her children away from school to place them at the General School, and gave as her reasons that though she was much pleased with the progress they had made, she did not consider the children who attended the Church Schools good enough to associate with her children."*[20] The perceived social divide between the Church and General Schools catchments is clear from Mrs Helyer's highly undiplomatic remark.

At this period the standard summer holiday took place from late June until late July, for three weeks; a period corresponding largely with the harvest. The children were given two weeks at Christmas, and a short holiday at Easter, as well as Bank Holidays, and various half and whole days for things like Bridport's April and October Fairs, Sunday School Treats etc.. Usually after the Inspectors had called and examined the children they also got a half-day off. In this particular year the summer holiday started on June 23rd and finished on July 16th.

"July 17th: Reopened school after midsummer holidays – Good attendance.

"August 9th: Very good attendance. Mistress heard that Selina and Bessie James had gone to the General School because she had told them they must pay their school money regularly. They owe 9d which their father refuses to pay."

Outbreaks of serious infectious diseases were a constant hazard at this time. On the 30th October, the Logbook records an outbreak of smallpox in the town. *"Small pox (sic) very much about. Mistress obliged to send away several children who have cases of small pox in their homes."*

In November the weather intervened. It was very cold and on 6th November the Log reports: *"A poor attendance – the children complaining greatly of cold, as the stove has not yet been put up."* Again at the beginning of the next year, 15th – 19th January 1872, the Mistress reports; *"Attendance poor through small pox being so much about – Mistress received very little assistance from Tryphena Brett (now a pupil teacher) who is a very lazy teacher".*

---

[19] Ibid
[20] Ibid

There were more problems with students in March: *"Heard that Mary Newman had gone to General School because Mistress kept her in to practise her arithmetic. Mistress went to her mother to ask her to allow Mary to return till after the examination. Mrs Newman refused to allow the child to return as she said she did not like her children 'punished and made to cry'"*. The stress caused to both staff and children of this annual examination is plain in this small incident. The government grant depended on good results, as well as on good attendance figures, and failure had grave financial implications. However despite all Emily Roberts' efforts, the Inspector's report for 1872 was not a good one:

"Summary of the Inspector's Report, April 1872:
<u>*Boys' School:*</u> *The School is not in an efficient state at present.* (This is the only reference to the Boys School in this Logbook. It had clearly not recovered from its period of closure.)

<u>*Girls Mixed School: (Girls and Infants together)*</u> *The Examination of the scholars was not satisfactory. The present teachers are not to blame for these discreditable results. H.M. Inspector again reports that the apparatus and furniture are defective. Unless this defect be immediately remedied a serious deduction (of the grant) will be incurred next year under Article 32(b)* (of the Revised Code).

I am to request your attention to Article 17(g) from which you will observe that the Grant to the whole school, not merely that conditionally due to the Infants, is endangered by an unsatisfactory report from H.M. Inspector on the Infant classes.

My Lords (presumably of the Privy Council, as education at this time was under the supervision of the Education Committee of the Privy Council – "Committee of Council" for short) *have ordered a deduction of five-tenths from the Grant this year from each Department (Boys', Girls' and Infants') for faults of Instruction and general inefficiency; and they will look for great improvement by next Inspection. The Registers appear to have been most irregularly kept, and the school is at present in a state of thorough disorganization."* [21]

After such a bad report it is not surprising that, by the end of March, Mrs Roberts had already resigned, and a new Mistress, Elizabeth Ann Morfee, had taken over as Mistress of the school in April 1872. Elizabeth Morfee's husband, Edward, was Master of the Boys School, so one husband and wife team was replaced with another. Her first report 2nd to 5th April states : *"Opened school with about 66 children. Found but a scanty supply of apparatus, no pens or pencils, books very few in number, dirty and torn. Girls very backward in needlework, no child being able to work a*

---

[21] Bridport National Girls' School Logbook 1870-1902: DHC

button-hole, or mark a letter-stitching – very inferior. No work prepared for inspection. Admitted one child. School visited several times by Rev G Brown, Misses Good & Newberry. The children attended well this week but had to complain of their not being punctual." [22] These regular visitors to the school were usually members of the Management Committee, whose job it was to oversee the work of the school on a regular basis.

The curriculum had by now greatly expanded from the basic reading writing and arithmetic of the early Sunday Schools. In one week Mrs Morphee records: *"Geography lesson, the openings into the land, and the mountains of England".* There were *"Object Lessons on the 'Beaks of birds' and on a 'Feather' and 'Slate'. Taught the children a school song – 'A Merry little Maiden', and the round 'London Cries'".*

Object lessons were part of the curriculum in the mid-19th century, and seem quite an enlightened way of introducing learning in an age when rote learning was so much the norm. The object chosen was used as the stimulus for learning a variety of things – perhaps to do with the material that the object was made of – or its use. Natural history, geography and other subjects could be approached through the object lesson. Accounts of similar lessons feature in the General Schools Logbooks.

Mrs Morfee seems to have been a very efficient teacher for by 1873 the annual report states: *"The School is improving and promises to become very efficient under its present mistress. More books should be provided in each Department."* [23]

However good its head teacher, the old Gundry Lane School was becoming more and more inadequate for the pupils to learn in. The 1874/5 Inspector's Report states: *" 'The Schoolroom is a dismal place, and it is very desirable that new rooms should be built as soon as possible'.* H.M. Inspector recommends the formation of a separate Infants Department under a certificated teacher. *'My Lords hope that the managers will carry this out before next year. The average attendance in the Girls' School must not be allowed to exceed 134, the limit prescribed by the conditions of Article 17(c) as to the area. A Bailey and T Brett (pupil teachers) must pass much better examinations next year.' "* [24]

By this time the Rev Melville Lee had been replaced as incumbent by the Rev Edward J L B Henslowe (1872-1891). It would appear from correspondence with the National Society in December 1874 that the plans for building a new school had been revived, and that a promise of a grant of £120 had been made by the National Society. By October 1875 the new school was in the process of being built and the Rev Henslowe expressed the hope that it would be completed *"within a very few months."*

---

[22] Ibid
[23] Ibid
[24] Quoted in Bridport National Girls' School Logbook 1870-1902: DHC/S.329

By 10th October 1876 Edward Henslowe can report that *"The new school buildings have been erected and are, with the exception of some minor details, complete."*[25] He is clearly hoping that the promised grant will be paid as soon as possible. However the land the school was built on was still glebe land owned by the church, and it would appear that Edward Henslowe, and presumably the churchwardens, were quite keen for this situation to continue, particularly as this would give the parish a source of income from the ground rent. In a letter dated 17th June 1879 the Rev Henslowe asks the Society if the land can remain the property of the church and if a yearly rent can be levied from the school managers. The answer is short and to the point. The Society will pay no building grant if the land remains glebe land. It must be conveyed to the trustees.

The deed for the transfer of the land by the Salisbury Diocese is dated 2nd February 1880. The deed makes slightly confusing reading, as it is worded as if the building of the school had not yet taken place, but in fact by the time the land was conveyed, the new building had been up and running for nearly four years. The document approving the final grant to the school shows that it cost £2067 12s 6d to build. Of this a surprisingly large sum, £1,872, was collected or subscribed by the parishioners, the Diocesan Board of Education gave £75 and the National Society £120.

By the time of the Deed conveying the land to the trustees, the Master of the Boys' School was George Henry Trott, doubtless the same George Henry Trott who witnessed the signatures on the deed. George Trott was probably not the first master of the newly built school. It is likely that Edward Morfee was still in post when the Boys' School opened, but George Trott probably took over in 1878, as his daughter Annie joined the Girls' Department as a pupil teacher in the July in that year.

Though he was born in Bideford in Devon, George Trott came to Bridport from Monkton Wyld, where it is likely he had been employed as a teacher. His wife Alice Trott is described in the 1881 census as "schoolmaster's wife", though there is evidence that she was also a teacher. However, she was obviously not employed at this time. The 1881 census records George Trott living three doors north of St Mary's Church in South Street with his wife and their six daughters and four sons, ranging in age from Annie, aged 18, to 4-month-old Ethel. At this time, Miss Annie Stickland was already Infants' Mistress. She joined the school in 1879.

On the resignation of Mrs Morfee in June 1878, the Girls' School went through a short period of mild instability as there were four mistresses in as many years. The Logbook records the arrivals and departures. Adelaide Cutenore took over in June 1878 but only served until December

---

[25] National Society's School File on Bridport National School held at the Church of England Record Centre

102

of the same year. Miss Emmeline Naunton took over in January 1879. By April 1880 she had also gone leaving the school in the temporary care of Miss Martha C Mitchell who managed the school until August 1882 when Miss Maud Craig took over. Martha Mitchell is yet another link with the Trott family for she lodged with them when they lived in South Street. Maud Craig was only in post for a matter of months before handing over to Miss Lucy James in October 1882, but although Lucy James served until April 1890, real stability was not established until May 1890 when Miss Mary Maud Winifred Reed took over. She was to serve the school until 1929.

The 1880 Trust Deed for the school gives an interesting insight into the management of the school. The deed required that while *"the principal officiating minister for the time being of the said Parish (St Mary's Bridport) shall have the superintendence of the religious and moral instruction of all the scholars attending the school"*, the setting of fees and the appointment and dismissal of teachers was to be in the control of a committee consisting of the minister and *"Ten other persons who shall be contributors every year of 20 shillings at least to the funds of the school."* They were also required to be members of the Church of England and resident, or with an interest in the parish.

The Committee listed in the deed is as follows: Joseph Pearkes Fox Gundry Esq.; William Hounsell Esq.; Alexander Broadley,Clerk in Holy Orders, Bradpole Vicarage; John Dunham: Ironmonger of Bridport; William Kerridge Brown described as retired tradesman of Bridport; William Townley Whetham and Stephen Whetham both described as merchants; Charles Tucker, chemist; Gerard Alexander Samson, another ironmonger, and Charles Newbery, draper. Four meetings a year of this management committee were to be held in the School House.

The site given for the new school was relatively small by today's standards, but about average for the period. It did not *"exceed one acre"* being 48 yards in extent north/south and 38 yards east/west.[26] In 1877, once the new school was completed, the old school building opposite was sold, and in 1879 was leased by the Bridport Borough Council. It became, in time, Assembly Rooms. The sign in stone can still be seen over the main door. On 24th June 1875 the foundation stone for the new school was laid, and a year later the new school opened. The Girls' School Logbook merely mentions the stone-laying, and is equally undramatic about the move into the new school in July 1876. This was the beginning of the new autumn term and the school moved across the road from the old to the new school. The entry reporting this is very brief: *"July 24th to 28th: Recommenced work in the new school with an average of 222. Admitted several new scholars.*

---

[26] I am indebted to Mr D England for the opportunity to study the original deed conveying the land to the school.

H Hawker came on Monday morning on a month's trial as P.T. (Pupil Teacher). *Miss Good visited."* [27]

The final Inspectors' Report for the old school for the year ending March 31st, reads: *"The Order and Discipline are very good and the instruction sound and accurate. The plain needlework shown to me was exceedingly well done."* [28] The staff at the time were: Elizabeth Ann Morfee . Certificated teacher; Miss A Bailey, a Pupil Teacher in her 5th Year, Tryphena Brett, a Pupil Teacher in her 4th Year, and Ellen Sprake described now as a "Candidate" (to become a pupil teacher). In addition to these teachers there were six monitors.

The absence of an extant Logbook for the Boys' School at this period means that the crisis that hit that school in the early 1880's is not detailed. It is clear that George Henry Trott left the town in the summer of 1881, as the reason given for his daughter resigning her post as pupil teacher in the Girls' School was "through her family having left the town". The next master of the Boys' School was a Mr Webb. At this time Fulbrook Lane [29] was a pupil at the school, having transferred from the Infants at Allington. He recalls Mr Webb's moustache, his propensity for wearing *"small checks"*, presumably checked trousers, and also recalls a caning episode that he witnessed which clearly burned itself on his memory. Interestingly he recalls the source of the schoolmaster's canes as being *"Cook's toyshop in West Street"*. Mr Webb left Bridport in 1883. Whether this precipitated the closure of the Boys' School is not clear. The reason given by the Rev Henslowe was *"a lack of funds"*.[30] Doubtless the numbers had fallen so low, and the inspection reports were so poor that the school lost its grant. On its closure Fulbrook Lane recalls moving to Allington School, as doubtless did the rest of his schoolmates.

What is quite remarkable is that this event passes with no comment at all in the Girls' School Logbook, even though the boys occupied half the building. The Boys' School remained closed until 1891, though not for want of effort on the part of the Rev Henslowe and the school managers to reopen it. In a letter written six years after the closure in January 1889, Henslowe asked the National Society for help and advice with his plans to re-open *"a Boys' School of a higher class"* that would be able to charge between 6d and 9d a week. It would seem that little came of the Rev Henslowe's plans, particularly as the National Society had to impress on him that they did not offer maintenance grants to schools. Moreover, the

---

[27] Bridport National Girls' School Logbook: 1870-1902 DHC/S.329
[28] Ibid
[29] "Bridport in the Nineteenth Seventies and Eighties (sic)" by Fulbrook Lane publ. 1934
[30] Letter 19th Jan. 1889 from Rev. Henslowe to National Society. National Society's School File on Bridport National School held at the Church of England Record Centre

proposed fees would have been a considerable burden on parents in a relatively poor parish. This is not so many years after the period when staff at the General School were recording, as a reason for a pupil leaving school, that the parents were unable to find the 1d or 2d required for the weekly fees, so 6d or 9d would have been very hard for parents to afford.

Whatever happened to this plan, the funding crisis which caused the closure of the Boys' School clearly dogged the managers of the Bridport National Schools for seven or eight years. A report in the Bridport News of January 10th, 1890 shows that eventually they turned to a solution well-known in educational circles today - namely fund-raising events. It reports a *"Drawing-Room Entertainment and Dance"* held in the school, which was suitably furnished and decorated for the occasion. The still empty Boys' schoolroom was transformed into a *"concert room"* and another large schoolroom into the ballroom, while the major part of the Girls' School became, for the night, the *"retiring and refreshment room".* The newspaper report states: *"The Bridport National Schools are an institution which must certainly deserve well of the town, and it is only just and right that churchmen in the neighbourhood should do their best to remove the stigma of debt which at present hangs over the schools."* It goes on to say, *"It has long been felt that the schools ought to embrace a branch for the education of boys, and no doubt when the present debt is extinguished.... which may now be looked forward to... in the near future, the managers will doubtless see their way to add something of this kind."* The fund-raising was obviously successful, for in March 1891 the Boys' Department did re-open with twelve pupils, under the care of 22-year-old Henry Saloway, of whom much later.

Weather and disease still plagued the schools through the 1880's. In October 1882 (by which time Miss Maud Marion Craig had taken over as Mistress) it was storms and floods. By early December in the same year *"so few children were present on Thursday morning in consequence of the snow that they were dismissed and the register not marked."* The following January once again stormy weather: *"The attendance yesterday and today has been very poor in consequence of the wet weather."* And again, *"attendance not good yesterday and today, on account of the rough weather."* Hot weather could be a problem too. In August 1884: *"The weather has been so warm this week that most of the children have taken knitting during the needlework lesson – the white work would have been much soiled."* [31]

---

[31] Bridport National Girls' School Logbook 1870-1902: DHC/S.329

Mary Maud Winifred Reed took over as Headmistress of the Girls' School in May 1890. She was to be one of the longest serving head teachers of the school, finally retiring from her post in 1929. Her career almost precisely matched that of Henry Saloway, the Boys' Master, who retired after forty-two years at the end of March 1933. Between them they established the school's reputation and ensured its lasting success. On Miss Reed's retirement in December 1929, after thirty-nine years, a series of speeches recalled her long and devoted service. She came to the school directly from Salisbury College, the teacher training college for female teachers in the Salisbury diocese established in 1840. The Rector, Rev Spenser Hollins Viggar, in his speech, recalled that Miss Reed had come to the school *"at a time when* (it) *was very small numerically, but she loved the work, and so the school has steadily grown in numbers".* Miss Reed trained a great number of pupil teachers in her long career, among them was her successor as headmistress, Clarissa May Rendell. In paying tribute to her predecessor, Miss Rendell gave a description of Miss Reed's life as headteacher, and recalled her own training as a pupil teacher:

"All that time when (I) *was but 12 to 13 years of age, lessons* (for the pupil teachers) *were commenced at 7am winter and summer, and continued until 8am. Oftentimes Miss Reed forgot the movements of the clock and pupils rushed home to breakfast at 8-15 or 8-20 to return at 9 o'clock, when they taught until 12, had lessons until 1pm and after dinner taught again until 4-30pm. Miss Reed spent her evenings either at evening classes accompanied by the teachers or in preparing and correcting lessons for the following morning which often necessitated her remaining at her task until midnight."* [32] This was the demanding career that Miss Reed was embarking upon.

There is one very strange and unexplained entry from Miss Reed for August 15th 1890: *"Opened school last Monday Aug 11th with a very fair attendance. One girl, Emily Fursey, has left as her mother said her little sister was afraid to go to the Infant School owing to the ghost scare, and she has determined to send Emily to the same school* (probably Allington or the General School) *to take her little sister to school."* There is no further reference to this "ghost scare", so what it was remains a mystery.

Despite a new headmistress, the problems the school faced did not change overmuch. Disease and weather continued to plague staff and children alike. In 1891 again snow is a problem: *"March 16th: The snow was so deep in the playground that the children could scarcely make a footpath to the school door."*

In December 1895 a serious outbreak of diphtheria struck Bridport. In the week the school broke up for the Christmas Holidays, Miss Reed

---

[32] Quoted in Bridport National Girls' School Logbook 1925 – 1930 DHC/S.329

reported a sad little detail that brings home the deadly nature of childhood diseases before the advent of immunisation: *"December 19th: School has broken up this week for the Xmas Holidays of a fortnight. ....One little girl Mary Willson has died this week of diphtheria, which has been very severe among young children in Bridport. Mary Willson had not missed once, or been late once since coming to the school."*

On January 31st 1896 Miss Reed reported: *"This is the first week after the holidays. Diphtheria has been so prevalent among the school children, that by the Doctor's order, the schools throughout the town have been closed 3 weeks, making, with the holidays, five weeks. Opened School on Monday with a small school, the attendance continuing poor throughout the week."*

The sickness persisted into the Spring. On February 5th she reports: *"The attendance has not been good. Sickness has been prevalent among the younger children, and this has been the general excuse among the older ones."* After this, for about three or four weeks in March, Miss Reed was herself ill, though she does not say what her illness was. The small number of teachers employed in schools of this period could make absence through illness a real problem, and it is clear a conscientious teacher like Miss Reed felt the need to get back to the classroom, even if she was not fully fit. On her return she reports: *"13th March: The school has been managed as last week* (by Miss Annie Stickland, who was the Infant Mistress)*, but I have taught a little, and superintended the school nearly every afternoon. The attendance has been very bad all through many illness* (sic)*, although diphtheria has improved."*

Diphtheria struck again in the winter of 1896, but this time it was combined with an outbreak of measles. Once again the schools in the town were closed, but this time well before the usual start of the holidays: *"Dec 4th 1896: School closed by order of the medical officer until further notice."* In fact the outbreak was sufficiently serious for the Borough Sanitary Committee to order the closure of all the public schools in the town for six weeks in order to try and prevent further spread of the diseases and for *"disinfecting purposes, and, where necessary, carrying out sanitary improvements"*[33]. The schools did not reopen until Monday 1st February according to a report in the Bridport News of Friday 5th February. Miss Reed reported on that day: *"School reopened with a fairly good attendance especially among the upper classes. Admitted two children – but find that the scholars in the upper division have forgotten a great deal. The fifth standard have quite forgotten the lessons given them in Simple Proportion. We have also had 4 maps, but now we haven't any on Europe, which is very awkward."* By the 19th of January however: *"Diphtheria has broken out*

---

[33] Bridport News: Dec 11th 1896

again, and parents are so nervous, that even if children have only a cold in the head, they are kept home from fear of the probable consequences." [34] The fear engendered by these epidemics must have been intense.

What with so much serious illness, it was not surprising that attendance was a problem, but the constant harping on attendance was not just because the teachers felt it was important for children to attend school. The yearly government grant still depended on good attendance figures, as well as good results in the annual examinations. If either were not up to scratch the grant, which was usually about £60 - £70 a year, was cut. To encourage good attendance, prizes were given to all students who attended over a certain number of sessions in the year.

At the Prize Day for Bridport National Schools, reported in the Bridport News of May 15th 1896, prizes were awarded for attendance over 390 sessions for the boys and girls and over 360 for the infants. The total number of sessions for the year was 420 for the boys, and 424 for the girls. Twelve boys and five girls were rewarded for 100% attendance, but the two Hutchings brothers were singled out in the report for particular praise. Arthur the elder had not missed a single session over five years and his brother Robert had not missed once in three years. At the end of the ceremony the children were sent home, the Bridport News reports, with a bun and an orange *"the gift of the ever thoughtful and generous Rector"* [35] Rev H R W Farrer. It seems strange that the only reference to this event in the School Logbook is *"Holiday given on Thursday afternoon owing to visitation of the Archdeacon. Visitors Rev H Farrer and Mr and Mrs Northover."* Mr Northover was one of the School Managers.

Henry Saloway, already mentioned briefly, came to Bridport from Wilton near Salisbury.[36] (Fig 17) He was only twenty-two, when he took up the post of Master of the beleaguered Boys' School. He re-opened the school with only twelve pupils, and faced the Herculean task of getting the school back on track. The 1891 census records him as unmarried and living as a lodger in a house in Prospect Place. In 1893 he married Lily Courtney at Fisherton Anger near Salisbury. She was also a teacher, and as they both came from villages close to Salisbury it is likely they met as pupil teachers, possibly in Fisherton Anger, at the National School there. By 1901 he and Lily were living at 35 Victoria Road (Grove). Newly

[34] Bridport National Girls' School Logbook 1870-1902: DHC/S.329
[35] Bridport News and Reporter: May 15th 1896
[36] Wiltshire Census 1881

married, and already in charge of an improving school, by 1897 he had the help of a certificated Assistant Master, W.J.Osmond.[37]

The 1897 Parish Annual Report mentions two inspections, one by the Diocese and the other by Government HMI. The Diocesan Inspector, The Rev J Pulliblank is quoted as saying of the Boys' School, *"Great progress has been made, especially in tone and discipline"*, but perhaps significantly no mention is made of examination results though these are specifically mentioned in the report on the Girls' School, headed by Miss Reed. However the tests administered by HMI must have been satisfactory, as must attendance, as the report also records that *"the highest possible grant"* has been awarded to all three departments of the school. The HMI report on the three Departments states that the Boys' School was *"Most satisfactory"*, while the Girls' School was *"A most pleasing, well-taught school"*, and Miss Annie Stickland must have been delighted that her Infants School was deemed *"An Admirable Infants School".*[38]

The very tight finances of the school are clear from the financial report. Despite an overall income of £642 6s 2d, the accounts acknowledge a deficit of £26 18s 2d, with the added note that this is partly due to *"The prevailing epidemic* (entailing) *heavy expenses on your Managers during the year".*[39] The "epidemic" referred to was that outbreak of diphtheria and measles in the town already referred to.

As well as the Government grant of £251 2s 6d and local subscriptions of £63 5s 9d, the school was in receipt of money from two local charities. The Bull Charity gave £3 17s 4d and the Broadoak Charity £7 5s 4d. (See Chapter I) Set against this were the salaries of all the teachers, including pupil teachers, a *"temporary monitress"* and a *"Drill Master"*. These totalled £447 19s 4d, which left very little for *"Books, Apparatus and Stationery"* (only £34 8s 8d was spent on these). *"Repairs to the building, Replacement of Furniture, completion of scheme of Ventilation, Sanitary Work* (no doubt the result of the epidemic) *and 12 New desks to Infants School"* cost £88 19s 4d, so the building, though only just over twenty years old was already costing money.[40]

Chairman of the managers at the time of this report was the Rector of St Mary's, Rev Henry Richard William Farrer (1895-1916), and William Hounsell was still one of the managers. Also on the Management Committee were Mr John James Roper, and Mr John Cleeves Palmer, so despite earlier protestations about the wealthier townspeople being largely

---

[37] St Mary's Parish Church, Bridport: Annual Report containing the National School accounts for the year ending March 31st 1897. (Bridport File: National Society Records held at the Church of England Record Centre)
[38] Ibid
[39] Ibid
[40] Ibid

non-conformist, it is clear that, certainly from the building of the new Gundry Lane School, the Management Committee had continued to attract the service of some highly influential people. The roll of the Boys' School in 1897 was 122, a remarkable turn-round from the low numbers in 1891. There were 124 girls and 126 infants.[41]

Attendance at school however, particularly after 1880, remained an issue, and here a short digression is in order. The 1870 Forster Education Act had set up School Boards around the country, and although these were not particularly influential in Bridport, elsewhere they had been so successful in ensuring that elementary educational was available across the country that in 1880 the Government was able to pass an Education Act making school attendance up to the age of ten compulsory. Now that school attendance had a legal framework, local school attendance committees were set up to monitor the local schools. Bridport's School Attendance Committee was made up of attendance officers and the relieving officers. It met on the first Thursday in each quarter at the Surveyor's Office and the Clerk in 1889 was a Richard Cornick. It was supposed to solve the problem, but, as ever, theory and practice did not always cohere. Complaints about the effectiveness of the Attendance Committee were common. It seems even the combined efforts of the School Attendance Officer and the Magistrates were often ineffective where persistent truants were concerned. No wonder teachers became exasperated.

Miss Reed expresses her frustration in the Logbook, August 1896: *"Attendance is still very poor and it remains the same girls who are so poor. Nothing frightens them or their parents. The Attendance Officer comes in, takes the same names every time and goes away. They do not improve, and when they are brought before the magistrate they are never convicted. Every time each case is adjourned to see how they attend the next month. Of course, during that time, they are sent regularly, and come just as badly after it. Now the attendance is even worse than usual, as the girls often go away after the holidays to the sea-side on bright half days, and there appears to be no way of stopping them."* In March 1897 another form of reward was tried to boost attendance. Miss Reed reports: *"We have had a banner with "This class has attended the best in the school" on it. It has already had a marked effect on the attendance, each class trying to obtain it."*[42]

Attendance was not the only problem, however. By September Miss Reed is clearly feeling dissatisfied with the senior girls' progress. She goes

[41] Ibid
[42] Bridport National Girls' School Logbook 1870-1902: DHC/S.329

on in her next entry: Sept 6th: *"I gave the 4th and 5th Standards a reading lesson instead of sewing Tuesday and Wednesday afternoons. They are progressing slowly, but are the most irregular in the whole school. At the usual monthly examinations I find that carelessness is responsible for many careless errors, especially is this the case with the 3rd Standard. Writing is greatly improved, and they take a pride in possessing neat tidy pages. Spelling by word building was good generally in all classes."[43]*

Poor Miss Reed - with all her other troubles that year, she was also having difficulty with the caretaker. July 9th 1897: *"The (pupil) teachers have not received their lesson this morning in school, as the caretaker had not swept the school or classroom, and in reply to a question whether he had swept out under the desks, he rudely replied, "Of course I have." I have had to speak to him about the dusting. It is badly done. In fact, the window sills, and pictures are hardly ever touched in the morning. The children have done it dinner times. When spoken to, Keech is invariably most insolent!"* However the following day the caretaker came to make amends– *"He came and apologised for his rudeness today."[44]*

It is quite surprising what uses were made of the Gundry Lane schoolrooms, many of the events meaning that the children had to have time off school. Apart from being used fairly regularly for polling in various elections, an entry for September 1897 reports: *"Holiday will be given Thursday, Friday and Wednesday afternoon, owing to the Agricultural show being held in these schoolrooms."* Perhaps the fact that the school was virtually next door to the livestock market in St Michael's Lane explains this.

The importance of needlework in girls' schools at this time is underlined by an incident recorded in December 1898. A Christmas Bazaar had been held at the school, but once the rooms were cleared *"the specimen box containing all the sewing which the 1st class girls have done as specimens, since last April, is gone, and according to Keech, the man who cleans out the school, everything in the shape of rubbish was burnt, and these specimens were considered as such, because they were all separated in paper bags, each girl having her own. The children had been particularly proud of these patches etc., and had procured new bags, when the old ones were broken, because at the end of the year they are all examined and the best put in a special box to be shown to visitors."[45]* The children must have been quite upset to lose their cherished work, feelings Miss Reed clearly shared.

Improvements were still being made to the schoolrooms: *"May 3rd 1899: Yesterday Mr Northover's men had taken the classroom door away*

---

[43] Ibid
[44] Ibid
[45] Ibid

to have glass put in at the top, and this has now been done, which supplies a long felt want, as younger teachers can take a class there. There is a great need of better ventilation in the class room, as the air gets most foul after the children have been there a little while. Miss Aplin has covered with brown paper about 100 books for the PT's and the children's library. A large number of text and other books have been ordered for the PT's who now have a nice lot of books for reference."

Children in this period were encouraged to be patriotic. National events were usually the occasion for celebration. The Logbook says little about Queen Victoria's Jubilee in 1897, which probably fell in the school holidays, but two years later, in May 1899, the school put on a special celebration, this time for the Queen's 80th birthday. *"May 24th 1899: "Teachers and some children decorated our schools. And brought pictures with them dealing with her Majesty's life – School assembled earlier in the afternoon and was dismissed at 4 instead of 4-30 in honour of the Queen's 80th birthday. The flags were hoisted over the buildings, and in the afternoon the girls danced round the Maypole* (Fig 21) *before all the three schools who were gathered together in the Infant room, after which the boys, girls and infants sang the National Anthem. The Master, Mr Saloway, briefly addressed them, referring to the death of the Queen's father, (the Duke of Kent, brother to both King George IV and King William IV) who was brought to Bridport and whose body remained in St Mary's Church one night; and dwelt on the progress of Education especially during her long and prosperous reign. Before the children were dismissed, the boys spontaneously gave 3 hearty cheers for Her Majesty."* [46]

The South African War against the Boers was one reason for the feelings of patriotism that the children clearly felt at this time. The report on November 3rd 1899 states: *"The children and teachers are taking great interest in the war out in the Transvaal. The latter have mounted maps cut out from the daily papers, brought in by Miss Brooks, and the children eagerly give any information, which they have heard at home. Every Wednesday afternoon, the first lesson throughout the school is devoted to conversational lessons on recent events, and the children like it. Rudyard Kipling's verses on "The Absent-minded Beggar" has(sic) been recited, and the sad side of the war was shown up."*

On January 12th 1900 Miss Reed reports: *"The girls are making garments for the soldiers in South Africa, more especially for the Dorset regiments. A letter has been sent to each lady of the Committee* (the Ladies Committee who helped to oversee the school), *and one from Mrs Farrer* (Rector's wife) *asking for monetary support to buy material. The*

---

[46] Ibid

112

children have also responded most liberally, enabling us to make, or buy, over 50 garments, so far. One widow woman sent to the Mistress's house on Saturday asking for the pattern of a Tam O'Shanter hat that she may make it in the afternoon. She is making a shirt, but she would like to give something herself. She only has one half holiday a week, and has to work very hard to bring up her children. The garments will be sent to Miss Hebe Templer, who is sending them to Mrs Law, the Colonel's wife, and will be despatched with the troops on the 31st.

"March 1st: On receipt of the news that Ladysmith has been relieved, the children who were out to play, were assembled and sang God Save the Queen. In the afternoon they had holiday in honour of the event.

March 2nd: This afternoon at 4-10 all three schools assembled in the Infant School, where a Union Jack was displayed, and the National Anthem was sung vociferously followed by three cheers for Roberts, Buller and White". (Commanders of the British forces.)

"June 1st: Holiday was promised to the children by the Mayor, who presided at our prize distribution – It was to commemorate the relief of Mafeking, the news of which we heard on the previous Saturday, & consequently the children couldn't have a holiday – They were very excited over the event, and as May 31st the following Thursday was the Music Festival at Salisbury, at(sic) which the teachers of the boys' school were going, and many of the choir boys, the holiday was postponed till yesterday. News of the fall of Pretoria was published yesterday. On May 12th we had our annual May Day Festival, when all the children of the three schools were assembled in Miss Stickland's room (the Infant Room), and the girls danced round the May Pole(sic) The queen was chosen by ballot by the whole school. Her qualifications were to be 'the most lovable and most loved girl in the whole school'. Annie Pearce had the honour of being chosen." [47] (Fig 19)

"1901: Jan 22nd: The National Anthem was sung this morning and yesterday prayers were offered by the children on behalf of Her Majesty the Queen – who is very ill." Then an additional note: "She died today Tuesday at 6-30pm. Jan 25th: Today I have read some anecdotes to the children on the Queen, and this was the first morning lesson after Scripture. The children from the smallest were very interested."

Still national events affected the life of the school. On June 1st 1902: "We heard today that peace in South Africa was declared. The children assembled all together in Miss Stickland's room, boys, girls and infants and sang God Save the King. Then they were addressed by Mr Farrer; Mr Northover, the Mayor, coming in for a minute. Then he went to ask for a whole day's holiday for the other schools, as Mr Farrer had

---

[47] Ibid

already spoken of giving our children that. Our flags were hoisted quickly by the boy Pupil Teacher Hounsell, and 'The Soldiers of the King' was played as a march. The children were very excited as were we, the teachers. So after returning each school to its own room, Mr Northover said a few words on the advantage it would be to have peace, and as he hoped the children would enjoy their day's holiday. They cheered heartily at this, and gave vigorous 'claps' to testify their thanks, both to the Rector, and the Mayor."[48]

In 1902 the Attendance Banner was still in operation and clearly still having the desired effect. It seems the prize for winning the banner was a school outing. On August 28th 1902: *"Yesterday Miss Hansford's class went to Eype in the afternoon to study the objects and things by the sea. The children brought 1d each and one of the parents offered a tent down there to boil the kettle, so they have had a most enjoyable day as an encouragement, and Mrs George kindly gave Miss Hansford some cakes over what she bought with the children's pennies."* Eype seems to have been a favourite place for outings, as other classes who won the banner also had visits there. It was also a favourite destination for Sunday School outings.

On January 15th 1904, long-serving Infant teacher, Annie Stickland, (Fig 17) was presented with gifts to mark her 25 years' service. The Rector and the Managers gave her a silver tea service, and Mr Northover a personal gift of an oak tray. She finally retired from the Infant School in March 1920 after forty-one years. Her successor was Millie Austin Lawrey, who served until 1934, when Mrs Rosa Walker took over the Infants' Department.

One final quotation from this Logbook shows just how much attitudes have changed since the Edwardian period, particularly in attitudes towards girls. In her entry for February 10th 1905 Miss Reed writes: *"The ordinary routine of the last few weeks has been broken today. We all assembled in the Infant room just after 9. Then 4 Managers came in: The Rector, Messrs Roper, Northover and Collins. The Rector, after a song from the boys, made a speech mostly to the boys of the future of themselves and the National Schools. He dwelt on the grand future in front of the poorest boy, and laughingly remarked that they might become Archbishop of Canterbury, or if their tastes were not that way, then they could become Lord Chancellor. But the girls too must qualify themselves to be the helpmeet of the ambitious boy – or boys – They must be young ladies – and able to appreciate education by making the best use of their life now, and becoming gentle and modest......This speech was followed*

---

[48] Ibid

by a song from the girls, after which Mr Northover gave each child a medal and the best had books. Then with 3 cheers for everybody the children were dismissed for the day – which was an ideal day for them, I think – and the weather was beautiful."[49]

---

[49] Ibid

VIII

ST MARY'S SCHOOL INTO THE TWENTIETH CENTURY

At the beginning of the twentieth century the Gundry Lane school was already nearly thirty years old, and the accommodation that had been deemed suitable in the 1870's was now growing more and more out-dated. For a start the old system of teaching many children all together in one large room had given way to a demand for individual classrooms for the different classes. Schools needed facilities for games, and nineteenth century sanitary arrangements were often primitive. The history of the Gundry Lane school in the twentieth century is one of a constant battle to try and upgrade the school, and make the best of the limited site and increasingly cramped buildings.

In 1910, in an attempt to remedy some of these shortcomings, a further grant of glebe land was made, providing a long narrow strip down the western perimeter of the site, presumably to provide for a toilet block as one of the improvements described is for *"Sanitary arrangements and Drainage"*. The improvements included the lengthening of the east wing of the building and the total cost of the work was £936-1s-9d.[1] Though these improvements might have satisfied the standards of 1910, by 1934 in a report for the Dorset Education Committee the sanitary arrangements at the school were described as *"very unsatisfactory"*.

The first years of the new century presented many challenges. The 1902 Education Act had devolved responsibility for schools to the Local Authorities, who were required to set up Education Committees to oversee the schools in their areas. The new funding arrangements meant a new Education Rate. This gave Miss Reed an unusual problem to deal with.

"Sept 11th 1902: Today I have learnt that a Passive resister to the Education Rate has removed his child from here and sent her to the General School. In an interview she had nothing to find fault with, the child really preferred to remain at her old school, but her father, a Baptist, is a staunch supporter of his clergyman, Rev Haynes who refuses to pay this rate."[2]

---

[1] Deed 1910 in the possession of Mr D England.
[2] Bridport National Girls' School Log 1902 - 1906: DHC/S.329. The National Passive Resistance Committee was set up by John Clifford as a result of the campaign conducted by non-conformist supporters of the Liberal and Labour parties against the 1902 act. By 1906 over 170 men had gone to prison for refusing to pay their school taxes.

But by far the most traumatic event of these early years was the outbreak of the First World War.[3] 1914 began with a bad epidemic of measles that lasted from January to March. The outbreak of war on August 4th fell during the summer holiday so the first reference is to *"A very large number of old boys* (who) *have joined the various branches of the Imperial Forces, and one, H Warr, was in the famous Lancer charge"* (Sept 14th 1914). Ten days later Henry Saloway reports: *"I regret that H Warr is variously reported killed and missing"*, though by November better news had come of his being a prisoner of war in Munster. Some past students returned to Dorset from the colonies to serve in the War: *"H Holley, No 4 on the books of this school has come over with the Canadian contingent."* (Nov 5th 1914). *"A Wadham, an old boy, has come over with the Australian contingent."*

From this point on Henry Saloway sets himself to record in the School Log, each item of harrowing news that he received regarding former students. This sets his account of the war years apart from all the other school logbooks for the area that I have studied. In addition to recording the news of past pupils as it came to him, at the end of the 1906-1933 Logbook, he wrote out what he called his "Roll of Honour", which lists in his own handwriting the names of all those students he knew who had died in the Great War. He read this Roll of Honour at the school Armistice services each year after the war.[4]

For the girls this was a period of intense activity making woollen garments: *"socks and scarves for the sailors and soldiers"* and by December they have delivered a great number of *"knitted garments and woollies"* to the Mayoress to be sent to fishermen in the North Sea. In March, the girls sent Lieutenant H B Farrer, the Rector's son, forty garments for the soldiers at the front. *"This is the 3rd parcel,"* Miss Reed comments, *"and on average every 1st class girl has made 5 garments. The children often put their names and addresses inside the garments sent and several received letters from the grateful recipients".*

Miss Reed records on June 11th 1915: *"May Spiller came down to show me a letter received by her from a motor driver at the front. In it he said that he had just returned from the trenches soaking with wet, clogged with mud, and had nothing clean to wear, if he changed his socks. Then he remembered that he had received from 'home' a pair of socks, which he had put aside at the time. He took them out, found her name and address on them and wrote to tell her how grateful he was. As her father is a motor driver, she answered him..."* She goes on to instance several other letters

---

[3] The account of WWI on the following pages is drawn from Bridport National Girls' School Logbook: 1906-1925, and Boys' School Logbook: 1906 - May 31st 1921: DHC/S.329
[4] See Appendix D

117

and concludes. *"I need not say how proud the girls were to get these letters of thanks."*

There were also refugees to deal with. A large influx of Belgians who had fled Antwerp and neighbouring cities presented particular challenges for the town. That Bridport rose so well to the challenge is indicated by the fact that, after the war, the Mayor and Mayoress, Mr and Mrs Cornick were awarded respectively "The Medal of Queen Elizabeth" and "The King Albert's Medal with ribbon" by the King of the Belgians. The Catholic Convent whose roots were in Flanders made the Visitation Convent available as a reception centre and the refugee families were housed in available empty properties in and around the town. The girls of St Mary's collected food for the refugees and in return several of the Belgian girls came to the school to give French lessons. One lasting legacy of the refugees' arrival was the tactful change of name for the prominent inn in the town from the King of Prussia Hotel to the King of Belgium Hotel, and King of Prussia Lane became King Street.

Inevitably the children joined local schools. Henry Saloway records: *"On Monday admitted Francois van Utterbeck, an intelligent young Belgian who speaks Flemish – one of the Belgian refugees now in the town."* (Dec 4th 1914). Then in December the first death: *"J Jeanes has died of his wounds – this is the first old boy to give his life for the country in the present war."* (Dec 11th 1914)

The school was affected by events on the home front. *"Jan 13th 1915: The yard is being used as a drill ground by the Naval Brigade."* And after the Easter Holidays in 1915, he has to report: *"Haymaking has somewhat interfered with the attendance this week."* The loss of men to the front left the farms short of labour. Inevitably this meant that their young sons ended up helping with the harvest. The girls' families were also victims of the events in France. In June 1915, Miss Reed records: *"One of my old girl's husband has died of gas poisoning; another child's father has committed suicide having, it seems, a dread of going to the front."*

The children were helped to feel involved in the war effort by making small sacrifices of their own. During the Whitsuntide holiday, the girls, instead of going out and enjoying themselves, collected and sold flowers to raise money, and in July Miss Reed reports: *"Nearly all the (Sunday) schools of the town except the Baptist and the Unitarian have decided not to have a Sunday School Treat this year, but to give the money saved to the soldiers from this town who are serving their country in France."* The children were actively involved in the war effort. In March 1916 Henry Saloway records, *"collected 16 eggs and sufficient money to buy 5 dozen eggs for wounded soldiers and sailors."* And by June 1915 the girls had collected 333 eggs. Sometimes enthusiasm overtook practicality. In 1916 a week's holiday July 26th – 30th was authorised by the County

Education Committee to take the place of the Whitsun holiday, thus officially sanctioning the need for children to help with the haymaking. But as the majority of the children were town, rather than farm children, this does not seem to have been very successful, as Miss Reed reports that *"Few farmers cared to avail themselves of child labour,"* no doubt feeling that inexperienced children were likely to be more of a hindrance than a help. The following year 1917 no haymaking holiday was given.

In October 1915 Henry Saloway received more reports of casualties: *"S Barrett of the 5th Dorsets reported wounded at the Dardanelles."* (Oct 15th 1915) and more old boys are called up: *"Cecil Major another old boy has been awarded a commission for services at the front."* (Oct 23rd 1915).

Young teachers were also drawn into the conflict and Henry Saloway had to contend with losing his young assistants. Nov 5th: *"Mr Strawbridge is applying for a commission in the RFA* (Royal Field Artillery) *and will most probably soon be leaving in order to go into training – It will be difficult to fill his place and the TT (*Saloway's shorthand for timetable*) will have to be considerably recast in order to get the work done."* In May 1916 Mr Strawbridge went to Plymouth to join the Royal Field Artillery.

In the autumn of 1916 there was news in the Log of two former pupil teachers: Lieutenant Tom Rowson, who had also been a pupil at the school, was reported killed at Ginchy, and on Sept 29th Pt H Hounsell called at the school to say goodbye as he was about to embark for France.

1916 was a bad year for casualties. Right at the beginning of 1916 another old boy was killed, *"I regret that John Ellery of the 5th Dragoon Guards, an old boy, has been killed in the Persian Gulf operation."* [5] On June 12th 1916 Henry Saloway records: *"I regret to record that William Abbott, an old boy, went down in the 'Black Prince' during the North Sea engagement, and Ernest Turner, on the 'Hampshire' was drowned when it was mined off the Orkneys. Lord Kitchener being aboard."*

In July news came of two former pupils. R G Symes had been killed, and later that month, C H Stone died of his wounds in France. In August, Captain H.E. Kitcher, serving with the 5th Dorsets was also killed. 1917 is little better. In February the Log records that George Oxenbury was killed by a bomb dropped from an aircraft in France and W Travers was drowned *"in the destroyer which went down in the Channel last week."* (Feb 16th 1917). On February 23rd he records that *"J Fowler, 5th Dorsets is, I am sorry, 'missing' in France. He recently won the DCM. In June, H Marsh... was killed in France.....he was a most promising young fellow."* In August 1917 Joseph Bartlett was killed in France and in September Arthur Gale

---

[5] In fact he seems to have been killed in France according to Henry Saloway's eventual "Roll of Honour"; see Appendix D

was reported missing in Mesopotamia, while William Wheadon was missing in France. The year ends with the news of the death of Sergeant Saddler J Rowe who was killed in France. It is not difficult to imagine the effect on Henry Saloway of this relentless recording of the loss of his former pupils. At any rate in July 1917 he fell ill, and did not return to school until after the summer holidays.

There were various visits made to the school by former pupils, and those connected to the school who were serving with the forces. Lieutenant Farrer visited the school on 28th January 1916 and brought with him a collection of *"war relics"* to show the boys *"in the shape of rifle, swords, shell-cases etc. and gave a most interesting account of life at the front to the children."* In September 1917 Lieutenant Hounsell visited the school, as did Private Welch from the Flanders front.

Life in Bridport was also becoming more difficult. The County Council were putting pressure on the school to conserve coal, and there were blackout restrictions ,*"lighting orders",* in place that mean the school room could not be used for evening meetings *"as the darkening of windows would cost too much."* In both winters 1915/16 and 1916/17 it is cold and there were constant outbreaks of disease: *"March 3rd – More heavy snow over the weekend";* March 10th – outbreaks of scarlet fever and colds *"caused by the very bad weather".* In March the school has to be disinfected because of the outbreak of scarlet fever.

In February 1917 the temperature was regularly below freezing, and given the very inadequate means of heating the classrooms: a stove in the middle of a very large room, it must have been almost impossible to operate. Miss Reed gives a graphic account of the situation: *"The fires are dreadful - The children have cried with the cold, and they can't hold their pens correctly, nor write owing to having such cold hands".* Still the children continued to do their bit for the war effort. In October 1817 *"We have sent to Mr Bates over 5cwt* (hundredweight) *of chestnuts which the girls have gathered together for the Munitions Minister,"* (these for additional food for munitions workers) and perhaps the strangest request of all: *"An appeal has been made by the Government for acorns to make cordite."* (Miss Reed: Oct 24th 1917)

In November 1917, as a result of the bombing of London in that year, there was a large influx of children from the Capital, which pushed the numbers in the Boys' School up from an average attendance of 117 to 173, but by the end of November many of the London children had gone home and the average dropped to 153. *"This does not cause overcrowding"* Henry Saloway records. In February 1918 Mr F Brooks of the RAMC, a former pupil teacher at the school, visited and took several lessons which must have given Mr Saloway some relief, but the shortages caused by the war were making life difficult. *"Stock is getting very short indeed."* Mr Saloway recorded on March 10th 1918, and Miss Reed lamented in July of the previous year: *"We find it very difficult to make the old books do, as the children are tired of them, and they are very torn. The allowance for each child has been cut down to about half."*

In April 1917, to try and combat the effects of the growing food shortages the school started supplying school dinners *"at 2d each... and a number of the children have taken advantage of the same."* The canteen was set up in the Artillery Drill Hall next to the school. This large stone building used to stand facing onto St Michael's Lane until it was demolished to make way for the Rope Walks car park. It was built in 1866 to provide training quarters for A Company of the First Dorset Rifle Volunteers. All that remains of a building that was once integral to the social life of the town, providing the venue for various entertainments, as well as facilities that were used from time to time by many of the schools, is the inscription that once graced the front of the building, now built into the perimeter wall of the car park.

In May and June, Henry Saloway records awards for bravery given to two former pupils: William Legg was awarded the Military Medal *"for bravely keeping telephone connections intact in spite of great personal danger",* and F Brooks, so recently a visitor to the school was *"awarded the Military Medal for services at the front during the recent battles".*

The state of desperation in the country by 1918, in the face of the losses suffered in all the theatres of war, is underlined starkly by the fact that Henry Saloway, at the age of fifty, was himself required to go to Dorchester for a medical examination for possible National Service. It was no doubt to his relief and that of the school managers when he was told by the President of the Medical Board that he would not be called up but should remain at his post. He adds *"Mrs Saloway took charge during my absence."* It was fortunate that Lily Saloway was also a qualified teacher for she often stepped into the breach to supply for absent staff, not just in this emergency, but throughout Mr Saloway's time as headmaster.

Still the news of old boys being killed comes in: Albert Marsh had died in April in France; Sergt B G Hallett died of heat-stroke in India, and in September, Percy (Arthur?) Ward was killed in France. Labour shortages in 1918 mean that a number of the boys in the school were required by the Flax Production Dept *"for the purpose of pulling flax and the attendance has this week suffered in consequence."*

As early as July 1918 the outbreak of Spanish Influenza hit Bridport and was playing havoc with the attendances. By September 1918 the influenza epidemic really began to take hold, and the school was closed until mid-October, but by November the influenza had still not abated. It is therefore perhaps not surprising that the Armistice, when it came on

November 11th was greeted by a rather subdued entry in the Boys' Logbook: *"Today news of the Armistice arrived – school was dismissed for the rest of the day. The flag was run up and the children attended a Thanksgiving service at the Church."* Miss Reed adds with a little more enthusiasm: *"there was great excitement. The children went home after attending Church. They had holiday the rest of the day"*. On December 6th Henry Saloway reflected in his Logbook entry that twenty-three old boys *"have laid down their lives for their country during the Great War."*

In February 1919 he and Lily Saloway finally succumbed to the flu, and although he was back at his post by mid-February on the 17th of that month Dr Robinson, the MOH ordered the school to close because of the influenza epidemic, which was still raging. School did not reopen until March 14th. The very last entry referring to the war records the departure of the Belgian refugees in April 1919. *"I am very sorry to record the loss of the Belgian children who have attended the school during the war. They have mastered the language in a wonderful manner and were among the most promising pupils in the class"*, Henry Saloway reports.

As so often, the war gave impetus for reform. In 1918 another major Education Act was passed. The 1918 Education Act required that all children should remain at school until the age of fourteen, and more significant for the schools, no pupil could leave during a term. Gradually life returned to normal after the war, but further upheaval was in store. In 1920, in response to the 1918 Act, plans were drawn up by the County Education Committee for a reorganisation of elementary schools in the Bridport area. The proposals envisaged the amalgamation of the National and General schools into three infant schools, two boys schools one for 7-11 and one for boys over 11 and two girls schools to cater for the same age groups. It had been proposed that religious instruction in the new schools should be on the same lines as that offered at the Bridport Secondary School. In effect what was being proposed was secular education with religious instruction as part of the curriculum. The outcome in practice would have been to make all the Bridport schools "County" schools and end the link with the church, although this was not the stated intention of the Education Committee.

Not surprisingly Canon Joseph Coulter, the Rector of St Mary's, strongly opposed the plans on the grounds that the religious instruction could not be guaranteed as the General Schools were non-conformist, and worse still *"very largely Unitarian"*. The old prejudices still held sway! He felt that the strength of religious education at the Secondary School was largely due to it having a very excellent headmaster, and by implication suggested that he did not have similar confidence in the orthodoxy of the headmaster of the General School. In something of a panic he wrote for advice to the

National Society and must have been relieved to be told that under the 1918 Act the Local Education Authority *"has no power to compel groupings of schools except they are of the same denomination."* He was urged to resist and work closely in the matter with the Diocesan Voluntary School Association.

Even if this put Canon Coulter's mind at rest there were other problems to contend with. In 1922 HMI condemned the boys school as unfit and insisted that the managers make improvements to the fabric of the building and the facilities. By 1925 it would appear that the money had still not been found for Canon Coulter again approached the National Society for aid. His letter shows that he had already put the work in hand as he states that it must be carried out in the summer vacation of that year as *"managers are obliged, owing to report (sic) of HMI, to carry out alterations to the Boys' School"* by putting in *"a new floor, a folding partition and a fireplace."*

In an earlier letter dated 16th June of the same year Canon Coulter again betrays the almost siege mentality that seems to have gripped the members of St Mary's parish at this time as they continued to perceive the better-endowed non-conformist schools as a constant threat. *"It is important"*, he reminds the Society, *"to keep the Church schools in a town like this where there is a non-conformist school as an alternative, and when we are educating some 300 children."* [6]

By the 1930's all the Bridport elementary school had developed senior classes (Standard 7) for those pupils who did not manage to get into the Grammar School, but who wanted to continue their education. In order to rationalise this tendency and make proper provision for senior pupils, in 1933, the Bridport CE School, as the three Departments of the National School had come to be called at this date, was reorganised, and amalgamated with Allington National School.[7] The Senior School, now a mixed school, was to be at Allington, and was to be led by Mr Theodore Walker, with Mr Penrose, and the Misses Beams and Kingman from Gundry Lane. The Gundry Lane schools became a Mixed Junior and a Mixed Infants: the Juniors under the headship of Clarissa May Rendell, who was, by this time the Girls' School Headmistress, having taken over from Miss Reed in February 1930. Miss Rendell had spent most of her career, both as a pupil, then a pupil teacher and finally assistant teacher at St Mary's with only a brief period away from the school from 1907 to 1909

---

[6] National Society's School File on Bridport National School held at the Church of England Record Centre
[7] This was part of a comprehensive reorganisation of elementary education in Bridport carried out by the County Council Education Committee. Extracts from DCEC Reports File: reorganisation of Schools (Bridport District): 1934, (DHC/ S117/12/15)

presumably to attend college. She returned as a certificated teacher. She was to continue to lead the Junior School and later the Primary School until April 1949.

The Infant School was to be in the charge of Miss Lawrey with Mrs Rosa Walker, as her assistant. In fact in September 1934 Miss Lawrey left and Rosa Walker took over as Infant Mistress. The upheaval did not just affect the school; there was a good deal of opposition from parents, particularly of the younger children. To mollify them, it was originally proposed to run a bus from Allington to transport the Allington infants to their new school. The reorganisation inevitably meant a lot of extra work and uncertainty for the schools involved. Mr Saloway complained on March 10th in the Boys' School Logbook: *"There seems to be some doubt as to the time when the proposed union with Allington is to take place as, as yet, no 'official' notice has been sent"*. But by March 31st the notice must have arrived for Mr Saloway records a meeting of the Allington parents and plans to amalgamate the managers of the two schools.

There is an understandable note of sadness both in Miss Rendell's and Mr Saloway's end of term entries in 1933. Miss Rendell reported in April: *"We have been turning out all cupboards as reorganisation takes place after the Easter Holidays. This afternoon I say farewell to all my senior girls - we have had a happy time together. A farewell party was held in the Church House on the evening of April 7th. The senior girls presented me with a silver calendar and an address book, also bouquets of flowers were given me and also to Miss Kingman and Miss Beams. We indulged in games and dances etc. until 9-30 when we all left tired but happy."* [8]

For Mr Saloway the sense of the end of an era was even more acute, for he was to retire: *"April 7th: Today is the last day of the School's (Boy's School) life. I retire today and the school ceases to exist"* [9]. (Fig 20) He had been Headmaster for just over forty-two years. His long service to the school was recognised at a gathering of former and present pupils and clergy at Church House on May 26th 1933 when he was presented with a gold half-hunter watch. Miss Eva Spenser, a member of staff at the time who had served with him for a number of years, spoke at the ceremony. She reminded everyone that *"Mr Saloway opened the Boys' School and Mr Saloway closed it. The school knew no other head."* [10] A statement that conveniently forgot the former unsuccessful Boys' Department that closed in 1883, and that everyone seemed anxious to consign to oblivion.

The preparation for the reorganisation of the school necessitated yet more repairs particularly to the Boys' School, but this time the National

---

[8] Bridport National Girls' School Log: 1930-1933 (In same volume as the Mixed School Log 1933-1977): DHC/S.329
[9] Bridport National Boys' School Log: 1921- April 1933: DHC/S.329
[10] Bridport News: June 2nd 1933

Society was only able to contribute £5 towards the £70 needed. The Diocesan Board granted £25, but the rest had to be raised locally. A former pupil of the Girls' School from 1925 to 1934, recalled the layout of the Girls' and Infants' Schools. She was unable to describe the Boys' School, as she only once ventured into the building with a message from one of her teachers. At this period the former Girls' Schoolroom was divided into three classrooms by means of one glass-panelled screen and one calico screen. It occupied the east wing of the building, while the Infants' Department, also formerly one large room, was divided into three rather smaller rooms with calico screens. This was at the rear of the building. The Boys' School occupied the west wing, and the toilets were on the other side of a corridor that ran across the back of the school.

The three girls' classrooms accommodated seven classes. Miss Kingman's room, which housed Standards 1 and 2 was at the rear of the east wing, next door to the Infant Rooms. Miss Beams taught Standards 3 and 4 in the middle section, and at the front of the building Miss Reed had her classroom, where she taught Standards 5, 6 and 7. The girls and boys had separate playgrounds, divided by a stone wall, and the boys had a separate entrance from that used by the girls and infants. Until the reorganisation of 1933, only the Infants' Department was mixed. The sheer discomfort of the school in winter is underlined by the fact that, even as late as the 1920's, only two "Tortoise" stoves, situated in the central classrooms in each Department served to heat the entire Girls' and Infants' Schools.[11]

The interwar years saw great changes in the elementary school curriculum, particularly for girls. The academic rigour of their education increased; physical education was introduced with netball and rounders teams, and interschool matches. The boys were playing football, and also taking part in competitions such as the West Dorset Cup. The opening of the St Mary's Playing field in September 1928 made such outdoor games a real possibility for the first time. Country dancing had been a favourite activity for the girls since just after the period of the First World War and in 1921, when Cecil Sharpe, the pioneer of the folk music revival, visited Bridport, fourteen St Mary's girls were involved in the accompanying display of folk dancing in the Drill Hall. Miss Reed also introduced Maypole dancing which was a particular feature of May Day celebrations, and which features in a number of photographs taken of St Mary's School. (Figs 21&22) Cookery classes were also added in the 1920's, and the boys went either to the Grammar school or to Allington for woodwork classes.

Gardening was also an activity introduced for the boys by Henry Saloway. The General School Boys had plots of land attached to the

---

[11] I am indebted to Christine Vlieklig (née Burt) for these details.

Grammar School site in St Andrew's Road. In 1927 St Mary's acquired a plot of land near Folly Mill and Mr Strawbridge FRHS was given the job of teaching the subject. It was not without difficulty for the plot of land was very overgrown when the school took it over. As it was close to the river it was subject to flooding. However the subject proved popular and the boys raised vegetables on their plot. There were the inevitable accidents: *"Albert Trevett while gardening in the school gardens this afternoon pushed the fork he was using through his boot and into his big toe."* [12]

Swimming was introduced, but before being allowed to swim at West Bay beginners had to show their competence in the water, and in June 1928, Henry Saloway proposes to *"again use the* (River) *Asker as a bathing pool."* In August 1929 the school Boys' Team took part in the swimming relay race at West Bay presumably during the annual Regatta.

In 1936 the separate Junior and Infant Schools were finally merged into one school, and Miss Rendell took charge. The Infants occupied two of the former Girls' School classrooms at the front of the west wing and the Juniors took over all the rest of the building. Even with this reorganisation of the facilities, the Gundry Lane site offered increasingly cramped conditions. This problem was not to be rectified until well after the Second World War. In the 1938 HMI report the addition of a Nursery class for the under fives is greeted with approval:

"The lowest class of Infants now consists entirely of children under 5 years of age. The room in which the class is placed is most suitable for the purpose, as it is the brightest and sunniest. There are a sufficient number of beds (most of which it will be noted were supplied by the Managers) and there is also a growing supply of large toys, and certain other suitable apparatus. Thus the class begins to approach an effective Nursery Class." [13]

Sadly the Nursery Class was short lived, as it had to be closed in the early years of the Second World War. It is interesting to note that pupils who attended the school in the early 1940's remember the camp-beds in the Infant School, and the fact that on fine days the beds were taken out into the sunny playground for the children to have their after-lunch rest in the fresh air.

Bridport was not immune to the economic depression of the 1930's. There was much unemployment, and short-time working in the staple industries meant that pay was very low and many families had a struggle to make ends meet. It was not until 1938 with war looming that the industry in the town began to recover.

---

[12] Bridport National Boys' School Logbook: 1921-1933: DHC/S.329
[13] All the information above and following is taken from the Bridport National Mixed School Logbook: 1933-1977: DHC/S.329

In September 1939, war was declared and almost immediately the school was faced with accommodating the first wave of evacuees. On the 18th September 1939 Miss Rendell reported *"I have admitted 33 children mostly evacuees from danger zones."* By 29th September total numbers in the school had risen to 246, and by the end of October two rooms in each Department, Infants' and Junior were occupied by evacuees *"which prevents normal working"*. The school was operating mornings only for the local children, so the evacuees could be taught in the afternoon, and the total number on roll had risen again to 254. At last matters were eased when, at the end of October, the evacuees were transferred to the Baptist Sunday School. *"All available furniture has been lent to seat our visitors in their new buildings"*, Miss Rendell records.

At last in mid-November the remaining evacuees from the Infants had been transferred and afternoon school recommenced, but it was only a temporary respite for on the Monday following *"one class of another London school (St Peter's) was transferred here and the two upper classes of infants must now occupy the room. Normal lessons can now be carried on but the room is rather crowded and restricts activity for the young ones."* In 1940 the numbers of evacuees continued to rise and by June 1940 the school's role had risen to 298, and by July it stood at 307. A casualty of the pressure of numbers was the recently established Nursery Class, as, from September 1940, all children under five were excluded from attending school.

Trenches were dug on the opposite side of the river, near Skilling for the use of the school children, though no one seems able to recall exactly where they were. Too far from the school, they were only ever used for one practice, as this immediately demonstrated the impracticality of getting nearly three hundred pupils to the trenches once an air-raid warning had been sounded. *"The staff were all agreed that it would take too long to get under cover and that a mass of children would be a good target for enemy aeroplanes-"*. It was agreed that the children would stay inside the school in the event of an air-raid. To increase safety inside the building the windows were all stripped with brown paper *"to prevent splinters of glass flying."* Also in 1940 the two cloakrooms were converted into shelters for the Junior children, though what precisely this involved the Logbook does not indicate. Ultimately an Anderson Shelter was built in the playground alongside the wall that had formerly divided the playgrounds. A former pupil remembers that it was about twenty or thirty feet long and the base must have been excavated to a depth of several feet for several past pupils remember hitting their heads on the entrance.

Though there were many air-raid warnings and the sirens frequently interrupted school, the first actual bombing was not until the summer of 1942. The bombs that fell behind West Street and seriously damaged the Lily Hotel and adjoining buildings, causing several fatalities, happened during the school holidays and, mercifully, only caused minor damage to the school. *"Shortage of labour"* meant this was not repaired by the time the children returned to school in the September, but that was a small price to pay. The air raid on 16th December in which a number of houses in East Street were destroyed, killing their occupants, and which narrowly missed the General School, was far enough away to leave the Gundry Lane school unaffected. It caused understandable panic in the town, and as soon as they could get to the school after the bombing, *"many parents called to see if their children were safe."* Finally, and one cannot help feeling a little belatedly, in May 1943, the Infant Department of the school was provided with three Morrison Shelters, one for each room. These could double as tables, and at least one pupil recalls one being used as the teacher's desk.

Once again a school meals service was set up, probably that established at the Grammar School, and the WVS (Women's Voluntary Service – later the WRVS) sent helpers to serve the meals *"as 60 to 70 children stay daily."* However it may well be that later on the canteen was rather nearer to the school, possibly once again in the next-door Drill Hall for, by 1946, Miss Rendell was in charge of employing canteen assistants. Past pupils of the time remember eating lunch in the school at this period, whereas before the war only milk was on offer: a third of a pint, the bottles often warmed by the stove on cold days.

Once again war precipitated the demand for reform and the Butler Education Act of 1944 was by far the most radical change in education that this country had so far seen. It was therefore bound to cause considerable upheaval in an area that had in truth seen so little real investment in education over the last half century. Even at this stage, with education nationally high on the political agenda, the discussions that took place at County level over how to reorganise the schools to fulfil the requirements of the act, seem more often to have focused on ways of saving money by re-using existing building stock, than on a really radical commitment to the provision of new buildings.

A number of proposals for the reorganisation of Bridport schools to comply with the new tripartite system were put forward. Bridport already had a Grammar School, and the Senior School at Allington was redesignated Bridport Secondary Modern School. There was also still a Senior Department at the General School in King Street. This left two primary schools, the church school still in Gundry Lane, now increasingly known as St Mary's Primary School, and the Juniors and Infants of the General School also at King Street.

In the 1947 County Development Plan drawn up by the County Council Education Committee, St Mary's School was to be adapted as a "Voluntary Primary Infants School"[14]. The original plan had Juniors (7-11) on the Old Grammar School site and Infants (5-7) at Gundry Lane. This suggestion provoked strong opposition, particularly to the siting of the Infants' School at Gundry Lane. A letter written by the managers of the General School to the Minister of Education in Whitehall expresses grave reservations about making the Gundry Lane site the school for *"all the infants from the town"*.

The managers state in their letter: *"This site, bounded on two sides by narrow streets, without pavements on the side adjoining the school, is both unsuitable and dangerous. There are garages, also premises used by motor haulage contractors, agricultural engineers, furniture depositories etc, discharging onto Gundry Lane, and on Wednesdays this thoroughfare is exceptionally busy with vehicular traffic of all kinds for the cattle market in St Michael's Lane and the Produce Market opposite the school premises."*[15] They went on to urge that neither this nor Allington School be used as a site for Infants. Despite all this the Infant Department of St Mary's School, which had already occupied these *"unsuitable and dangerous"* premises for over seventy years continued to occupy them for a further forty-three years!

In 1948 the HMI report on the Gundry Lane school was uncompromising about the shortcomings of the buildings - particularly the lack of good outdoor facilities: *"The provision for Physical Education throughout the school consists of two playgrounds with a considerable slope and the use of a playing field for games. (St Mary's Field) There is no indoor accommodation for use in wet weather. Some of the playground space is taken up with air-raid shelters and it is hoped these will be removed as soon as possible. The playing field is on low lying ground and is unfortunately frequently too wet for use."*[16]

In 1949, Miss Rendell retired and, in the September of that year, Mr Roy Pethen took over as headmaster. (Fig 23) Mr Pethen was a native of Blandford, and an experienced teacher and headmaster, having been a teacher at both Dorchester Boys' School and at a school in Sidcup in Kent before serving as Headmaster of Badminton School in Gloucestershire for ten years. He was a keen cricketer, having played for St Alfred College in Winchester as well as teams in all the towns where he worked. He captained Bridport Cricket Club for a number of years from 1952.[17]

---

[14] File: Reorganisation of Schools (Bridport District): DHC (S117/12/15)
[15] Ibid.
[16] Quoted in Bridport National Mixed School Logbook 1933-1977: DHC/S.329
[17] Bridport News: "West Dorset Notebook": July 6th 1956

By the time Roy Pethen took over as headmaster, St Mary's Primary School had become a Voluntary Controlled Church of England School, under the provisions of the 1944 Education Act. This meant that while the parish and the diocese kept primary influence over the religious life of the school, and a proportion of the governors were appointed by the diocese – to all intents and purposes the school became a Local Authority school, funded and "controlled" by the Local Education Authority. New buildings and repairs to the existing ones would now be entirely the responsibility of the LEA.

Almost the first thing Mr Pethen had to deal with when he arrived at St Mary's was a collapsing ceiling in one classroom that happily did not cause any injury. The school had by this time created a remedial class, and managed to house it in the school proper rather than in the Drill Hall next door. Still the buildings and playgrounds needed attention. A visit by LEA officials in 1951 recommended a new toilet block, which was built in the following academic year starting in September 1952. In March 1953 the school started to make use of the Salvation Army Hall in Priory Lane as an extra classroom, which enabled a class of sixty Year 2 pupils to be divided into two classes. More work, decoration, and work on the windows continued and in September 1953 Mr Pethen recorded that *"School reopened, a much more attractive and comfortable building than it was a year ago"*.

The shortcomings of Gundry Lane as a site for a school were emphasised in May 1954 when the school gateway was knocked down by a lorry, and still by April 1955 the problem of overcrowding had not been solved. Mr Pethen records in April *"The beginning of the summer term finds the school with the first class of 40 that it has had since 1949."* At last in 1956 some relief was in sight. The *"new secondary school"* had opened *"at Bradpole"* and reorganisation could really take effect.

On 10th Sept Mr Pethen records in the Logbook: *"On 27th August County Hall notified me that the Allington building, vacated by senior children now going to the new Alfred Colfox School, would be available as extra accommodation for this school for the next three years."* He transferred the senior three classes to Allington and kept the younger children, the five to nine-year-olds, at Gundry Lane. The extra space meant that they could now use the large Infants' room as a Hall, *"with new dining furniture and new kitchen facilities"*.

The Allington school was in a poor state of repair and so refurbishment and decoration had to be put in hand, and the frequently criticised toilet facilities were still considered inadequate. On 8th October 1956 Mr Pethen remarks *"School has settled down reasonably. The Allington building has its disadvantages, having been neglected for so long, but apart from the lavatories it is reasonably comfortable."*

130

In 1957 central heating was finally installed in the Gundry Lane building, and the old stoves could be consigned to history. By the end of July 1958, the Allington school building was finally closed as a school and St Mary's three top classes were moved to King Street. For a while they had to share the accommodation with Alfred Colfox School pupils, and it was not until the autumn term of 1962 that the Colfox pupils finally vacated the remaining rooms, and St Mary's had the use of the whole building. Within three years however part of the former Girls' School building had been earmarked for the new Bridport Teachers' Centre, and by January 1966 the Centre was decorated, furnished and fully functioning.

By now, St Mary's School had assumed the shape many local people remember best. It became a split-site school, with all the disadvantages that entails. The Gundry Lane site remained as the Infant School and the Junior School took over the King Street site in its entirety. For more than thirty years the school had to contend with all the difficulties of operating in old dilapidated and cramped Victorian buildings. Just how poor the accommodation got is indicated by a 1974 news item in the Bridport News reporting on the collapse of part of a false ceiling in the King Street building. The false ceiling panels had been installed in an attempt to conserve heat in the old high-ceilinged rooms. No one was injured, fortunately. However, despite the difficulties of operating across two sites some distance apart, and in old Victorian buildings, the school thrived. By Sept 1969 the roll had grown to 317. In the 1970 New Years' Honours List Roy Pethen was awarded the CBE. In the same year he retired and Mr Roland C Potter took over as Headmaster.

It was not only in school buildings that Bridport was deficient. It also lacked a swimming pool, and increased pollution in the river and a greater awareness of the potential hazards, had made swimming in the harbour unacceptable. All the schools in the years after the war would fund-raise to build their own small pools. In 1971 after intensive fund-raising by the St Mary's parents, a learner pool was erected behind the school, staff were coached in swimming instruction and in July of that year the pool was officially opened.

By April 1972 the school roll had risen to 404, but this seems to have been the high-water mark for numbers as by September 1972 the numbers had fallen back to 395. Nevertheless proposals for a new school were by now being discussed and Mr Potter estimated that any new school should be built large enough to cater for 450 pupils. However far from rising, the numbers in the school began a gradual decline down to 351 in 1977, and Mr Potter records in the Log *"no new building as yet envisaged."* The school had a further thirteen years to wait.

The Gundry Lane/ King Street School finally closed in 1990 and the new St Mary's School opened on its present site on Skilling Hill in the academic year 1990/91. The new school was officially opened on June 26th 1991 by the Bishop of Sherborne the Rt Rev John Kirkham, and the guest of honour was the well-known children's writer, Dick King-Smith. The school was designed to be open plan and the history of the school and to some extent of primary education in Bridport is still commemorated in the four "pavilion" areas into which the school is divided. These are "Miss Gundry's", "Gundry Lane", "King Street" and "Allington". Appropriately enough "Miss Gundry's" was designed to house the infant classes, although in fact St Mary's has no historical connection with Miss Gundry's School which, as we have seen, was originally a Wesleyan school. "Allington", as befitted the erstwhile Senior School, housed the older pupils.

The old building in Gundry Lane was sold, and is now used by a variety of businesses including appropriately enough a day nursery, a Christian bookshop and a shop selling equipment and toys for babies and young children. The connection of church and early years education also persists at the King Street site. Part of the two-storey building is now occupied by St Ronan's Nursery, and the single storey building, facing onto Folly Mill Lane, is the home of the Bridport Christian Fellowship.

IX

MORE CHURCH SCHOOLS

The child population of Bridport and its neighbouring parishes was considerably higher, vis-à-vis the adult population, in the nineteenth century than it is today. Although we now tend to think of Allington as simply the west end of Bridport, its parish, now part of the Team Ministry of Bridport, had, in the nineteenth century, a very distinct identity, not least because of the physical boundary drawn by the River Brit. Bradpole parish was much larger than it is today; its boundaries coming as far south as the north side of Rax Lane, and including all of the area from just north of West and East Street, which included Victoria Grove and much of Barrack Street and St Andrew's Road. The need to provide for the children of Bradpole and Allington bore as heavily on the clergy of these parishes as it did on the Rectors of St Mary's, and they too turned to the National Society for help in establishing schools for the children of their parishioners.[1]

Bradpole National School

In April 1848 the Rev Alexander Broadley, Vicar of Bradpole, wrote to the National Society: *"Rev Sir, There is, I fear, some probability of a little delay in my getting matters forward in respect of my contemplated School Buildings. A favourable opportunity having presented itself, I have come to the determination of proceeding at once with a National School in the Cottage which at present I rent for the purpose of carrying on the Sunday School".*[2] He had only been in possession of the benefice for four years, but this graduate of Wadham College, Oxford, like so many of his generation, was determined to improve the education of the children of his parish.

He had already put in an application for a grant to build and fit up *"one School-room for Boys and Girls, together with a residence for a teacher"*. By March 1848 he is apparently having second thoughts about the teacher's house for he writes asking whether a teacher's residence is *"insisted upon"* and whether *"if it be so the residence need be attached and contiguous to the School-room."*[3] This is the first intimation of the financial problems the parish was to encounter. However Hutchins, in the edition of 1863, describes the village as having *"A good modern National School*

---

[1] The schools of the more outlying villages: Loders, Shipton Gorge, Burton Bradstock, Symondsbury, Powerstock, though close to Bridport are outside the scope of this history and their stories will need to be told at another time.
[2] National Society's School File on Bradpole National School held at the Church of England Record Centre
[3] Ibid

adjoining the churchyard, with teacher's residence attached," so whatever difficulties there were about erecting a house seem to have been resolved.

The grant application gives a picture of a large and somewhat scattered parish. The total population of the parish at the time was 1,245, but of these some 400 lived more than a mile from the church. Rev Broadley seemed to feel that the children of those living more distant would not attend the school as the application is to cater for the remaining population which he adds is *"chiefly agricultural and manufacturing".* He states that the existing Sunday School has a hundred pupils, sixty boys and forty girls, and daily scholars are already being catered for, sixty-five in all, thirty boys and thirty-five girls. All are *"very much crowded in a cottage rented for the purpose".* He adds that a *"Dame's School in the parish caters for about 10 or 12 scholars".* Possibly this was the Misses Harts' School transferred from Bridport.

The new school for which the grant was being applied was to consist of one room for 105 boys and girls. He intended to charge fees of 1d per week with an additional 1d for extras such as writing and arithmetic. He estimated the cost of schoolmaster or mistress to be £32 per annum, which cost would be met out of the school pence and subscription. The building was to be constructed of stone under a slate roof and with a floor of Watchett Tile. The estimated cost of the building was £352, of which locally raise funds totalled £122, the Committee of the Privy Council for Education would provide £120, and he hoped the National Society would make up the deficit of £110.

The schoolhouse was completed in 1848, but the conveyancing of the site was not. Problems arose because the site chosen for the school, that of the former Parish Pound, belonged to the Poor Law Guardians of the Bridport Workhouse, and it appears they required certain conditions before they agreed to convey the land to the parish for use as a school. On May 24th 1848 a proposal was put before the Vestry that *"The site of the Parish Pound be converted to the purpose of a building site for a Parochial School Room and another site below the church be prepared for the said Parish Pound".*

The minutes of the July Vestry Meeting are more precise and give the exact location of the piece of land owned by the Poor Law Guardians that the parish wanted for their school. It was *"bounded in the north and west by a field called Court Close – the property of Mr E B Bishop – and in the east by the churchyard and on the south by the Parish Road – being in extent forty feet square or thereabouts, and under the provisions of an Act passed in the fifth year of the reign of her present Majesty (1842) entitled 'An Act to afford further facilities for the Conveyance and Endowment of Sites for Schools'."* The meeting hoped the Guardians of the Poor of Bridport would convey the land *"to the Minister, Churchwardens and*

Overseers of the Poor of the Parish of Bradpole for the purpose of the said Act, and to be applied as a Site for a School to be under the management and control of the Minister of the Parish for the time being, and of such persons being members of the Church of England, to be hereafter named, and submitted for the approval of the Committee of Council on Education, and to be conducted upon the principles of the Incorporated Society for Promoting the Education of the Poor in the Principles of the Established Church, (The National Society) and to be open to the inspection of the Inspectors, or Inspectors appointed or to be appointed by Her Majesty."[4]

It was this last stipulation that caused the trouble. The Vestry Minutes of a meeting held on February 26th 1850, give some insight into the battle that had clearly been going on for the best part of two years between the Vicar and Churchwardens on one side, and the Poor Law Guardians on the other. The issue that divided them was this matter of government inspection. The Vicar and the Churchwardens wanted no kind of interference with the school; the Poor Law Guardians had made the inspections a condition of their conveying the land. Also dependent on accepting regular inspections was the Government grant. The upshot was that the Vestry declined the grant, which put them into severe financial difficulties.

Just how deep their financial difficulties were appears from a letter written by Alexander Broadley to the National Society dated June 1849, Rev. Broadley states: *"having built my school buildings in the hope of* (assistance) *from the Society..... and having declined the government grant on the grounds of the management clauses which myself and the parishioners did not choose to accept, I have contracted a debt of nearly £110 for which I have made myself responsible."[5]*

At the Vestry Meeting on February 26th the churchwardens formerly rescinded the approval of the terms of the Conveyance, and debated two new proposals: firstly that as the *"Parish School"* has been erected *"without the aid of the Committee of the Privy Council"* that they rescind the formal resolution to allow HM Inspections, and secondly, *"That the Poor Law Board be solicited to approve the Conveyance of the said School Site, without insisting on the inspection".* Both proposals were passed unanimously by the vestry but, unsurprisingly, the Poor Law Board and the Guardians declined to proceed with the conveyance.[6] The matter of the school site was only resolved by going over the heads of the Poor Law Guardians and appealing to the representative of the *"late Lord of the*

---

[4] Minutes of the Bradpole Vestry Meetings from 1848 - 50 : DHC/MIC/R/327
[5] National Society's School File on Bradpole National School held at the Church of England Record Centre
[6] Minutes of the Bradpole Vestry Meetings from 1848 - 50 : DHC/MIC/R/327

135

Manor, J H Browne Esq[7] who conveyed the land to the Vicar and Churchwardens without any stipulations. Precisely how this was achieved is not clear from the Vestry Minutes, but the fact that *"a Pound was placed in its present situation under the churchyard wall"* once the school had been built might suggest that a trade-off of parcels of land was achieved, and resolved the impasse. Things now began to go ahead and the Trust Deed for the school was executed on 23rd July 1850.

The school which stands next to the church in Bradpole and is now a private house, is a small compact building under a pitched roof, constructed in soft honey-coloured stone, and in such a position, facing south, to catch the sun almost all day. It takes little imagination to visualise it as it would have been when it was full of children. It opens onto a raised pavement with a handrail, and well-worn steps lead down onto the roadway. Today there is the hazard of emerging onto a road used by many cars, but then, the road would have been quiet and safe. The building was later enlarged to take 150 children, which may or may not have been over-ambitious as by 1885 the average attendance was only 100, about the same as the original Sunday School. At this time the master was Mark Edwin Johnson, who was Master from the mid-1860's until the early 1890's.

In 1878, no doubt in response to the 1870 Forster Education Act, a School Board was set up in Bradpole. They seem to have been an officious bunch for their activities elicited a rather agitated letter to the National Society from Alex Broadley: *"Kindly instruct me as to the best course Ministers can take in a parish where the School Board has been appointed who desire to occupy the National School for the purpose of education under the Elementary Education Act. All that the Trustees want is to satisfy their consciences on the religious point"*; in other words the matter of religious education. This threat of interference must have seemed like the dispute with the Poor Law Guardians all over again. The Society's reply must have been a relief, for they assure Rev Broadley that the School Board could make no legal claim to the use of the National School. *"The School is held in trust for Church Education and with this trust the School Board has nothing to do."* [8]

The school was further enlarged in 1895 to admit 165 pupils, though the average attendance never seems to have approached this

---

[7] "About 1790 the manor or royalty (of Bradpole) belonged to Mr William Browne of London, who possessed considerable property in the parish. John Herbert Browne esq. Of London and Weymouth, at his death bequeathed his estates in undivided moieties, to James Frampton of Moreton, Francis Brow of Frampton esqs and General Grant, by whom they were afterwards parcelled out, and sold in various small lots." The History and Antiquities of the County of Dorset by John Hutchins M.A. Vol 2 (3rd Ed.) 1863.

[8] National Society's School File on Bradpole National School held at the Church of England Record Centre

136

number, peaking, according to Kelly's Directory, at 120 in 1903. Edwin Johnson was replaced by Miss Alice Garner, and in 1895, the year of the enlargement, the average attendance, according to Kelly's, dropped to the alarmingly low figure of 51. Whether this was the result of the upheaval of the building works or the fact that there was only a mistress in charge, is not clear. By 1898 a husband and wife team, John and Clara Morton were in charge of the Mixed School and the Infants respectively, and they remained in charge until just after the turn of the century, when Thomas Hervey Beams took over. He was still in post in 1927.

Four more teachers served the school in its final years. Miss Gertie Bonfield, was Infants' Mistress in the 1930's and into the war years. Miss Emily Sutton, who was also organist and choir mistress at Holy Trinity Church, was Junior Mistress at the same time. The last headmaster of the school was Mr William Bayne-Cole, assisted by Miss A Woodhead as Infant Mistress. These two steered the school through to its closure in 1959. "Billy" Bayne-Cole transferred to the staff at the Alfred Colfox School, where he taught until his death in 1974.

Much the same issues affected Bradpole School as affected all the elementary schools in the area: the same problems with epidemics; the same difficulties imposed by two world wars. In 1939, like the other Bridport schools, they had to try to accommodate what for such a small school was quite a large influx of evacuees. Thirty-one children, mostly from the London Boroughs, from Plymouth and Southampton, are listed as being at Bradpole School in that year, though most had gone home by 1944. The school finally closed on 23rd July, 1959. The children who were not old enough to go up to the Alfred Colfox School were all transferred to the "Bridport General County School" (later designated Bridport County Primary).[9]

A final grand concert was given on July 21st to mark the closure, which was appropriate considering the strength of music in the school. The school's Junior Choir had not only won the Junior Schools' Premier Award at the Dorset County Festival, but had also been selected to represent Dorset choirs in a West of England BBC series on music in the region, according to the Bridport News of 17th July 1959. The following week's edition of the paper recorded the final concert. As it was attended by *"the whole populace of Bradpole,"* it was held at the Alfred Colfox School, where, according to the paper, the Assembly Hall was filled *"almost to overflowing"* to pay tribute to *"this humble little 'seat of learning' "*. Mrs Violet Bayne-Cole, who, as well as being the headmaster's wife, was also a

---

[9] Bradpole School Admissions Register 1944-59 DHC S74/3/3

137

noted local amateur singer, contributed several songs to the programme, and conducted the choir. There were formal presentations. Mr Bayne-Cole received a barometer, and Miss A Woodhead, his assistant was given a travelling clock. Fittingly for such a nostalgic event, Miss Emily Sutton, the former headteacher, received a bouquet of flowers to mark her *"long association with the school, first as a pupil and later as a teacher"*.

Allington National School

The first reference to Allington School is in 1831 when an application was made to the National Society for aid towards *"the Erection of a Sunday School for Boys and Girls at Allington in Dorsetshire"*. The application was made by the Rev Henry Fox, who seems to have been another of the very energetic clergyman whose efforts were so important in providing local children with an education, often in the face of considerable difficulties.

In the application he describes the parish as consisting of about 1,330 inhabitants of whom between eighty and ninety were children between the ages of seven and thirteen. The application was to provide a purpose-built school of two rooms to accommodate at least eighty boys and eighty girls, to be supported by annual subscription. The initial proposal was to build a stone, slate-roofed building in one corner of the Churchyard of the newly completed St Swithun's Church in Allington

Whether there was resistance in the parish to this proposal is not clear, but what is clear is that the Society was not keen on the location. Unsurprising really, as the site chosen was in the lower corner of the graveyard! However the idea was persisted with, and again in 1834 Henry Fox wrote to the Society, this time enclosing an architect's plan of the proposed site. The tone of his letter is slightly defensive: *"We have no prospect of being able to procure a different site and there seems no reasonable objection to the school being built in the Churchyard, as it was consecrated in the year 1827, and contains ample space for present and future generations, besides which the school will be so erected as to leave the churchyard distinct and private."* [10]

The matter rumbled on for another year with letters going back and forth. Not only was the Rev Fox having trouble over the site of the school, he was also having difficulty raising money locally and in October 1835 he wrote again with an estimate of the probable costs of building the school. He expected it to cost £220, *"to meet which a subscription has been raised now amounting to about £60 and I think it likely a further £30 may be*

---

[10] National Society's School File on Allington National School held at the Church of England Record Centre

138

advanced." He anticipated a government grant of £80 and therefore asked the Society for £50, but by September 1837 there was still no school, and it appears that, by this time, the idea of using the churchyard site had been abandoned.

On Sept 19th 1837 he wrote once more: *"The impediment in our way has been the difficulty of procuring a suitable site, which however is now overcome by my having the opportunity myself* (of) *giving a piece of land for the purpose, belonging to the glebe of the Impropriate Rectory of Allington of which I am the sole and lawful owner."* He goes on *"I would wish the Deed of Gift* (to be executed) *as briefly and plainly as possible and at the least possible expense."* The foundation stone was duly laid in 1837 and a further letter dated Nov 2nd 1838 indicates that *"the Schoolhouse for the use of the Sunday School in Allington is now nearly completed."*

Where was it? The only clue in the letters to the National Society is that it was built on glebe land belonging to the Rectory. However, in a memoir of the period, the writer recalls an earlier school which he attended as a small child *"at the corner of Fulbrook Lane in a building now occupied by a bakery".*[11] The bakery certainly existed and was indeed on the corner of Fulbrook Lane in the building now occupied by St Swithun's Stores. Further corroboration comes from the 1871 census return which clearly lists next door to Fulbrook House, a *"School House"* for a *"Day and Sunday School"* and in the same property James and Harriet Cleal (or Cleel) *"Master baker employing one boy"* and *"baker's wife".* It is therefore clear that the bakery did not follow the schoolhouse, but the school and bakery occupied the same building, the bakery probably occupying the rear of the building.

Fulbrook Lane (the man, not the place) recalls *"a large square room with hat pegs round the four walls, and, on one day a week, in addition to the hats and cloaks, loaves of bread here and there between the pegs. These were brought to the school by the relieving officer for distribution to those children whose parents were needy".* Bearing in mind the bakery next door, probably they were not brought very far! (It is interesting to note that the building immediately on the opposite side of the road to the National School, housed the Industrial Branch of the Girls' General School, which also provided meals for the poor labouring classes: See Chapter X.) Hutchins mentions this first Allington School, and describes it as a parochial school for 160 children located in two rooms one above the other, built in 1838 by subscription, with aid from a government grant and the National Society.[12]

---

[11] "Bridport in the Nineteenth Seventies and Eighties" by Fulbrook Lane,1934 (BMS/19)
[12] "History and Antiquities of the County of Dorset": by John Hutchins Vol. 2 1863

The original school clearly served a pressing need. A later grant application dated 17th December 1861, this time for money for books and equipment, gives more details of the building and the school. Each schoolroom was 30ft long and 16ft wide. The school employed two paid teachers, both men, and eight voluntary teachers, no doubt mostly women. The school was entirely dependent at this time on the school pence to defray the teachers' salaries. There seemed to have been no or few subscribers, the school being funded in addition to the children's pence by collections made from the parishioners. The number of children in attendance at this point was 110. However *"in attendance"* meant not daily attendance but attendance after work, for in an earlier letter, Herbert Williams, describing himself as *"Curate of Allington"* indicated to the Society *"that we had only an evening school as the children get employment during the day in the Flax Warehouses."*[13]

In his efforts to jolt his wealthier parishioners into becoming subscribers Rev Williams enlisted the aid of the local newspaper. An extract from the Bridport News which he copies out on the back of his grant application reads:

"We are glad to find that the school is in a very prosperous state. Upwards of 100 scholars attend every evening. Not a tenth of these are able to attend school during the day, a fact which is of itself sufficient proof that the parish wanted an evening school. Some articles of school furniture and other things, which cost money, are badly wanted and we feel sure that the well-to-do inhabitants of Allington will not allow their active Curate – the Rev H Williams – and his assistants to labour very long under disadvantages which a subscription of a few pounds would remove." What exactly the Bridport News means by *"a very prosperous state"* is unclear, as to a modern reader the school's state seems quite the reverse of prosperous, but perhaps they were referring to the state of the buildings which in another letter the Rev Williams describes as "good" and he also refers to the very many children who were being educated. Technically the school was still a Sunday School, though to us it was operating much more like an evening institute. With the 1870 Education Act however, it became incumbent on parishes to provide proper elementary education and if they did not then the secular School Boards would do it for them. The pressure was on to rebuild.

Although it was the Revised Code on 1862 which had stipulated the keeping of Logbooks, the first extant Logbook for Allington School is dated 1870.[14] The first entry for 7th November 1870 simply says rather testily: *"School troublesome - the children not being settled down".* The entry for

---

[13] National Society's School File on Allington National School held at the Church of England Record Centre
[14] Allington Mixed School Logbook: DHC/MIC/R/890

140

January 9th 1871 gives some idea of the number of children attending the school at this point, though not the roll, which always at this period tends to be larger than the attendance. There were fifty-four children present and the master admitted eleven new pupils. It would appear that Allington School was, from the outset, a mixed school, unlike the Bridport National School.

The Summary of the Inspector's Report for 1872 gives a clear indication of the urgent need for new buildings. *"My Lord's (sic) trust that every effort will be made to complete the new buildings now in contemplation before the next visit of HM Inspector, for it is very doubtful whether they will be able to frank any further aid to the school in its present premises. (Article 17(c)). In particular, the arrangement by which the Infants are taught on a different floor to the elder children is one that cannot be sanctioned by the department, except as a temporary expedient".*[15] The Master at this time was Alexander Parkin. He is described in the Logbook as a certificated teacher. He served until February 19th 1873, still in the old school. He was replaced by Henry Short, also a certificated teacher. The school obviously used the monitorial system as in March 1871 William Munden was engaged as a monitor. He was paid 2s a week. The school was also training pupil teachers. Two are listed for 1870: J W Munden, and Sarah Guy.

A letter to the National Society of 6th March 1873 fills in a little more background, for in that year an endowment of £44 had enabled the parish to set up a National School, in other words a daily school under a certificated master, *"in a building hitherto used for Sunday School purposes only, but which we felt certain would not be passed by the government inspector".* The report quoted above shows how right they were in that supposition.

In 1871 plans of the new school were sent to the National Society for their approval and on 8th March 1873 a formal application was made for grant assistance. The new school would have an Infants' Schoolroom measuring 34ft by 20ft, and two Mixed schoolrooms, one of 49ft by 20ft and the other of 17ft by 12ft. There was another room, described in the Logbook as "Class" which was to be 20ft by 17ft, though precisely what this was used for is not clear. Once again no teacher's residence was proposed. School pence was raised for the junior pupils to 2d, though for infants it remained 1d. The estimated cost of the new school was £1444 5s 8d, of which £585 8s had been raised locally, £62 10s had been granted by the Diocesan Board of Education, and the Government grant was likely to be £203 15s 6d. It was intended to sell the former schoolhouse for a sum of £200. The old materials on the site were deemed to be worth a further £58.

---

[15] Ibid

The total number of scholars to be catered for would be 275, 190 boys and girls and 85 infants.

The site, close to St Swithun's Church, was purchased for £320, but all did not run smoothly. The Vicar, Rev Edward May wrote to the National Society *"then commenced the difficulty of answering the demands of the Committee of Council, who after repeatedly returning the plans, enlarged them to such an extent as proved quite beyond the sum we had been able to raise"*.

His letter is full of the anxious urgency created by the need to build a school *"so there may be no incentive for establishing a School Board in our midst."*[16] The Society obviously moved fast for by 20th March 1873 they had approved a grant of £203 15s 6d, but matters were still not entirely resolved. The foundation stone for the new school was formally laid on Tuesday August 12th and the occasion was marked by the children being given their Annual Treat.[17]

At last, by the summer of 1874, the building was complete. The new school opened for lessons on 24th July and was described by Henry Short, who was still master at the time of the move, as being *"well filled with desks"*, though by October he was lamenting *"school sadly in want of books and other apparatus"*.[18] The Inspector's Report for 1874 was also less than fulsome in describing the school's new accommodation. A drain was already giving problems. Curtains should be put up to separate the classes in the Mixed School, and the Inspectors deplored the aforementioned shortage of books and apparatus. Emily Jones, who was Infant School Mistress at the opening of the new school commented: *"The room well adapted for teaching with the exception of the small gallery which is very inconvenient at present."*[19]

In July 1875, Henry Short resigned and twenty-two-year-old James Blamey from St Blazey in Cornwall took over as Master. His wife, Kate, also taught at the school for a few years from 1877. James Blamey did not retire until 1918, joining Henry Saloway and John Beard as yet another long-serving headmaster of the period. In all, he was headmaster of the school for forty-three years. Fulbrook Lane, in his memoir, recalls being taught by James Blamey after being transferred to Allington on the temporary closure of the Bridport National Boys' School in 1883. It seems the pattern of part-time schooling was still in place, for he refers to it as *"the Allington adult school"*. Though we would certainly not regard children often as young as twelve or thirteen as adults, the school clearly catered for children who could only attend either mornings or afternoons as they were

---

[16] Letter dated 6th March 1873 National Society's School File on Allington National School held at the Church of England Record Centre.
[17] Allington Infant School Logbook 1873-1900: DHC/MIC/R/890
[19] Ibid

working the rest of the time. For this part-time education the school levied a charge of 2d per week.

Fulbrook Lane gives a vivid picture of the relative deprivation of these part-time students, who were however *"heroes to the others, and 'What do you do at the factory?' was the question. More often than not the answer was 'Carry size'."* [20] He goes on to observe: *"An indication of the nature of that occupation was in many cases afforded by the appearance of a boy's clothing which not infrequently cracked asunder upon the hard seats of the benches. One thing which impressed me were the chapped hands in winter time and the habitual use of the coat sleeve for a handkerchief by ill clad boys. Allington was a poor community,"* he comments. Despite its financial problems, Allington Mixed and Infant Schools must have been successful, as by 1885, the average attendance had reached 271, no doubt inflated by the closure of the Gundry Lane Boys' School.

In 1894 shortcomings in the sanitary arrangements seem to have been detected, just as they were at the Bridport National School at around this time. Government Inspectors demanded that the school increase what is coyly described as *"outside accommodation".* The Rev S.S. Keddle appealed to the National Society for help as *"the managers have been obliged to put up* (the extra toilets) *during the summer holidays".* He goes on *"This is a poor parish and it would be very difficult ... to raise the amount: between £40 and £50."* [21] In his second letter dated 15th September, Rev Keddle is more specific: *"we must have more closet accommodation for the girls: six instead of three".* Also *"The offices* (toilets) *must have separate approaches for each sex (Rule 13a of Schedule VII of the Code) or the grant will be endangered."* Who says only modern education is bedevilled by regulation. A grant of £43 3s 6d was made by the National Society the following October.

This grant application, like the Bridport National School report of 1897 gives us a snapshot of the school at this time. The number of children in attendance was 165 boys and girls and 69 infants. The School's income for the year totalled £364 18s 8d, the bulk of which came as a government grant of £208 10s 7d. The staffing costs were £307 18s. It is instructive to compare these accounts with those of the Bridport School. It was a smaller school of course, but its income was comparable. Neither School, it seems, was particularly well-off. In his covering letter with the grant application, Rev Keddle copies out some quotations from a recent inspection report:

"Mixed School: The school has passed a very satisfactory examination, the Arithmetic and needlework deserving special

---

[20] Size was a gluey substance used to stiffen textiles
[21] Letter dated Aug 24th 1894 in National Society's School File on Allington National School held at the Church of England Record Centre

143

commendation. The tone and behaviour of the children is also praiseworthy.

Infants' School: There is much that is pleasing in this School. The children are bright and happy and the teaching, which is appropriate, is given with considerable skill. A few large natural history pictures are required. Some better sitting accommodation should be provided for the babies class, and the gallery is so improved as to render it more suitable for kindergarten and other exercises.[22] I am not quite sure what this last comment means, but it was also apparent that the school was continuing to train pupil teachers for the report refers to a number of them passing parts of their training.

For a number of years Allington National School, and Bridport National Schools in Gundry Lane existed side by side providing elementary education for the children of the two parishes. However, as already mentioned, after the 1902 Education Act that made possible the setting up of secondary education, a number of the elementary schools began to develop what were called Higher Classes for secondary age children. Both the Gundry Lane Schools and Allington had well-developed higher classes by the 1930's, as had the General Schools, and it finally dawned on the County Council that provision of secondary education in Bridport was somewhat haphazard, so in 1934 a report of the Dorset County Education Committee proposed reorganisation in Bridport and the neighbouring villages to cover the National Schools of Bradpole, Allington and Bridport as well as the Bridport General Schools.[23]

The initial proposal was to close these schools and build a new "Central School". However this idea, as with so many grandiose schemes proposed through the pre and post-Second World War period was abandoned and the more pragmatic (and cheaper) solution was arrived at and implemented in 1934/5. I have already dealt with these changes through the experience of the staff at the Gundry Lane School, but it is worth enumerating them from the point of view of the county administrators.

The proposals were as follows:

- That the Boys' and Girls' Departments at the General School should reorganise as Junior Mixed and Senior Mixed, the former occupying the Boys' School and the latter the Girls' School premises. Presumably the Infants stayed put in their existing schoolrooms.

- That the managers of the Bridport C E and Allington Schools should amalgamate and carry out a combined reorganisation of their schools. Allington School, which was a Mixed School for

---

[22] Ibid
[23] Report of DCEC 21st November 1934: Reorganisation of Schools (Bridport District) 1934: DHC (S117/12/15)

children of all ages becoming a Senior Mixed School, and Bridport C.E School which had been three departments for Boys, Girls and Infants respectively becoming a Junior Mixed Department, and an Infants Department, giving up the older children to Allington School and taking the Allington Junior and Infants' Departments to become later one Department for Junior Mixed and Infants.

The report goes on rather testily: *"it is absurd that in a small town like Bridport there should be two senior schools"*.[24] It was further observed in the same report that if all the outlying schools of Bradpole, Pymore, Symondsbury, Loders, Askerswell, Salway Ash, Chideock, Burton Bradstock, Shipton Gorge and Powerstock were to be closed and central provision made for all their children in Bridport, the County Education Committee would need to provide a building large enough for 600 places. (The size, in fact, of the Alfred Colfox School when it was first built in 1956.)

The history of Allington School from the reorganisation of the 1930's is the history of a very different school to the one set up a hundred years before. It became the *"Senior School (Mixed) for St Mary's Bridport and Allington"* to give it its full title.[25] It drew its pupils from St Mary's Junior School, largely those who did not manage to pass the scholarship exam for the grammar school, or who did not want that form of education. The school built up a fine reputation alongside the Grammar School, as did the Senior Department of the General School.

The job of setting up the Senior School fell to Theodore E Walker. (Fig 24) He started the Senior School with a staff of three: Mr A. W. Penrose, Miss Beams and Miss Kingman. He had succeeded James Blamey as Headmaster in April 1918, and served the school for nearly twenty-two years, retiring in September 1939. Some nine years after his retirement, A. W. Penrose wrote a short memoir of Theodore Walker for the Dorset Year Book of 1958. He conveys a picture of a robust, yet kindly man. His choice of the well-known pilgrim hymn "He Who Would Valiant Be" as the school hymn, gives a flavour of his moral aspirations for his pupils. But school-life should also be fun. There was the annual picnic on Eggardon Hill and summer excursions to places as various as Windsor, Oxford and Hampton Court. Christmas celebrations involved a visit from Father Christmas who made full use of the latest technology, announcing his arrival at the school by telegram. Once he was there, each child received a present. No doubt the boys benefited from the fact that Mr Walker was a keen cricketer. He was also a prominent member of the

---

[24] Ibid
[25] Theodore Walker in the Allington Mixed School Logbook: DHC/MIC/R/890

County Historical Association. On his retirement, he and his wife, Rosa, (former Infant Mistress of St Mary's Junior School), left Bridport and moved to the South East.

The schools last Headmaster was Richard A Inkpen. He took over in January 1940 and saw the school through the war years. On its closure in 1956, he moved with his pupils to the Alfred Colfox School, where he joined the staff.

Bothenhampton Village School

Whereas in Bradpole and Allington, School Boards were successfully resisted, the reverse was the case in the village of Bothenhampton on the eastern outskirts of Bridport. The local School Board was set up in 1872 to administer what had formerly been a church Sunday School built in 1868 on the site of four cottages hitherto known as Bothenhampton Poor House and transferred for the purpose of educating the local children to the Minister and Churchwardens of Bothenhampton by the Guardians of Bridport Union. The schoolhouse was in Church Lane, very close to the Old Church of Bothenhampton. The 1874 Directory "Dorsetshire Towns" lists the School Board for Bothenhampton. The Chairman was the Rev W. P. Bennett, and the other members of the Board were J Gundry, J Hounsell, J Matthews and W Denziloe.

In 1911 the Education Committee of Dorset County Council took up a 99-year lease of the property at a nominal rent payable to the Vicar and Churchwardens and the school had another change of status ceasing to be a board school and instead coming under the control of the County Education Committee. The connection with the church was kept by maintaining in the indenture that the premises should still be available for the Sunday School.[26] The attendance declined in the early twentieth century and the school closed in 1923, though a photograph taken not long before the school closed shows twenty-eight children ranging in age from tots of about four to boys and girls in their early teens.[27] The headmistress at the time, still dressed in the long skirt of Edwardian fashion, is Miss Shilton. The building still stands in Church Street and is now a private house. By comparison with the other church schools Bothenhampton was tiny and of quite short duration, but it is remembered with affection in the village and by those who attended the school. (Fig 25)

---

[26] Information taken from "Bothenhampton and its Churches" by Cyril Kay. Publ. by Bothenhampton District Church Council.
[27] BMLHC Education File

146

Pymore National School .

Pymore School was built to serve the children of the mill workers at Pymore Mill. As such it was quite late in establishment compared to the other National Schools. It was also different in being owned by the Mill and endowed by the Gundry family, and therefore its reliance on the National Society was very slight.

The first recorded mill at Pymore was in 1317. By the nineteenth century the Pymore Mill Company had been established to process hemp and flax, and a thriving industrial community grew up round the mill. By 1812 the original linseed oil, grist and bolling mill had been converted to a spinning mill. Pymore was also involved in the manufacture of sailcloth as well as twines and thread, ultimately specialising in shoe and saddler's thread, mattress and upholsterer's twine, and seaming and roping twines. In 1833 the proprietors came from three families, all well-established in the staple trade of Bridport: Gundry, Templer, and Stephens.

The school was built in 1870 to cater for eighty children. According to the inscription on the gable wall of the little building, the school owes its foundation to a sad event. On 29th January, 1869, Edward Cameron Gundry, the younger son of Joseph Gundry, was drowned at Bridport Harbour in a tragic accident. He was only twenty-five. A popular local figure and a keen sportsman, he held the rank of Lieutenant in the Dorset Militia, and also in the 3rd Dorset (Bridport) Volunteer Artillery Company.

According to a contemporary account of the accident [28] he and a group of friends went down to the Harbour, at seven o'clock in the evening, to see the wreck of a ship, the Demetrius, that had been driven onto the shore. A high sea was running, with waves breaking over the East Pier. Edward and one of his friends, Alfred Dammers, decided to see if they could reach the "King Pile" at the end of the pier. Both were washed off their feet by an unexpectedly large wave, but while Alfred Dammers managed to hang onto a beam at the end of the pier, Edward was swept off into the sea and drowned. His body was recovered from the sea under the East Cliff by two local men, Job Gale and a man called Hutchings, and taken to the Neptune Inn.

His mother, Mrs Mary Gundry, who was devastated by his death, had the school erected in his memory. The small school building, now a private house, still carries the memorial inscription: "Erected in Memory of Edward Cameron Gundry by his Loving Mother. 1870". Looking at the building today it is difficult to work out how eighty children could ever have been accommodated in such a small building, but nominal roll and

---

[28] Report of the accident, inquest and funeral: Bridport News 6th Feb 1869: copy also in DHC/ D/BTM: F20/1

147

attendance were never the same in these years, and most school-rooms were expected to accommodate far more children than would be considered acceptable today.

The school was described as an "Elementary Church of England School", and the managers were to be responsible for overseeing the religious instruction of the pupils. Despite the fact that from time to time a sizeable proportion of the children came from non-conformists' homes, the Bible was taught according to the syllabus arranged by the Diocesan Inspector, and the children also had to learn the C of E catechism. In 1898, according to Kelly's Directory, Miss Jane Chubb was mistress of the school. The average attendance in that year was only twelve. By 1903, Mrs Jane Davey had taken over as Mistress and raised the attendance to forty-five.[29] (Frontispiece)

A pupil who attended the school from 1922-1925, recalled one big room and a small room which contained at that time a small sandpit for the younger children. Mrs Davey was still the teacher. Her husband apparently used to bring her to school in his motorcycle sidecar. There was a very small playground outside the school and outside toilets that were *"very rough"*.[30] Most of the children came from the Mill and lived nearby. When precisely the school closed I have, so far, been unable to ascertain. It seems likely that it closed before the Mill as it was being used as a social club for the village from about 1941. It certainly did not survive WWII, but may have closed even before war broke out.

The Catholic Mission School, later St Catherine's School.

Bridport was, from the seventeenth century, a strong dissenting town, unlike the neighbouring village of Chideock where the influence of the Roman Catholic Arundell family had been strong before, during, and after the Civil War. Even after the slighting (demolition) of Chideock Castle, the seat of the Arundell family, at the end of the civil war (all that now remains of it are a few mounds in a field to the north of the main street), Catholic influence endured in the village, centred around the Manor, which came latterly to the Weld family who were descendents of the Arundells. For many years it was their chapel, attached to the Manor that served the Roman Catholic community. There was a small Roman Catholic community in Bridport, but until quite late in the nineteenth century they had no church or school. The church came first, built between 1845 and 1846. It was dedicated to the Blessed Virgin and St Catherine, though initially it was referred to as "The Mission", as it was not at first an independent parish,

---

[29] Kelly's Directory of Dorsetshire 1903.
[30] Mildred Larcombe: Taped interview for Dorsetshire Schools: BMLHC: BMS/SCH/06

148

but an offshoot of the Catholic Chapel attached to the Manor, at Chideock. It was not until 1848 that the then priest Rev Edward Kenny started an independent baptismal register for Bridport.

In 1863, Rev Remigius Debbault arrived in Bridport from Spetisbury to take up the role of Parish Priest. He seems to have been an enormously energetic man, originally from Flanders in Belgium. When he arrived there was no presbytery for the priest and initially he lodged with a Mr Wright, a catholic bandmaster who lived at number 2 Bedford Terrace. However he was determined to build a priest's house and by June 1866 he had managed to get the shell of a building erected to the south of the church. He set up home in it though it was at first without a staircase or doors. In April 1866, even before the presbytery was finished, he began the building of a school and schoolhouse on land purchased for £250 to the north of the church, where the modern church now stands. The school, initially called The Mission School, opened with eight pupils on 14th February 1867. A further piece of land was bought by one of the congregation, a Mr Roney, north of the school for the sum of £123 10s. The aim of this further purchase was to allow for expansion of the school and a Mr Elwood donated a field near the sea at West Bay, yielding a rent of 5s, which was to go towards the upkeep of the school. The school was extended onto the extra land and in 1882 it re-opened as the St Mary and St Catherine Catholic School catering for forty children. The first schoolmistress of the larger school was Teresa Cavanagh. The school continued on this site until 1902 when it closed and catholic elementary education was transferred to the newly built Convent of the Visitation in Pymore Road.

The Convent was yet another of Remigius Debbault's initiatives. In 1888 he was installed as a canon of Plymouth Cathedral Chapter *"As a due recompense after all his labours and earnestness at Bridport"*.[31] Whether this gave him renewed impetus is not clear, but the very next year, in 1889, he arranged for Sister Mary Bernadine and two other sisters of the Visitation Convent in Ghent to come to Bridport to establish a boys' boarding school. With them came their Director General, Canon Jules Biacq of St Bavon's Cathedral in Ghent. They bought three Georgian houses: numbers 30, 32 and 34 Victoria Grove, to the south of the Presbytery for £850 in 1890, and their school, known as the School of the Sisters of the Visitation, opened in 1891, sadly just too late for it to be recorded by the census of that year. The school remained for some years under the supervision of Sister Mary Bernadine.

This school continued in Victoria Grove until 1899, when it moved, with the community of nuns, to the newly constructed convent building in Pymore Road. This building which was finally demolished in 2002 was a large and imposing three-storey, red-brick building, big enough to house both the community of nuns, the boys' boarding school and the St Mary

149

and St Catherine's day school, which became known colloquially as the "Convent School", though it was actually known, according to a copy of a fees' receipt which survives from 1941, as the "Day School conducted by The Sisters of the Visitation". The fees for a day scholar at that period were £3 a term. Up to the end of the Second World War the school taught girls up to fourteen years of age, but in 1944 the new Education Act divided primary and secondary education and in 1945 all the secondary-age pupils had to transfer to other schools in the area. The school continued as a private fee-paying primary school up to the opening of St Catherine's Primary School on the opposite side of Pymore Road.

A picture of the Day School – largely a school for girls at this period, though they did educate some young boys – has been recalled for me by Jennifer Ackerman, who attended the school from 1935 to 1945. The Day School occupied the south wing of the Convent and consisted of *"two large, light airy classrooms divided by a folding door.... on the ground floor."* The Convent chapel was above. There was also a *"Babies' Class"* on the ground floor with its own entrance through a side door. There were good cloakroom facilities for each class. She recalls the *"smell of wet gabardine raincoats"* on wet days. A statue of St Theresa of Lisieux stood at the entrance to the main school. Of the teachers she recalls Sister Christine who taught the infants for some years and Sister Georgina who helped the gardener in the convent gardens, milked the cows and looked after the turkeys, hens and ducks.

Sister Bernadine, who was a Bridport woman, formerly a Miss Hibbert, and who probably took her name from the founding Reverend Mother of the Convent, was recalled as being very strict, but an effective teacher. Jennifer Ackerman recalls Sister Agnes-Christine joining Sister Bernadine from time to time to teach craft to the younger children. These occasions must have been infrequent as Sister Agnes-Christine was, at that time, already Headmistress of Chideock RC School, a post she had held since April 1922. In their craft lessons the girls were taught needle-crafts which included darning as well as embroidery.

As it was wartime by the time Mrs Ackerman reached the senior class, she recalls the maps of war-zones on the walls and khaki wool being supplied so the girls could knit scarves, balaclava helmets and socks for the troops. The school formed a choir, which joined other schools in the area to perform at the opening of special fund-raising events in the town, such as Spitfire Week, and War Weapons Week. She recalls: *"The massed choirs stood on the pavement opposite the Town hall and were conducted from a wooden dais erected for the occasion in the roadway.....a large 'Barometer' was fixed to the front of the Town Hall, and as the money was raised so the 'Mercury' rose accordingly on an almost daily basis".*

150

The last of the teachers Mrs Ackerman recalls is Sister John Mary She was a university graduate and came from Belgium *"full of new and progressive ideas"*. She taught the very senior examination class who were called the "Aquinians" after St Thomas Aquinas. To distinguish them from the rest of the school the Aquinians wore *"a black-and-white dog-tooth check dress modelled on a gymslip with sleeves. Three red buttons adorned the front at the neck, and red bias-binding bound the cuffs and collar. The girls had to sew these garments themselves, under supervision, the result being nicknamed 'Sackcloth and Ashes' "*.

The children joined this class at the age of eleven or twelve, and their curriculum expanded to include, English Language and Literature, French, Mathematics, History, Geography as well as RE. Folk Dancing was also taught, and took place in a room known as "The Playroom" which was in the part of the building occupied by the Boys' Boarding School. (Fig 26) This was at the northern end of the building. Other than using the Playroom, the girls had nothing to do with the Boys' School.

Other forms of physical activity were the usual playground games of hopscotch, skipping, fives and ball games, though the latter were discouraged due to the risk of broken windows and the annoyance caused to the neighbours in the house adjoining the school. Sports Day was held in the hayfield once the hay had been cut.

The religious life of the school, as with most catholic schools, revolved around the festivals of the Church Year. The Feast of Corpus Christi in May was celebrated by a procession from the Convent down Victoria Grove to the Catholic Church. The girls were dressed in white for the occasion and *"strewed flower petals taken from the Convent gardens"*. The procession also involved the clergy with alter boys carrying censors dispensing incense. Many of the parishioners joined the procession *"carrying sacred banners and singing appropriate hymns."* On special feast days the girls attended Mass in the Convent Chapel, *"a very lovely place with its stained glass windows, smelling of beeswax polish and fresh flowers."* And on St Cecilia's Day (patron Saint of Music) all pupils being taught to play the piano by Sister Gertrude were given a small gift of sweets or chocolate, to mark the day. In 1945 the new Education Act forced the closure of the senior classes and after taking examinations the older girls left to join other schools in the area, or, if they were old enough, to go to work. The school continued post-war as a primary school.[32]

The school's facilities were extended in 1958 to improve the accommodation, but the pressing need for better facilities was already apparent. The days when very small private school could be economically viable were coming to a close. This school and the Roman Catholic School

---

[32] Notes by Mrs Jennifer Ackerman: pupil at the Convent School 1935-45.

in Chideock, featured in the various reorganisation discussions and plans debated by the Local Education Authority in the post-war period, but it was not until more than twenty years after the 1944 Education Act that the issue of accommodation was finally resolved. By this time Chideock RC School had become, like St Mary's, a Voluntary Controlled school, and as such it fell to the Local Education Authority to provide new and more up-to-date accommodation.

As the intention was to provide Roman Catholic education for Bridport and the surrounding villages, a site in Bridport was preferred. At last, the site; probably that originally discussed in the 1930's as a possible site for an enlarged Grammar School, was selected and building began in the mid 1960's. By this time the headteacher of Chideock School was Mrs Cynthia Coatsworth.[33] She had taken over from Sister Agnes Christine in 1955. It was under her headship that the school transferred to Bridport, and formed the core of the new St Catherine's Primary School. The new building was finally completed in 1967, with the Local Education Authority providing 75% of the money, while the Diocese of Plymouth providing the other quarter. The Convent Day School closed and the pupils moved the short distance across Pymore Road to take possession of their new modern building

The School was formally opened on Thursday June 22nd 1967 by the Bishop of Plymouth the Rt Rev Cyril Restieaux. Also in attendance at the ceremony was Lt Col Weld, who recalled at the opening ceremony that it was just ten years since he had attended the opening of the new wing of the Visitation Convent.[33] It was fitting that he should be an honoured guest at the opening of the new school as he had been Chairman of Governors of the Chideock School; his ancestor Mrs Christina Weld had laid the foundation stone of the original Catholic Church in Bridport in 1845; and the Weld family had been considerable benefactors of the original Mission.

The nuns of the Visitation Convent did not entirely lose contact with their Day School pupils, as several of the nuns were appointed to teach in the new school. However this arrangement did not last long, effectively the nuns' involvement in primary education was at an end. The Visitation Convent Boys' Boarding school also closed in 1967 and the nuns converted the former schoolrooms and dormitories into residential care facilities for the elderly. Cynthia Coatsworth continued to lead St Catherine's until her retirement in 1985. (Fig 27)

---

[33] Cynthia Coatesworth (née Fleming) was married to Ronald Coatsworth, Head of Rural Studies at the recently opened Alfred Colfox School.
[33] Bridport News: 30th June 1967

152

Fig 28
The General Girls' School around 1906. The groups in this and Fig 29 are posed in front of the King Street Girls' and Infants' building in King Street.

Fig 29
The General School Infants' Department about 1906.

Fig 30
John Beard as a young man. John Beard was appointed headmaster of the Bridport Boys'
General School in 1854. He served until 1894, retiring after forty years' continuous service.

Fig 31
Bridport General Infants' School: Winners of the Choral Competition about 1929.
(L-R) Back Row: Sidney Bowson / - / Colin? / - / Daphne Hawker, Don?, Ruth Powell, Alec Williams, Mrs Norman. Middle Row: Kenneth Davey, Dorothy Mab(b), Mary Dennett, Joan Edwards, Tommy Wells, Jean Hutchins, John Humphries. Front Row: Chrissie ? / - / Joyce Gale, Enid ? / - / Lloyd Hansford / - / Nina Gale / - /.

Fig 32
Victorious Bridport County Primary Boys' football team with the Kenway Cup, around 1979, with teacher and coach David Thomas. Back row, third from left: Paul Cross. Front row (L-R) Andrew Tolley, / - / Matthew Thomas, Richard Studley, / - / - / Creighton Pitcher.

Fig 33
Memorial plaque to the
boys and staff of the
Bridport Secondary School
who died in the Great War.
It reads: "In Proud and
Grateful Memory of Those
who Gave their Lives for
King, Country and
Humanity."
Staff: E.G.Rees
Pupils: H Coppock, F.G.
Easton, W.M. Edwards, C.
Hannam, A. Masters, J.H.
Medcalf, C.E.T. Patten,
W.T.Perrot, H.C. Quarrell,
J.S. Read, T.H. Rowson,
W.G. Russell, K
Winterflood.

Fig 34
Bridport Secondary School staff, probably about 1925.
(L-R) Back Row: Mr J.R.Spenser, Mr T.J.Taylor, Mr R.T. Alston. Seated: Miss A Broughton,
Miss Edith M. Bickford, Mr Walter Ferris Hill (headmaster), Miss B.A.Witham, Miss Butler.

Fig 35
Bridport Secondary School 1st Annual Sports' Day June 1912. Fifth Year Boys 100 yards flat race. The result was: First: R Beams, Second: G Nicholl, Third: W Studley.

Fig 36
Bridport Grammar School Violin Class, about 1937. (L-R) Back row: Joyce Roberts, Grace Wrixon, Muriel Fowler, Daphne Ahrens, Betty Simmonds, Christine Lovell, Kitty Hawkins, Joyce Kenway. Next row standing: Margaret Hill, Joyce Gale, Ralph Long, Fred Eveleigh, John Humphries, (Dorothy?) Wadham, Gladys Studley, Nina Gale, Evelyn Reed, Joan Edwards. Next row sitting: Mary Dennett, Ruth Humby, Joan Humby, Florence Dommett, Mr Francis Tighe (Music and Art master) Joyce Gale, Jane Westmacott, Ruby Richards (Down?), Ivy Stickland. Front row: Marjorie White, Margaret Whitemore, Eileen Powell, Enid Fooks, Barbara Kay, Joan Scadden, Phyllis Conway, Jose Mabb.

Fig 37
A Colfox family gathering at Rax House in about 1872. The photograph shows William and Thomas Colfox and their families with members of the Wansey family to whom they were both related, having married the two Wansey sisters, Anna and Louisa.
Seen (L-R) back: Blanche Wansey standing next to her husband Arthur Wansey who was brother-in-law to both William and Thomas Colfox. Next to Arthur is his sister Anna, Mrs William Colfox.
Seated, middle row: Aunt Ellen Wansey, Mrs Thomas Colfox (née Louisa Wansey), and seated together on the bench are the two Colfox brothers Thomas, the elder brother, who owned Rax House, and William, who lived at West Mead. Thomas died in 1886, and William carried on the family firm.
Seated on the ground in front are Harriet Colfox, Thomas's daughter, and William's three children, Margaret (Minnie) Colfox, Alice Lee Colfox, and lying at his father's feet, Thomas Alfred.

Fig 38
Croquet Game at Rax House about 1872. (It is possible that this photograph was taken on the same occasion as the last as Harriet is wearing the same hat!) Seen on the extreme left is Chaffy, their coachman with other domestic servants. The two figures standing, middle of the picture are unidentified. On the right of the photograph are (L-R) Harriet Colfox, Alice Lee Colfox, her cousin, Thomas Colfox and his wife Louisa.

Fig 39
Lieutenant Colonel Thomas Alfred Colfox. In the Uniform of the Dorset Yeomanry, taken some time during the Great War.

Fig 40
Sir Philip Colfox as a young man, taken
probably sometime in the 1920's when he
was Member of Parliament for the West
Dorset constituency.

Fig 41
Sketch of the original Colfox School building around 1986, seen from the orchard.

Fig 42
Detail from the Colfox School staff photograph taken in 1979, showing Major Thornburn and some of his staff just before his retirement. (L-R) Back Row: Tony Simice, Chris Thorne, Alan Morris, Chris Nichols, Jimmy Holmes, Roy Chapman, Dennis Tackley.
Middle Row: Elizabeth Truscott, Gill Gallop / - / Gwyneth Brazendale, John Hilder, John Labrom, Rex Trevett. Front Row: Colin Wood, Robin Middleton (Deputy-Head), Sir John Colfox (Chair of Governors), Major Urwin Thornburn (Headmaster), Rev Lionel Brown (Vice-Chairman), John West and Frank Newing.

Fig 43
Hard labour in the
Colfox School
Gardens.

Fig 44
Colfox runners relax in the Square in Beaminster after the Bridport to Beaminster Fun Run.
Left foreground, Chris Tolley and John Foster, probably 1984 or 85.

.

Fig 45
The Colfox Sixth Form 1983/84 gathered in the Memorial Garden. The Sixth Form tutors with
Head Boy and Head Girl are sitting (L-R) in the second row from the front: Ed Hanson, David
Finbow, Peter Davey, Alan Morris, John Labrom (Head of Sixth Form), Vanessa Prideaux
(Head Girl), Carson Russell (Head Boy), Penny Cook, Tony Simice and Fiona Taplin.

X

THE BRIDPORT GENERAL SCHOOLS
BOYS', GIRLS' AND INFANTS': 1844-1900

While the focus of the Church of England and the Catholic Church was on establishing schools that taught the catechism and doctrine of their particular church, there were those who felt that education should be either totally secular or at least not tied to one particular denomination. It is ironic that the school in Bridport which quite deliberately sought to distance itself from the non-conformist British Society, and that was, by stated intent, non-denominational, was nevertheless seen by the headteachers of the main parish school, St Mary's, as being fully and firmly in the grip of the non-conformist congregations, particularly the Unitarians. Worse still, they saw the establishment of the General Schools as a direct challenge to their schools. The non-conformists in the town could have been forgiven for believing the boot was on the other foot, for the Bridport National School had already been in existence for nearly thirty years when it was finally decided to establish a boys' elementary school, organised on non-denominational principles, in the town.

A public meeting at Bridport Town Hall on September 10th 1844 chaired by Mr J.P.Stephens proposed the setting up of a General School *"to promote the extension of education generally, and especially of the rising generation of this locality on such enlarged principles as shall meet the views of all religious denominations"*[1]. This proposal had the support of three local non-conformist clergymen: Rev Thomas Clark, Rev R.E.B Maclellan, and Rev J Wallace.

Kelly's Directory of Dorsetshire of 1852 erroneously describes this establishment as a British School for Boys, but, while the committee set up at that inaugural meeting did consult the British and Foreign School Society in the matter of appointing a school master, their determination from the outset was that the school should not be tied to any organisation. However it is inevitable with the appointment of a British Society trained master that the methods used should be those pioneered by Joseph Lancaster. The first master was Benjamin Templar, and he was provided by the British Society, who at that time was one of the few organisations to train teachers.

The members of the Committee set up at this inaugural meeting to set about raising funds and finding a site for the General School were: Mr Joseph Hounsell, The Revs Clark, Maclellan and Wallace, Jas Williams, Mr

---

[1] The Minute Book of the Committee Meetings of the Superintending Committee: Bridport Boys' General School 1844-1864 (DHC/ S117 1/1/1)

J. P. Stephens, Samuel Bennett, Edwin Nicholetts, Mr Jefferies, Silvanus Stephens, Thomas Ewens and William Colfox.

As we will be meeting various members of the Colfox family in connection with this school and a number of later schools it is perhaps appropriate to digress here to introduce the family more fully. While many individuals were generous benefactors, both in terms of time and money to education in the town, no single family has done so much over such a long time as the Colfox family. It is perhaps right and fitting that some account of a family that has made such an important contribution to education in Bridport should have a place in this history. While they appear from time to time in accounts of fund-raising in earlier centuries, it is from the nineteenth century that their contribution is such, that many institutions might simply not have come into existence without their benefaction.

The Colfoxes seem to have been largely, though not exclusively, dissenters from the seventeenth century. In the early eighteenth century they were members of the Presbyterian Old Meeting, but the marriage between John Colfox and Mary Collins in 1748, firmly established the Colfox family link with the Unitarian congregation. Mary was the daughter of Rev Thomas Collins who founded the Unitarian Congregation in Bridport. (Chapter VI) From this point, the Colfox family became prominent members of that congregation, and various members of the family are buried in the small churchyard in front of the Chapel.

John and Mary Colfox were survived by two children, a daughter, Mary, who married William Hounsell, and a son Thomas Collins. It is Thomas Collins Colfox who established the family woolstapling firm in the late eighteenth century. He traded in English wool, Madeira wine and dried cod from the Newfoundland fisheries, establishing a triangular trade that took ships loaded with a half-cargo of wool to Madeira where they filled up with wine. The wool was then taken on to Newfoundland where it was traded for cod, and the ships returned loaded with wine and dried cod for the British market. He built St John's Wharf in London for the London end of his trade and acquired Rax House in Bridport for his family home. This now substantial house, was originally a cottage surrounded by a field and orchards. Thomas Collins first rented and then bought the house and developed the garden. It was convenient for the premises of his woolstapling business, Thos. Colfox and Son, which also opened onto Rax Lane. In addition to this business he owned shares in a number of ships (nine in all) operating out of the port of Bridport. By 1785 Thomas Collins Colfox had amassed a fortune of about £75,000.

Thomas Collins was left a widower at the comparatively early age of thirty-eight, and his unmarried daughter, Harriet, acted as a devoted companion and later his amanuensis after he had a stroke and could no longer manage his own correspondence. His eldest daughter Elizabeth, known to her family as Betsy, married a Captain in the East India Company, John Channon Lee. Captain Lee was a native of Lyme Regis, son of Simon Lee, who had also been a Captain with the East India Company.

The Lees lived for a time in London but after his retirement from the sea they retired to Camberwell, and John Lee carried on business at Carpenter's Smith Wharf in London. However they kept their links with West Dorset by keeping a house at Charmouth for some years. They had no children which is perhaps one reason for Elizabeth's close affection for her younger brother's sons, her nephews Thomas and William. On her husband's death she returned to Bridport and settled at West Mead, the second of the large Colfox residences in the town. Elizabeth was the first of the family to devote substantial sums of money to the education and welfare of the poor of Bridport, leaving money to set up the Industrial Branch of the Girls' General School which is dealt with later in this chapter. She was also interested in infant schooling, and may have ben instrumental in the establishment of Miss Gundry's School in West Street (See Chapter VI).

Her younger brother William was Thomas Collins' only son to live into adulthood. He married Hannah Abbot in the old Allington Parish Church just before it was pulled down and replaced with the new St Swithun's Church. William, like his father, was also an excellent businessman, and continued to expand the family business. William and Hannah had two sons: Thomas the elder and William. Both boys were well educated, having taken degrees at London University, but eventually both ended up back in Bridport, as part of the family firm. Thomas Colfox as a very young man acted for a short time as a teacher at the Unitarian Sunday School in the 1840's.

The brothers, unusually, married sisters, Louisa and Anna Wansey in 1855, (Fig 37) the year the Girls' General School was opened, by which time William was already involved with the Boys' School. Thomas died in 1886 leaving only a daughter Harriet, and the Colfox "succession" passed to his younger brother. Like her husband, Anna Colfox also became involved with education in the town as a member of the Superintending Committee of the General Infants' School. William and Anna had three children. The eldest Alice Lee never married. She lived into her eightieth year, dying in 1936 and was known in the family as *"our beloved Aunt Alice"*. She became a noted philanthropist in her own right. In addition to her work with the Unitarian Sunday School, and the Girls' General School, Alice became deeply involved in the welfare of children, who were, in the terminology of the time, *"mentally deficient"*. In her work in this field she came into close contact with many of those in the area who were leading the fight to gain appropriate provision for children with special needs.

A volunteer herself, she was instrumental in the establishment of a County Voluntary Association. The volunteers visited and reported on *"feeble-minded"*, or difficult children, as they were called at the time. The aim was to help mothers cope and out of this organisation grew the Dorset Voluntary Association for Mental Health. After her parents' death Alice lived at West Mead, and it was to West Mead that Katherine Bussell came, after she had retired from Thorneloe School, to act as Alice Colfox's companion.

Alice's younger brother Thomas Alfred, who was born in 1858 was to play probably the most significant role of any member of the family in the field of education in Bridport. This then is the family that will play such a large part in education right up to the millennium.[2]

The Bridport Boys General School

At the first meeting, on 16th September 1844, of the Committee, set up to enquire into the possibility of establishing a day school for boys, which included William Colfox, Mr J. P. Stephens was asked to correspond with the British and Foreign School Society *"for information as to the plan and probable cost of a schoolroom for 200 boys"*. By the meeting of Sept 23rd various plans for school houses had been drawn up and Silvanus Stephens and Edwin Nicholetts were set the task of finding a suitable site.

The following meeting held early in 1845 (the minute is not dated precisely) saw the Committee proposing that *"application be made to the Town Council for a lease of the South Eastern portion of a piece of land called Killingham, now used as garden grounds in the tenure of a Mr Joseph Hounsell for the purpose of erecting a Public School thereon, said lease to be for the term of 75 years."* [3] The fact that they all knew Joseph Hounsell who was a member of the Committee, and doubtless took part in the discussion, did not deter the writer of the minute from referring to his fellow committee member in this oddly formal manner!

Killingham is an area of land lying between Folly Mill Lane and East Street and bordering Prospect Place and King of Prussia Lane (now King Street). The Ordnance Survey street map of 1888 shows the schools sited next to "Drying Grounds". Joseph Hounsell, already mentioned in Chapter

---

[2] The quotations, and the information on the Colfox family, here and later in the book, comes from the "Colfox Papers" BMLHC/BRPMG/55, and the Colfox papers held by the Dorset History centre: DHC/D/Col/C49. I am also indebted to Sir John Colfox for additional material on his family.

[3] The Minute Book of the Committee Meetings of the Superintending Committee: Bridport Boys' General School 1844-1864 (DHC/ S117 1/1/1)

Two, lived in a property on the junction between East Street and Barrack Street, and was involved with the Unitarian Sunday School.

The next meeting was held on November 1845 and heard a report that the cost for providing a school for 200 boys would be not less than £500. The land at Killingham would cost *"not less than £300"*. The plot to be leased was *"75ft in breadth at the north-eastern extremity with a right of way from the King of Prussia Lane and 110ft at the South Eastern* (extremity) ..... *for the erection of a General School for the children of the labouring classes of all denominations of the town of Bridport and its neighbourhood."* At the meeting on December 22nd 1846 the committee heard that the lease of the land for 75 years had been agreed at a rent of £10 per annum, and the committee proposed laying out £300 on a *"substantial building"*.

In the following September 1847 it was proposed at the committee meeting of 7th Sept to hold a public meeting *"of the inhabitants of the town and neighbourhood at the Town Hall.... In furtherance of the object proposed, and duly on 20th September the public meeting was held with the Mayor in the chair to consider the proposal 'that a school to be called Bridport General School, for the education of 200 boys be now established'."*[4] The Superintending Committee for the School was now set up and consisted of the following: Mr James Templar, Mr S. W. Whetham, Mr Joseph Gundry, Mr Barnicott, Mr Joseph Hounsell, Mr Thomas Colfox, Mr James Williams, the Rev J. Wyld, Mr Samuel Bennett, Mr Jefferies, Mr Thomas Beach and the Rev J. L. Short. Subscriptions were now to be sought to fund the building.

At the Committee meeting nine days later it was decided that a 75-year-lease was too short and a request should be made to extend the lease to 99 years. This was finally granted in May 1848, at which meeting, on the 20th of the month, it was reported that the sum so far raised totalled £411-10s. The original lease between the Mayor, Aldermen and Burgesses of the Borough of Bridport and the Trustees of the school, for 99 years from 11th October 1848, was approved by the Education Committee of the Privy Council in Whitehall on 18th September 1848 and a final copy of the lease was issued on 9th November 1848.[5] By the Annual General Meeting of the Subscribers held in the town hall on Friday September 29th 1948, £511-15s had been raised. A further grant of £261 was provided by the Government towards the provision of a school and schoolmaster's house.

A meeting on October 24th 1849 settled the master's salary at £40 with a house provided free of rent and taxes. The salary would be augmented if the number of boys exceeded one hundred.

---

[4] The Minute Book of the Committee Meetings of the Superintending Committee: Bridport Boys' General School 1844-1864 (DHC/ S117 1/1/1)
[5] DHC/ S117/12/8

157

At this point the school still did not have a schoolmaster and at the meeting on November 2nd of that year it appears they had applied to the Irish Education Society in Dublin for a teacher but this society had been unable to help and so the application was made to the British and Foreign School Society for *"such master to be ready to come here either the 1st or 2nd week in December".*[6] They offered Benjamin Templar. He was cautiously engaged on a trial period of 4-6 months, but in fact stayed for four years leaving in 1854 to take up a post in Manchester.

The formal opening of the school was on Monday 14th January 1850. This was celebrated with a grand public event. The Committee and the subscribers met at the Town Hall in the morning, then accompanied by the Mayor and Town Council, everyone processed along East Street to the school house where there was the formal opening at midday. In the evening there was a public meeting to explain to all interested parties how the school would operate. Two days later, the School Superintending Committee set up a system of monthly meetings. They agreed to meet on the second Wednesday of each month in the Council Chamber of the Town Hall. From this point on the Minute Book provides an invaluable record of the month-to-month running of the school. By April 23rd 1850 it was reported that the building works were finally completed. The total cost was £905-16s-2d, of which £644-14s-2d had been paid, leaving the sum of £261 which was the amount of the government grant. Despite the school having been built for 200 boys, the meeting in May 1850 decided that the maximum allowed on roll should be 212.

The Boys' General School opened in 1850 in the one storey building that can still be seen fronting Folly Mill Lane. It is a handsome building in the Victorian gothic style that became standard for school buildings of this period. To the east of the schoolhouse is the adjoining schoolmaster's house. In 1909 the accommodation in the building is described in the Logbook as: *"Large Room - 47 ½ft x 30ft x 30ft; Classroom (1) - 18ft x 18ft x 20ft; Classroom (2) - 20ft x 15ft x 30ft, and Classroom (3) - 20ft x 15ft x 30ft."* This obviously takes account of later partitioning of the area, but gives nevertheless a goods sense of the dimensions in which, by 1883, 337 boys were being educated.

The Minute Book of the Superintending Committee throws some interesting light on education in this period. For example the Committee agreed at a meeting on June 13th that the summer vacation should commence on Thursday 20th June and school should open again on Monday July 8th, giving the students all of 2 ½ weeks. In July 1850 a request was sent to the Council on Education *"for papers relative to pupil*

---

[6] The Minute Book of the Committee Meetings of the Superintending Committee: Bridport Boys' General School 1844-1864 (DHC/ S117 1/1/1)

158

teachers", and at the August meeting (14th) the decision was taken to appoint four pupil teachers. In the nineteenth century, the elementary school year ran from the beginning of April to the last day of March, following broadly the financial year, so most major teaching appointments were made from the beginning of April and resignations were dated March 31st, unless the sudden departure of a teacher meant that an appointment had to be made within the year. The Logbooks follow this pattern, and it is not until the late nineteenth century that the modern pattern, of the academic year starting in September, became the norm.

Life in Bridport for the working population was not easy in the mid-century years. Poverty was endemic, and problems arose for the Committee to deal with, such as that reported to the Committee in April 1850 that *"one of the scholars has been imprisoned for theft – the master is requested to admonish the boy and to inform him that on a repetition of such misconduct he will be dismissed the school."*

School premises were clearly in demand by the wider community even in the mid-nineteenth century and in April 1853 a request from the Bridport Choral Society for use of the schoolroom twice a week on Tuesdays and Thursdays from 8-00pm–9-30pm is granted. Whether it was this increasingly public role for the building, or simply that standards had moved on, it was decided, only seven years after it opened, that the school needed improvements to make it more habitable. When it was built the schoolroom simply had a bare brick floor, which must have been very cold and damp in winter. At the meeting in September 1857 it was decided to replace the brick floor with a wooden board floor. As this would necessitate the evacuation of the building while the work was done, an approach was made to the Churchwardens of the Unitarian Chapel for the use of their Sunday School Room for the duration of the alterations.

By this time the school had a new Headmaster. At the meeting on July 12th 1854 it was reported that Mr John Beard (Fig 30) had been appointed to succeed Mr Templar, and had commenced his duties on July 10th. Thus enters onto the Bridport scene a gifted teacher who served the Boys' General School as headmaster for forty years, not retiring until 1894. John Beard is not unique in Bridport for his length of service as a headteacher in the town, for Henry Saloway, Mary Maud Reed and James Blamey all served their schools for long periods, but there was clearly something special about John Beard, for his death was marked in the town as no other teacher's death has ever been marked: first by what was in effect a civic funeral attended by the Mayor and most of the prominent citizens of the town, many of whom were former pupils. The cortege included fellow teachers Henry Saloway and Alfred Edward Champ, and as the cortege passed through the town, blinds were drawn in private houses

159

and the shops put up their shutters as a mark of respect.[7] In addition, a memorial brass plaque, subscribed by former pupils, was formally unveiled in the General School on August 31st 1911 by the Mayor William Edward Randall. It now adorns the walls of the former Grammar School building in St Andrew's Road where it was moved on the closure of the General School in the 1950's. The plaque reads:

"TO THE HONOURED MEMORY OF
JOHN BEARD.
BORN AT BRISTOL MARCH 20TH 1833,
DIED AT BRIDPORT DECEMBER 30TH 1910.
HEAD MASTER OF THIS SCHOOL FOR 40 YEARS
Of the multitude of scholars who came under his influence during this long period, many from far and near join in this memorial in thankful recognition of their indebtedness to him for wise discipline, sound and thorough general instruction, and above all for the inspiring example of love of justice and devotion to duty which was ever set before them."

Bridport was not John Beard's first post as a teacher. Having commenced as a pupil teacher at the Red Cross School in Bristol which used the Lancasterian monitorial system, he trained at the Borough Road Training College in 1852/3. The College originated in 1798 as Joseph Lancaster's School in Southwark and became, due to the influence of Lancaster's monitorial teaching system, the first teacher training college in Britain. The school moved to Borough Road, Southwark in 1804, where it became known as the Borough Road College. In 1814 control was assumed by the British and Foreign School Society. Both John Beard's pupil teaching experience and his training at Borough Road would have meant that, like Benjamin Templar, he was fully immersed in Joseph Lancaster's methods, and no doubt employed them when he came to Bridport.

On the completion of his training, as a certificated teacher, John Beard started his career at a school in Chatham. He was still only twenty-one when he came to Bridport to take up the post of master of the Boys' General School. In 1858, four years after he had taken up his appointment, he married Ellen Swain in the Congregational Church in Bridport where he was a member of the congregation. She was the daughter of Captain Swain who was Bridport Harbour Master. They went on to have three sons, William, Ernest and Frank, and two daughters, the younger of whom was called Kate.[8]

---

[7] John Beard - A Brief Biography. Published by the John Beard Memorial Committee 1911: BMLHC.
[8] Ibid

160

It may seem that twenty-one was very young for a man to take full charge of a large elementary school, but at this time such responsibility at a young age was not that unusual. Henry Saloway was the same age when he took charge of the National School. However, Mr J Pike, who was the Hon Secretary of the Management Committee on John Beard's appointment, clearly aware of his youth, observed that he was little older than some of the pupil teachers at the school, to which John Beard is reported to have replied: *"If you give me the chance I shall soon get over that defect."* In the same biographical note, written about him and published by the John Beard Memorial Committee in 1911 to accompany the unveiling of the plaque in his honour, the writer states *"it is worthy of note that during the whole of the forty years, he was absent from his post in school but three or four days when illness compelled him to remain in his room."*

It is clear from his entries in the earliest School Logbook that not just the academic, but also the moral welfare of his pupils was a very high priority. The General School Logbooks are virtually complete all starting in 1862, and they give a fascinating insight into the life of the schools over a long period. A stern moral tone runs through many of John Beard's entries for 1863: *"An umbrella stolen - read the Commandments: stated that a boy had broken the eighth".* Again in July: *"A shilling picked up in the playground:- gave the school to understand that the boy had only done his duty in bringing it to me"* and the very next day, July 29th: *"Cautioned the boys against plucking wheat - stealing".* It is clear that John Beard lost no opportunity to give the boys moral guidance. But it was not just behaviour in school that he felt he had jurisdiction over: *"August 3rd 1863: Cautioned the boys against mis-behaviour (sic) at Sunday School."*

The following year it is the moral welfare of the pupil teachers that is concerning him: *"Jan 25th 1864: Cautioned pupil teachers to be careful in the selection of their companions,"* a sentiment possibly inspired by his observations of the behaviour of young people around the town, for on Jan 27th he writes: *"The behaviour of boys and girls, young men and young women in the streets at night is very sad. I told the school how sorry I was at this and hoped when they became young men their conduct would be far different."* But it would appear that John Beard was equally good at inspiring high academic standards in the school. The first inspection conducted under the Revised Code in 1864 praised the school for the *"high character for attainment which it has long possessed under Mr Beard, and the discipline is admirable."* [9]

---

[9] Bridport General Boys', Girls' and Infants' Schools Logbooks: 1862-1956: DHC/MIC/R/893/894

Despite the straightjacket of the Code, that forced many school to narrow their curriculum and teach to the tests, it would appear that John Beard kept to the ideal of a broad-based education. In September 1865 he introduced *"a drawing class under a master connected with the Department of Science and Art".* This was the drawing class that first encouraged the juvenile talents of Francis Newbery, who would go on the become an internationally acclaimed painter (See Appendix A). John Beard mentions the drawing class regularly, observing in February 1869 that *"the School of Art inspector visited the School."* Doubtless this was the Bridport School of Art that had been set up just across the main road from the school in 1865.

He was keen to promote technical education for the boys and, although a plan to build a technical instruction facility on land adjoining the school never got off the ground, he did include in the Boys' School curriculum, surveying, *"mensuration"* and any other subject that he considered would fit the boys for the kind of career ahead of them. In addition to practical subjects he also taught Physical Geography, often at the time called Physiography, and Animal Physiology. After 1869, on the instigation of Mr Montagu of Downe Hall, John Beard studied for certificates in science, and science teaching was added to the curriculum as a supplementary subject. In addition, being the first qualified teacher of science in the town, and only one of three in the County, he was also in demand to teach science in some of the private academies in the town. He wrote two textbooks: one on English History and another entitled "Outlines of the English Language."[10]

Like so many other teachers of his generation John Beard had to fight against poor attendance and truancy. In 1863 he laments: *"Although I have converted some truant players into regular attendants I still have two or three confirmed truants".*[11] Various demands took the children out of school. In August 1863 it is *"gleaning".* This was the time hallowed custom of farm labourers and their families being permitted to scour the fields after the harvest had been taken in to pick up the remaining wheat left lying on the fields. This would be ground by hand into small amounts of flour, and by this means poor families got a little free food.

Local events were another problem. The Bridport Regatta was a hugely popular afternoon out for the whole town. It was held at the Harbour, in the middle of August, which in those days was after the annual school summer holiday. It drew so many children out of school that after battling the non-attendance for several years, John Beard pragmatically declared a

---

[10] John Beard - A Brief Biography. Published by the John Beard Memorial Committee 1911: BMLHC.
[11] Bridport General Boys', Girls' and Infants' Schools Logbooks: 1862-1956: DHC/MIC/R/893/894

162

half-day holiday and closed the school for the afternoon. Such pragmatism was no solution, however, during periodic visits of the circus. In 1867 *"a travelling circus reduced the numbers* (one) *afternoon to 118"* from the usual total of round about 280.

All the local schools had their particular Christmas customs. The one John Beard established throughout his time as master was the *"Christmas letter"* to their parents, which the boys were given time to write in the week or two before the Christmas holiday and which they took home with them. Even when the school was closed for Christmas a week early in December 1871 because of an outbreak of smallpox in the town, John Beard observed: *"Nearly every boy took home a Christmas letter."*[12]

In 1874, possibly inspired by the Winter School being run by the Girls' School staff, John Beard started a Night School at the Boys' School which attracted between 150 and 200 pupils throughout the winter months. Even this however was not proof against the occasional distraction. In November 1876 he laments *"Owing to Guy Fawkes day being kept on Monday the attendance at Night School was very poor."* He also gave occasional lectures to the Working Men's Institute, which, at that time, occupied the present Museum Building in South Street. In addition to all of these activities, he assisted many youngsters by coaching them and helping them prepare for examinations, and generally encouraging them to aspire to achieve their ambitions. It is clear that John Beard touched the lives of many young boys and men in Bridport, and this alone would account for the extent to which he is uniquely remembered in the town. That said it seems all the more remarkable that his retirement from the school after forty years is marked in the Logbook by the simple entry: *"Sept 29th 1894: This is my last entry in the Logbook as Master of the Bridport General School."*

John Beard retired from the school in 1894, and died on December 30th 1910. He is buried in Bridport Cemetery. In addition to the brass memorial which was erected in his honour, Charles Edmunds former Mayor of Bridport was inspired to write the following short poem in his memory:

"THE SCHOOLMASTER
'Neath Bonham Wood, where often lovers walk,
Admire the prospect, or on prospects talk,
A modest schoolmaster his home has found,
And midst the young pursues his daily round.
No mean ambition moves his gen'rous heart,
His aim alone how best to do his part.
Around his house no tulip beds are seen,

---

[12] Ibid

No shrubs to ornament, or lawns of green.
He ne'er announces in the local Press
His rare attainments or his school address;
Yet through the neighbourhood his fame is known,
From year to year his influence has grown,
His early pupils, now in man's estate,
Are never tired his praises to relate;
And the young school boys oft are proud to tell
How soon they learned to read and wrIte and spell.
Should e'er a stranger chance to pass this way,
Let him awhile within the school-room stay,
He'll find a teacher to the lads endeared.
A noble man; his title - plain "John Beard."[13]

A rather different poetic effort is a piece of doggerel recalled by a former pupil, that the boys apparently used to chant no doubt out of their master's hearing:

"Oh, Johnnie Beard is a very good man,
He tries to teach us all he can -
Reading, Writing, and Arithmetic,
And when we fail he gives the stick!
And when he does he makes us dance
Out of England into France,
Right through France and into Spain.
Over the hills and back again."[14]

Whether the last lines are a reference to John Beard's summer trips to the continent is pure conjecture, but he brought back not just mementoes, but also accounts of his experiences to enliven his teaching, so the boys must have been aware of his travels. He was known as a stern disciplinarian, as he needed to be, but he was also a gifted and charismatic teacher. No doubt like most teachers of the period, he used the stick from time to time. After all this was the period when the saying "Spare the rod and spoil the child" was the accepted wisdom.

The Bridport Girls' and Infants' General Schools

To tell the story of these two schools it is necessary to wind the clock back to 1855. This was the year in which the Boys' School was joined on

---

[13] Published in "John Beard - A Brief Biography". Published by the John Beard Memorial Committee 1911: BMLHC.
[14] A handwritten note in the BMLHC

the Killingham site by a two-story building to house girls and infants. On Saturday 28th July 1855 the "Illustrated Bridport News" reported the "erection of a handsome and most convenient building for a Girls' and Infants' School contiguous to the Boys School" which "opened a few years ago". It went on: "The Girls' School was opened Monday last (23rd July) for the reception of the children who have been accustomed to assemble in Rax Lane. 105 girls (about the usual attendance) were present." The report adds, "The Infants' School will be opened some time in August when it is intended to hold a public meeting." The writer further adds: "These schools which are built in the Elizabethan style present a most handsome appearance."

The new building was two storey unlike the Boys' School which was single storey, and it was built to the north of the Boys' School. The infants had two classrooms on the ground floor, and the girls occupied a large classroom on the first floor which was 48ft by 25ft and nearly 12ft high. They were also provided with a "bonnet room" (cloakroom?), which was 25ft by 11ft and in the Logbook is described as a classroom. The schools were built to accommodate 168 girls and 250 infants, boys and girls. Attached were "convenient houses for each school mistress."[15] The first school mistress for the Girls' School was a Mrs Hodges, and of the Infants' the unfortunately named Miss Fear. School hours were a little longer at this time than today. The girls were expected to be in class from 9am-12pm and from 2pm-5pm in summer (March to October) and 9am-12pm and 2pm to 4pm in winter. In 1862, when the daily activity of the school begins to be recorded in the Logbooks, the Mistress of the Girls' School was Eliza Carter. She had three pupil teachers working under her: Selina Andress, Anna Jane Hall, and Elizabeth Warren.[16]

The annual report by the Management Committees of the Girls' and Infants' Schools, presented to the AGM held in the Town Hall on June 30th 1868, provides an interesting snapshot of the schools at this time, thirteen years after their opening. The news that Miss Eliza Carter is leaving her post to be replaced by Miss Margaret Saturley, recruited from Westbury British School, is mentioned. The report compliments Miss Carter on improving the performance of the girls, 84% of whom have passed the inspectors tests in Reading, Spelling, and Arithmetic.[17]

One of the drawbacks of the explosion in educational provision that occurred around the middle of the nineteenth century was that the cost to the government, who provided grants, began to spiral. In order to make

---

[15] Illustrated Bridport News: 28th July 1855
[16] Bridport General Boys', Girls' and Infants' Schools Logbooks: 1862-1956: DHC/MIC/R/893/894
[17] Annual Reports by the Management Committees of the Girls' and Infants' Schools 1868-1895: DHC/ S117/12/2

sure the money was being prudently spent, the government appointed the Newcastle Commission which recommended that all schools be required to undergo regular inspections. The students were tested by the inspector and the grant allocated to the school was based on the results of the tests and on the attendance rate. This system, generally known as "Payment by Results" was widely hated, and ultimately had a baleful influence on education, focusing attention on drilling in the three skills of reading writing and arithmetic that would be tested, and reducing the time given to the rest of what had been a widening curriculum. As in the National Schools this regime of payment by results and the rigorous system of inspection and testing, was a constant cause of anxiety. The regular inspections and the effects a poor report could have on the school's income has already been looked at in relation to the National Schools. It had no less an impact on the General School. As ever, one of the principle worries was poor attendance. (For a more detailed description of the Revised Code see Appendix C.)

In the 1868 Management Committee Report, the attendance at the Girls' School is causing understandable concern, having sunk from an average of 120 in 1862 to only 97 in 1868. Four girls are reported as having left school because their parents were two poor to pay the 2d per week fees. (Infant fees were 1d per week.) These must have been hard years in Bridport for the report goes on *"whilst the depression of trade must leave many children free to go to school, who might else have been prematurely sent to work, there are parents who may not be able, even with the most self-denying economy, to afford the needed weekly pence."*[18] The lower priority set on labouring children's education at this time, particularly that of girls, is reflected both in the low attendance figures for the school relative to the registered roll, but also in the very short time some girls and infants spent in education at all.

To set this problem in context it is important to recall that only twenty or so years before, a report into the employment of children nationwide, drawn up in 1841, reporting on the employment of children in the local rope and twine industry, found that children working for a master spinner could be employed from about seven or eight years-of-age and would be expected to work a twelve or thirteen-hour day (7 or 8am – 8pm) for a weekly wage of about 1s-8d. The report goes on: *"After three or four month they are able to 'tie the knots' and are fit for their business. Some go to 'penny schools' and some to Sunday Schools and some 'do read at their work'. In the twine yards children of as young as 6 or 7 years-of-age would work from 6am – 9pm in summer."* All this despite the Factory Act of 1833 which forbade the employment of children under nine in the textile industry

[18] Annual Reports by the Management Committees of the Girls' and Infants' Schools: 1868-1895: DHC/ S117/12/2

and restricted the hours of children under thirteen to nine hours a day and made schooling obligatory for two hours a day or six hours a week. The evidence collected in 1841 set in train a series of Acts of Parliament to limit the age and hours children could work, and to extend control beyond the narrow confines of the textile industry. The Factory Act of 1844 raised the amount of schooling to three hours a day, or five hours on alternate days, but as the evidence of the 1841 survey suggests there was widespread infringement of the existing law, and it would be some time before more enlightened attitudes prevailed, especially as households often depended on the money their children could earn, or, in a cottage industry like Bridport's, their labour.

While the average attendance at the Girls' School in 1868 was ninety-seven, the number on roll was 162. The low attendance figure was partly, though not entirely, accounted for by the fact that some children were part time, having to work the rest of the day or week. The other factor was the low priority working families placed on their daughters' education at this period.

The teachers' work must have been made more difficult by the shifting population within the schools. In 1867/8 sixty-six girls were admitted but eighty-two left. In the Infants' School, of the 117 girls on register, sixty-three were admitted but fifty-seven left, while the Boys' School, with 126 on register, recorded fifty-seven arriving and seventy leaving in the course of the year. Reasons for leaving varied. Apart from those who could not afford the fees, and the deaths recorded of two Infant boys and two Infant girls, some girls who lived in outlying districts found it too far a distance to travel; some left because their families had moved out of the area, but the vast majority left to start work, *"going into service or a trade".*[19]

The statistics also indicate just how few years the average student spent in education. Although infant education started at two or three years old, few attended for the full five years. At seven the children moved into the Boys' or Girls' Schools, where they could remain until the age of fourteen, and latterly as the school began to develop Higher Class schooling, beyond that age. But in 1868 there were only fourteen girls in the school over the age of fourteen and the bulk of the girls left school at between ten and twelve years-of-age. Only six girls in all had attended the school for more than six years, the majority staying only about two or three years and some managing less than a year.

The School syllabus shows a heavy emphasis on training God-fearing children, useful in the domestic arts, able to read and write

---

[19] Annual Reports by the Management Committees of the Girls' and Infants' Schools:1868-1895: DHC/ S117/12/2

accurately, and calculate. The girls studied Scripture and Bible reading; Writing, including Writing from Dictation; Arithmetic, Sewing, Fixing work and Domestic Economy; Natural History with Object Lessons, and a few could study History and Geography. The Infants learned Reading and Writing on Slates as well as Writing in Copy Books; Arithmetic; Natural History and Object Lessons, Scripture, Sewing and Lessons in Form and Colour. (For a description of the Object Lesson see Chapter VII.)

The 1868 Report gives an interesting insight into the funding of the school at this time. The figures quoted relate to the Girls' School. The income came from three sources: subscriptions, government grant, and the penny fees or "school pence". These were respectively £25-18s-6d; £49-1s-4d and £44-8s-4d. Out of this income the managers had to find the various salaries. The school mistress's salary was £47-3s-4d in total made up of a basic salary of £36-19s-9d, plus £12 for teaching the pupil teachers, and £8-3s-7d which represented a sixth of the government grant. This is interesting, as the Revised Code stopped the system whereby teachers' salaries were augmented by a direct government grant which had been introduced in1846. Grants were now paid direct to managers, but it is clear that the managers of the Bridport School felt that a percentage of the grant should still be earmarked to augment the mistress's salary. Possibly they were encouraged in this by the good results from the Inspectors' tests.

The pupil teachers' salaries came to £21-17s-6d, and the monitors cost the school managers £4-1s. How many monitors there were is not stated. The mistress of the Infants' School got a higher salary, no doubt reflecting the larger number of pupils in her charge. The Infants' School was also in receipt of money from the Daniel Taylor Charity to the tune of £20. In this same year the Boys' School received £40 from the Daniel Taylor Charity, but there was no payment to the Girls' School. The Daniel Taylor Charity was aimed at boys' education, not girls'.

The management of the Girls' and Infants' Schools was undertaken frequently by the wives and daughters of those on the Superintending Committee of the Boys' School. Anna Colfox, wife of William, served on the Superintending Committee of the Infants' School, and the family were subscribers to the schools. Mrs Henry Hounsell also served on the Infants' School Committee. Other families actively involved in supporting the schools, either as subscribers or managers were the Newbery family, Mr Beach and Mr Barnicott, chemists, Mr and Mrs John Dunham, ironmongers, Mr and Mrs William Townley Whetham. Mr Joseph Pearkes Gundry is also listed as a subscriber. He was also on the Committee set up to manage St Mary's School. Other individuals and families subscribing to the General Schools were Mr J. M .P. Montagu, the Hounsell family, The

168

Whetham family and Mr Knight of the Knights Bull Hotel who in 1868 contributed 2s-6d.[20]

In 1871, during Margaret Saturley's time as Mistress, the Annual Report acknowledges changes produced by Forster's Elementary Education Act of 1870. While the report states that *"no grant is made in respect of any instruction in religious subjects"* the Government grant has increased to £53-17s-4d to the Girls' School and £91-0s-6d to the Infants'. In response to a concern over the poor health of the country's children, all schools were now required to provide some time in the school week for physical exercise. The report states that a Sergeant Matthews had been engaged on the recommendation of the Ladies' Committee *"to drill the girls for two half-hours a week".* Infant numbers were on the increase, up to 196 in 1870, rising to 209 by 1871.[21]

The Winter School

In the winter of 1870/71 an evening school known as the "Winter School" was opened for young women over the age of fourteen. It fell to Miss Saturley to organise and teach at the Winter School – the Logbook refers to it as the *"Evening School"* [22] – with the assistance of some of her pupil teachers and some volunteer ladies. There were forty-eight meetings and the average attendance was forty-one. At the end of the year the students were examined in reading, writing and arithmetic *"as required by the Government".* There were only fourteen failures out of 132 tests taken. Nine more official sessions completed the Winter School year, but Miss Saturley must have been a very devoted teacher for she extended the meetings, running a further seven meetings for about eighteen pupils unpaid. The need for this evening school is stressed in the report. *"This Evening School helped to meet a palpable want. Many girls stop too short a time at school to derive much benefit, and, when they go to work, are apt to forget the little they have learnt."*[23] However, despite its success, it seems the Winter School was not to continue, as the Government's Revised Code meant that to qualify for grant aid the school would have to have eighty meetings and this would place too great a burden on teachers who were already working all day in the day school.

The Winter School was a brave attempt to improve the education of older girls. How much this was needed is clear in the Report for the Girls'

---

[20] Annual Reports by the Management Committees of the Girls' and Infants' General Schools:1868-1895: DHC/ S117/12/2
[21] Ibid
[22] Bridport General Boys', Girls' & Infants' Schools Logbooks:1862-1956:DHC/MIC/R/893/894
[23] Annual Reports by the Management Committees of the Girls' and Infants' General Schools: 1868-1895: DHC/ S117/12/2

School of 1878. By this time Mr William Colfox was acting as Treasurer to the Committee. The report of that year contains the ritual complaints about parents not sending their daughters to school. Though the numbers on register have risen to 236, the average attendance is barely half, only 124. Thirty scholars are described as half-timers. This Report refers to the establishment in the Borough of *"one new school"*. This is probably a reference to the newly-built Gundry Lane school for St Mary's, though this was scarcely a new school, nevertheless it is clear from the Logbook that it was succeeding in recruiting girls from the General School.

The Industrial Branch of the Bridport Girls' and Infants' General Schools.

One other attempt to further the education of older girls was attempted not long after the Girls' School was built, though modern readers would be more inclined to describe the Industrial Branch of the school as providing vocational training rather than education.

Barely a year after the General Girls' School opened in 1855, the future benefactor of the Girls' Industrial Branch, Elizabeth Channon Lee, was already floating the idea of an Industrial School in a letter, partly addressed to her nephews, Thomas and William Colfox. The letter does not appear to be written solely to William and Thomas as it is addressed "Dear and Valued Friend". Who the friend was is open to conjecture. However, whoever the letter was principally addressed to, she is obviously writing in the clear knowledge that William and Thomas would share in the reading of the letter. She goes on:

"Dear and Valued Friend,

Knowing the interest you feel in having an Industrial School established in Bridport, also your kindness in endeavouring to further my wishes respecting it, ... I wish to inform you that I have decided on giving a Thousand pounds for the purpose and if you, my nephews, with me and two other gentlemen, will determine on what plan to proceed, I shall be obliged to you all. If on consideration this school be not likely to succeed which I cannot imagine to be the case (at all events I hope a trial may be made) then should it prove a failure you will please to appropriate the sum specified to some other purpose you may approve of for the advantage and comfort of our more needy Brethren."[24]

As it turned out this letter was written just two years before her death in 1858, and ultimately her bequest was administered by a trust set

---

[24] Colfox Papers: DHC/ D/Col C49: . An envelope filed with the letter in the DHC file cannot belong to this letter as it is addressed to "The Masters Colfox", at Kings Down House, Bristol, which was the Rev J R Wreford's Seminary, the last school the boys attended before going on to London University. The letter is dated 1856, which was a year after the two brothers were jointly married to the Wansey sisters and well past their school-days.

up on her death. It was left to the trustees to set up the school. The original trustees were her two nephews, Thomas and William Colfox, and the Rev John Lettis Short, and the terms of the trust made it clear that the money was to benefit the poor of Bridport. In addition to Elizabeth's bequest, the Industrial Branch was also supported by local benefactors, among whom was Elizabeth's sister-in-law, Hannah Colfox, who contributed £20 per annum to the school.

The idea of setting up a special training centre for older girls, both those destined for domestic service, and also those whose domestic duties would be in their own homes, seemed popular, and the school was established just a year after Elizabeth Lee's death, in 1859. Rather than a separate school, which is what she seems originally to have envisaged, it was set up as part of the Girls' General School. Its official title was "The Industrial Branch of the Girls' General School". It was short-lived, but gives a vivid picture of the enlightened utilitarianism of mid-nineteenth century education. While the "Academies and Seminaries" were educating young ladies in French and German conversation, painting, drawing and music, the daughters of the *"poor labouring classes"* were being taught to become good servants. Given that this was likely to be their sphere of employment, and no doubt offered better prospects than the factories and mills, the Industrial Branch at least tried to make sure that they learnt the skills they would need.

Although Kelly's Directory of Dorsetshire of 1867 describes this establishment as being *"in King of Prussia Lane"* with Miss Caroline Golding as mistress, in fact it operated from premises in North Allington from 5th December 1859, until it closed in March 1867. As these premises seem to have been purpose-built for the Industrial School, it is tempting to wonder whether, in fact, Elizabeth had put the wheels in motion before her death. The purpose of the school was for the *"training and instructing in household labour, and the arts of domestic life, the girls of the Bridport General School."* [25] The premises, a large house (now divided into three houses: 69-71 North Allington) stands on the west side of the road opposite Fulbrook Lane. (Fig 16) On the opposite side of the road was the original Allington National School, so once again educational establishments found themselves in close proximity with one another.

Girls, over twelve years-of-age, could be admitted free to the Industrial Branch as long as they had completed two years schooling either at Bridport General School or some other school approved by the School Management Committee. Each pupil received a present of a *"print dress of her own making"* each year and had *"the liberty of contributing to a*

---

[25] Rules of the Industrial Branch of the Bridport Girls' and Infants' General Schools, printed by T Male of Bridport: DHC/S117/12/1

171

Provident Fund at the rate of not more than 6d per week". Out of the funds saved she could receive a bonus and be allowed to purchase at cost price *"articles of clothing for herself to be made by the pupils."*[26]

Girls employed in the kitchen had a daily dinner provided free. The Industrial Branch was run by a Superintendent (Miss Caroline Golding?) whose job it was to instruct the girls in *"household work, causing them to keep the establishment and its appurtenances in good order."* The girls were also taught *"the art of economical cookery";* to wash, starch, iron and mangle the Superintendent's and their own clothes *"which they shall bring to the Wash-house every Monday morning"*. In the afternoons the girls attended the General School where they were to be instructed in *"plain needle work, cutting out any garment they may be required to make, dressmaking and mending."* The school also operated as a public laundry, hiring out the washing facilities to the *"labouring poor"* when the girls were not using them. The rules required the payment per hour for the use of *"washing box,...a compartment of the drying closet, the mangle, ironing boards etc."*

The Branch provided dinners to subscribers of 5s per annum and above. These "dinner tickets" were issued in the proportion of 40 for each £1 subscribed. (5s would entitle you to 10 tickets). Each ticket entitled the holder to a *"meat dinner, or to a plain rice, sago, or tapioca pudding, or to two quarts of good soup"*. In order to receive a dinner, application had to made to the Branch before 9 o'clock in the morning. Dinner had to be collected at *"1 o'clock precisely"* bringing a *"basin or dish in which to carry it away"*. It is also clear that the Branch sold dinners in addition to the subscribers' tickets.

The Branch was inspected by "Visitors" who were required to inspect the establishment *"at least once a week"*. The Branch received a government grant until 1864 which was then discontinued, and it is probably this, as well as the decline in pupil numbers which signed the school's death warrant. In 1864 it became necessary to seek a general subscription from the townspeople to raise money. This enabled the Branch to continue for a further three years but by 1867 it was felt that there was not sufficient proof that the money was being *"bestowed to the best advantage,"* for *" from the average of about 20 scholars, many of them from the country, the number has steadily declined."* [27] As the trustees of Mrs Lee's bequest were at liberty to devote the income of the trust to *"some other purpose which they shall deem to be for the physical, mental, or*

---

[26] Rules of the Industrial Branch of the Bridport Girls' and Infants' General Schools, printed by T Male of Bridport: DHC/S117/12/1
[27] Report by the Management Committees of the Girls' and Infants' Schools: June 30th 1868: DHC/ S117/12/2

moral benefit of poor persons of this town" they decided the funds would be better used to provide a cottage hospital for the town, and so the Industrial Branch duly closed in March 1967. On the closure of the Industrial Branch the building was converted to use as a Cottage Hospital. It was known as St Thomas's Hospital and the words "Hospital" are still vaguely discernible today on a stone slab between two of the first floor windows.

As the Industrial Branch had provided cooked dinners for distribution to a number of families in Bridport, it was a concern that this closure would cause some hardship, and so the Hospital Committee agreed to continue to issue dinner tickets to subscribers. Over the eight years and four months of the school's existence it had provided 14,600 dinners for scholars. 21,910 meals were distributed from the kitchens via subscriber tickets and 2,140 were sold to the public. The accounts for the final year of the Industrial School's existence show that, in addition to subscriptions, the Branch received £70-15s-6d from Mrs Lee's Trust; dinner tickets sold brought in £37-0s-6d; dinners sold: £5-13s-0d and boarders' fees were £11-19s-6d. Much of the financial outlay was for provisions for the kitchens.[28]

That this early experiment in vocational education aimed at girls largely failed is to be regretted, but the drive to educate girls continued and in 1878 the Girls' General School was in receipt of an increased government grant. There were further changes to the funding arrangements which would also benefit girls, for according to the Management Committee Report of that year, the Daniel Taylor Charity would no longer provide cash grants for boys, but had put a new scheme in place, approved the previous year by the Charity Commissioners, to provided scholarships. Twelve were provided, each of an annual value of £5. Boys and girls over thirteen, who had regularly attended elementary school for three years, and whose parents earned less than £2 per week, were eligible. In a major departure from the original terms of Daniel Taylor's endowment, three of these scholarships were specifically earmarked for girls to encourage their education at secondary level. The new charity also provided for prizes to be awarded for attendance.

Margaret Saturley continued as Headmistress of the Girls' School until August 1875, when she was replaced by Mary Collins. As is often the way when a new teacher starts in a school she is immediately reporting problems. The Logbook records: *"Oct 1st-The scholars have been kept several times for talking during class. This week several of the forms have been repaired"*. These were broken during the lunch hour and the suspects were the girls who stayed in school to have their packed meal. Miss Collins

---

[28] Ibid

duly *"spoke"* to the girls. There were no school lunches provided at this time and, as most children went home to lunch, the culprits must have been an easily identifiable group. Mary Collins only stayed at the school for one term and in January 1876 Kate E Lake took over and served until 1882. In 1882 Miss Annie Rendell took over as Mistress of the Girls' School and Mrs E Scadden was Infants' Mistress. In 1887 Thomas Alfred Colfox, joined his father, William, as a Superintending Committee member, and his wife, Constance, joined the Infants' Committee, as secretary, replacing her mother-in-law. [29]

The commitment, both of time and money that these middle-class members of the community gave to their voluntary roles is impressive. By 1887 the duties of the Superintending Committees had begun to involve a modicum of inspection. A member of the committee was required to go into the school weekly to inspect the mistress's report, and enter their name and comment in the Logbook. Through this period the Logbooks of all the local schools record the visits of managers, often several times in the week.

By the 1890's the old-style large classrooms were considered out-of-date. No longer was it appropriate to teach all age groups together in one room. Most schools had erected temporary screens of some kind to divide off the rooms, but the need for more permanent partitions was becoming vital. The 1894 AGM, which was held for the first time in the Liberal Hall in Barrack Street, with Thomas Alfred Colfox in the Chair, heard of the improvements which had been made to the Girls' classroom on the upper floor by the construction of a wood and glass partition to divide the room, *"whereby the efficiency of the teaching and the comfort of the school staff has been much increased"*. A savings bank had also been established.[30] The school was poised for the major changes that would come in the next century.

---

[29] School File: Bridport Girls' General School: DHC/ S117/12/2
[30] Ibid

XI

THE GENERAL SCHOOLS INTO THE TWENTIETH CENTURY

Up to the 1890's the three General Schools had operated pretty much independently of one another. The Boys' School site was completely separated from the Girls' and Infants' by a wall, and the Boys' School had a separate entrance onto Folly Mill Lane, while the Girls' and Infants' used a gate into King Street. (Figs 28 & 29) However, in 1895 the Management Committee recommended that *"the Boys', Girls' and Infants' Schools shall be united under one management"*. This change was made by 1897, with the three General Schools being brought under a joint management committee. The wisdom of this move was clear when, in 1897 the Government passed the Voluntary Schools Act, which attempted to bring the financing of the voluntary schools under a greater degree of control and it became necessary for the managers of voluntary schools to join some association in order to be sure of getting the full grants available. Bridport General Schools had so far resisted the School Boards, and had preserved their independence of state control. Clearly the managers wished to continue as before funded by a combination of private subscription, local charities and government grant.

The Voluntary Schools Act required voluntary schools, which were not under the umbrella of some organisation such as the Church of England, to band together in order to be able to access Government money. Various Associations were set up. At a meeting held in Yeovil on July 9th 1897, representatives of schools in Hampshire, Wiltshire, Dorset and Devon set up the South-Western British and Voluntary Schools Association. Fifty-six schools joined the Association including the Bridport General Schools, and 1901/2 Miss Gundry's Infant School. This enabled the schools to draw down more substantial Government grants than before and in 1898 the combined General Schools, with an average attendance given as 481, were awarded £122-5s-1d. In 1899 attendance having dropped to 441 the grant was £120, and in the academic year 1901/2 Bridport General Schools got only £98 (Miss Gundry's Infant School got the princely sum of £13 in 1901/2), but this dip probably reflects the imminence of the 1902 Education Act effectively starting a nationally funded system of state education.

There were further changes to the staff at the end of the century. By 1900 Annie Rendall had left the Girls' School and Miss M A Gordon had replaced her as headmistress and in 1894 William Edward Bates replaced the long-serving John Beard as headmaster of the Boys' School. It was probably just as well to have two relatively new headteachers in charge of the two schools as the new century was to bring new and testing challenges.

The 1902 Education Act, which devolved responsibility for schools to the Local Authorities, came into operation in April 1903. The changes to school funding, now under the control of the new Local Education Authorities, brought about by the Act meant that there was no longer any need for the South-Western Association which was dissolved. But the changes brought problems for the voluntary schools. The existing managers (with certain additional members nominated by the County Council Education Committee or other authority) had to *"continue to discharge their functions on condition that they provide the school premises* (to the local authority) *rent free, keep them in repair and make such alterations as may reasonably be required out of their own funds"*. Perhaps in response to these requirements, the School Management Committee decided in 1903 to spend *"not in excess of £225"* on improvements to the school, building a new cloakroom to the Boys Schools and asphalting the playground. However there were problems in the Girls' School as HMI Irvin reports in November 1913 that *"the floor of the main room has sunk a good deal and vibrates when in use. The Managers should assure themselves of its safety."*[1] Doubtless, as this was the upstairs room, they did!

By 1910, William Edward Bates had been headmaster of the Boys' School for sixteen years. He had continued to lead the Boys' School in the strong academic tradition that John Beard had established. He introduced the teaching of Chemistry for the older boys, and very quickly after his appointment had established a boys' football team. The Boys' School, at that time, had nothing more than a small playground, equipped only with some *"gymnastic apparatus"* and a swing, off which boys fell from time to time, on at least one occasion causing serious injury. St Mary's Playing Field was not in existence, so for the football team in their first year, Mr Stephens, one of the managers, loaned a meadow and they set up practices twice a week on Thursdays and Saturdays. The meadow must have been a little distance from the school for in October of the following year, 1895, the school *"engaged"* a field nearer the school at a rent of thirty shillings, and practices were increased to three times a week.[2]

William Edward Bates seems to have been just as energetic a Master as his predecessor. In 1894 he decided that monitors in the upper classes should be elected by ballot, the aim of this being: *"1) more methodical arrangements in the classes, 2) a training of the boys in the methods of parliamentary and other elections."*[3]

---

[1] School File: Bridport Girls' General School: DHC/ S117/12/2
[2] Bridport General Boys', Girls' and Infants' Schools Logbooks: 1862-1956: DHC/MIC/R/893/894
[3] Ibid

The facilities were not just limited outside the school, inside there were the usual problems of keeping their classrooms warm. In late November 1894 he complains: *"Commenced fires for the season. The stove in the large room smoked so much I shall not use it again until the pipe is altered"*. Fortunately for the boys they only had to shiver for just over a week until December 6th when the pipe was altered by *"taking it through the roof instead of horizontally into a large chimney."* Whether it was this alteration that caused the fire in the roof four years later is not clear from the Logbook, but on the morning of November 23rd 1898 when *"a heavy gale was blowing"*, a boy came to the door of the school *"with news that the school roof was on fire"*. Fortunately *"the fire was confined to the woodwork and straw between the slates and the plaster in the roof"*. Help was quickly at hand: *"Very great assistance was quickly rendered by a number of men with ladders and buckets, and by the time the Fire Brigade got to work the danger was practically over"*. There was minor damage: *"The slates had to be removed for a space of several square yards but the only damage inside the building was by dirt and water. Although a stiff gale was blowing the slates were replaced during the afternoon and the school reopened as usual"* the following morning, leaving the replastering to be done over the Christmas holiday.[4] It was just as well the fire left little damage as the greater part of the floor in the large boys' classroom had only been renewed three years earlier, and new dual desks purchased, giving seating for seventy boys.

In January 1895 Thomas Alfred Colfox presented the Boys' School with a *"museum cupboard"* so they could display their collection of fossils and minerals which up to that time had been *"out of sight in a cupboard"*. Encouraged by this facility many more interesting items were donated by friends of the school, and the boys were also encouraged to add to the collection *"their contributions... being principally minerals, fossils and foreign coins"*. William Bates states in his entry for January 10th 1895: *"This may be considered the opening day of the Museum."* In September 1901, the Museum was a major attraction at an exhibition held in the school over a weekend (Friday 20th and Saturday 21st September) at which work of all three departments was on show: girls' needlework, infants *"kindergarten work"*, and drawing and writing books from both Girls' and Infants' Departments. The *"many hundreds"* of people who visited the exhibition contributed £2-2s-8d to the Museum fund.

Like his predecessor and the various masters and mistresses of the National Schools, William Bates fought a continual battle against poor attenders, and was yet another headteacher to complain bitterly about the

---

[4] The straw "between the slates and the plaster" would have been insulation – a common method used in buildings at this period. Account of the fire in the Boys' School Logbook.

shortcomings of the School Attendance Committee, which seems to have become almost as great a source of frustration as the truants they were supposed to discourage. Things had obviously come to a head in 1895, for on November 8th, William Bates, representing the West Dorset Teachers Association, met with the School Attendance Committee *"to urge upon the Committee a more thorough exercise of their powers"*. He tells the committee that *"it is a fact, well known by the parents, that no action will be taken in the case of children making seven or eight attendances out of ten"*, and that *"while the Committee expresses its desire to secure better attendance"* this reluctance to prosecute in all but the most extreme cases was undermining everyone's efforts. The depth of the teachers' frustration is summed up in the picture William Bates paints of *"sending out boys to look up absentees"* and of writing two and three times a week to parents on the matter. How much difference his arguments made to the Committee's actions is unclear, but two years later, he is still making broadly the same complaint. He records in November 1897: *"Several prosecutions for non-attendance have had the effect of checking the very worst cases of irregularity, but nothing yet touches the common evil of two or three absences in the week."* [5]

Despite the problems however, the picture we get of William Bates, from the Logbook, is of an energetic and dedicated teacher. In addition to the main curriculum, he also encouraged an awareness of the history and topography of the local area through study visits. In 1907 on 25th April, he records: *"This afternoon I took the 1st class to Eggardon Hill, leaving by the 3.8 train for Powerstock and walking back. The chief objects studied were the ancient earthworks and the pit dwellings."*

It was William Bates' unenviable task to see the Boys' School through the rigours of the First World War. His Logbook entries are far less detailed than Henry Saloway's for the same period, but it is still possible to glean some sense of the difficulties the school had to face. One pleasant event however was a visit to the school by the painter Fra Newbery. Mr Bates records it as follows: *"Sept 22nd 1916. Mr F.H. Newbery, a boy in the school under Mr Beard, now Director of the Glasgow School of Art, visited this morning. He examined the drawing of the first class and offered prizes of £1-1s (one guinea) and 10s-6d to be awarded next July for not less than twelve studies in colour. He also presented to the school four pairs of studies executed in the Bridport Art School by the late Mr Broadly."* In fact the Francis Newbery Prizes continued to be awarded annually and joined the existing Daniel Taylor Prizes for Attendance as regular awards at the annual prize-giving in July.

---

[5] Ibid

178

In October 1917 the school was dealing with evacuees: *"A number of London boys (forty-one in all) who are staying in Bridport for a few weeks to get out of the neighbourhood of the German air-raids"*. It is clear that the plight of these children chosen by doctors in London for evacuation as they were suffering from *"nervous strain"* touched Mr Bates closely, for he obviously gave them considerable time, taking them *"each week a march and a nature study lesson on the beach at West Bay, on the cliffs etc."* Like the National School, the Boys' General School lost many former pupils in the "Great War", though little reference is made to the fact in Mr Bates' log, but due tribute was paid to those who died when, on the afternoon of March 8th 1924 a *" tablet to the memory of Old Boys who fell in the Great War, and subscribed for by the Old Boys of the School was unveiled"* appropriately by Mr Bates, who, having retired from teaching in 1923 was by then Mayor of Bridport. This "tablet" is now in the former Grammar School building in St Andrew's Road.

In 1914 the Girls' School acquired a new Headmistress. Edith Strawbridge took over in the September, and like Miss Collins before her, immediately had problems. She had to discipline one of the girls for *"fighting on the stairs,"* and she had struck her *"on the palms of the hands with the flat side of a ruler"*. She reports that *"the child has not attended since"*. In addition the girl's mother came to the school and *"abused me using most insolent language"*. In March 1915 Edith Strawbridge began gardening lessons for her senior girls in the school garden. *"Eight plots are being worked, one for each of the seven girls and one for demonstration"*. [6] I can find no other account of girls being given gardening lessons this early, though the boys were taught gardening from about this period. It seems Miss Strawbridge was ahead of her time. However so impressed was HMI Walsh that he suggested to her that gardening should be put on the school timetable *"as an article 2 subject."* And in April 1915 the girls, obviously fired with enthusiasm gave a concert in the Town Hall to raise money to buy gardening tools – and a sewing machine for the school, so the status quo was partly maintained!

Miss Alice Lee Colfox, elder sister of Lt Colonel Thomas Alfred Colfox, was a manager of the Girls' School at this time, but her work with the school went far beyond what was usually expected of a manager. Throughout the war years she made it her job to teach the girls, in a series of weekly lessons starting in Sept 1916. First she gave a series of lesson on Home-nursing to the Class 1 girls, and followed this with lessons on Domestic Science, and in May 1917, when food was really running very short, and all sorts of strategies were being considered to try and relieve the situation, she gave a lecture to Standards 2 and 3 on Food Economy.

---

[6] Ibid

As a further part of the war effort on food, the entire Boys' School was taken by the staff to pick blackberries on two separate occasions, netting a total of 164lbs of the fruit. As in the National School, there were egg collections to send eggs to the hospitals caring for wounded soldiers. The end of the war did not bring an end to the privation, and in February 1919 the Girls' School was closed because of the influenza epidemic and did not reopen until March 10th.

The shock of the First World War, and the enormous loss of life of so many young men, galvanised the Government into activity, and the result was the 1918 Education Act. Health was also a concern. The Chief Medical Officer of the Board of Education estimated in 1913 that the health of the country's elementary schoolchildren was poor: 10% having poor vision and 5% hearing problems. A horrifying 50% had serious dental decay, and a smaller percentage had such conditions as ringworm, enlarged tonsils and adenoids, and 2% were still suffering from tuberculosis. While these figures take into account city children whose condition was generally worse that their rural counterparts, the Logbooks of all Bridport schools report a significant amount of disease. The response was to begin a programme to visits to schools by doctors and dentists and the appearance of the Health Nurse to inspect children for infestations. While some of her visits to the General Schools result in the note: *"no exclusions"*, quite often one or more children were sent home.

The 1920's saw much the same expansion of the curriculum and in the activities available to children as are detailed in the National School Logbooks. Reference is made to children competing in the County Athletics Championships, to the schools closing for the annual Sunday School Treats and to the special visits to the Electric Palace to see patriotic films. The increased opportunities for children to progress in their education is reflected, not just in the development of Senior Classes, but also in the number of children passing the Scholarship examination for Bridport Secondary School. In March 1923 this was superseded by the newly instituted County examination for children over 11 (the 11+ as it came to be called) and a steady stream of bright children passed from the General Schools to Bridport Secondary, later Grammar School, throughout the inter-war years.

On Dec 20th 1923, William Bates retired, but continuity was ensured at the Boys' School by the fact that his successor had already served the school as an assistant master since 1911. Arthur G Spenser had served for nearly three years in the forces during the war. He took over as headmaster on Mr Bates' retirement and served until 1950. Like John Beard, he is also fondly remembered by his pupils. Reference is made in a historical note in a much later Colfox School prospectus, probably written by Major Thornburn, to the *"redoubtable"* Mr Spenser, and his excellent Senior School.

On his retirement in December 1923, tributes were paid to Mr Bates' long service to the school. In addition to his work in the Boys' School, he also ran evening classes in Science and Mathematics for boys and young men who needed the extra tuition. He was very involved with the Congregational Church, being both a deacon and Sunday School Superintendent. He was also a town councillor and was ultimately awarded the MBE for his public work. It is slightly ironic therefore, for such an active man, that his retirement present was an armchair, though as he went on to serve the town as Mayor in the year following his retirement, he obviously did not make much use of it.

In January 1933 the three schools were re-organised into Mixed Senior, Junior and Infant Schools. The Senior School occupied the former Girls' School on the upper floor of the two storey building. The Infants who, as they had always been mixed suffered virtually no change at all, remained on the ground floor in their original rooms, and the Boys' School became the Junior Mixed School. The reorganisation seems to have gone remarkably smoothly, and is hardly mentioned in the various Logbooks. All Mr Spenser says, in his entry before the Christmas holidays in 1932, is *"This is the last meeting of the school as a Boys Department."*

He took over as Head of the Senior School. Miss J M Orton who was already Head of the Girls' School by this time, took over the Junior School for two years until her retirement in 1935, and Miss Hounsell continued with the Infant School. Dorothy E P Abbott, generally known as "Dolly", who had joined the school in 1923, became Senior Mistress. In 1935, Ethel Batchelor took over the direction of the Junior School, and in 1936 a great loss to the school was the death of Alice Lee Colfox who had been such a tireless supporter of the school. The Logbook records that Miss Batchelor attended her funeral on 13th October.

Little was done to the buildings, and a report for the County Council 1934 observed that *"in the case of the General School, the premises occupied by the Senior School are cramped and unsatisfactory"*. It further went on to list the shortcomings of the accommodation that *"cookery and laundry work are at present taught at the Unitarian Sunday School and the committee rent premises for Woodwork and Metal work"*. A former pupil of the General School from 1931 to 1940, Tony Tiltman, who went on to become Mayor of Bridport, recalls attending woodwork and metalwork classes near Allington School. These were run by Mr Bernard Jolliffe, who later taught at Colfox School. In addition to the classrooms being described as *"passage rooms"* – that is without a corridor – the County Council Report states that *"the cloakroom accommodation is unsuitable ...."*

181

......*there are no staffrooms, the playground accommodation is inadequate.*"[7] Things had clearly not improved by 1935 when HMI reported that the Senior School was operating under the *"severe handicap"* of having a *"very small room in which the Headmaster teaches the oldest group"*. And going on to add *"it is very greatly to be hoped that the plans for unifying the Senior Schools of Bridport will be pushed forward with all speed."*

Nothing was done, and once again, in 1938, HMI were complaining about the building being inadequate: *"there are few amenities for the children and none for the staff"*. It goes on to say: *"A rearrangement of the children was brought about in 1933 with very little alteration of premises. This enabled the older children to have some advantage in classification according to age, but it is not reorganisation in the modern sense of the term as the Senior Department has no Science room, no Practical Instruction room, and no Hall, nor is there a playing field. The Bridport General School is, in fact, still a self-contained full-standard school of the old conventional type, and the seniors are working under conditions that can only be viewed with deep regret and an earnest desire that they may not endure much longer."*[8]

Sporting activities at the school in the thirties, though handicapped by the lack of facilities near the school, were as extensive as possible. The boys played cricket and football, like the children from Gundry Lane using the main St Mary's Playing Field. The girls played netball and were allowed, with Miss Alice Colfox's blessing, to use the tennis courts at her house, West Mead, in the summer. Also in the summer there were running, and swimming lessons, the latter conducted at West Bay in the harbour. Considering the number of schools, both state and private that took their children down to the Bay for swimming lessons as well as the existence of the swimming club, it must have been pretty busy on fine summer days.

Christmas was a time of parties: Tony Tiltman recalls one particular Christmas when he was about six or seven and in the Infant School. He was asked what he would like for a Christmas present. He asked for *"a train set"*, not really expecting to get one, but to his surprise that was exactly what he got. He believes that the teachers clubbed together to raise the money for the presents. The Girls' School Christmas Party was held for a number of years from about 1928 in the Liberal Hall in Barrack Street. Games and refreshments were followed by a programme of plays and carols. Each girl was given a cracker, the gift of Alice Colfox. Parents and friends attended and an entertaining evening was had by all.[9]

---

[7] Reorganisation of Schools (Bridport District): DHC/ S117/12/15
[8] Bridport General Boys', Girls' & Infants' Schools Logbooks: 1862-1956: DHC/MIC/R/893/894
[9] Ibid

182

The General School also had gardens, both up near the Grammar School and on land between the River Asker and the mill-leat for Folly Mill, In the area known as Back Rivers. Tony Tiltman recalls having to cross the mill-leat to get to the gardens which were later turned into allotments, and may well have been part of the same plot used by St Mary's School in the 1920's. However there may also have been garden plots on the school site near the King Street perimeter, which may have been the ones used by the girls.

Like St Mary's, the General School pupils celebrated Empire Day with parades and flags, May Day with Maypole dancing, and on Prizegiving Day, which was just before the summer holidays, Tony Tiltman recalls the boys doing a sword dance as part of the entertainment. Armistice Day was also observed with a special service in the Senior Schoolroom which was divided by partitions for normal day-to-day use, but which could be opened out into one large room for special occasions.

As Empire Day is only a dim memory for most people it is worth reproducing the programme for the Empire Day celebrations held on May 22nd 1931:

> *"EMPIRE DAY - A PROGRAMME*
> *1. Saluting the Flag*
> *2. Jerusalem - Boys and Girls*
> *3. Recitations - Boys*
> *   • "Our Heritage"*
> *   • "Rule Britannia"*
> *   • "Admirals All"*
> *   • "England, My England"*
> *   • "St George for England"*
> *   • "To English Boys"*
> *4. Songs - Senior Boys*
> *   • "The Children's Song"*
> *   • "The Stately Homes of England"*
> *   • "Land of Hope and Glory"*
> *5. Empire Play - Junior Boy*
> *6. A Pageant of Empire - Girls*
> *7. "Here's A Health" - Boys and Girls*
> *8. God save the King.* [10]

Most of the children at the school lived within walking or cycling distance of the school and most went home for lunch. School canteens were a WWII innovation as a response to rationing. Those who lived too far

---

[10] Ibid

to go home and brought a packed lunch, apparently had to eat their food sitting at a desk in the playground whatever the weather, according to one former student who attended the school in the late 1920's.

One of the more entertainingly bizarre clubs that the Junior School set up, driven it seems by the enthusiasm of one of the managers, a Miss Suttill, and the Headteacher Ethel Batchelor, was the "Bird and Tree Club". This was apparently an offshoot from an adult body, the Bird and Tree Society, of which Miss Suttill was a member. The junior members were known as Bird and Tree Cadets. The first event seems to have taken place in July 1937 when *"16 of the top class"* sat for a competition organised by the Bird and Tree Society in which they had to complete two essays, a Bird Essay and a Tree Essay. The following July, 1938, a Bird and Tree festival was held in the school at which the prizes for the previous year's essays were awarded and an entertainment of appropriately themed items was given in front of an audience of parents and friends. The programme was as follows:

1. *Songs by the School Choir: "The Cuckoo" and "The Lark in the Morn".*
2. *Recitation: "If I were a Fir Tree"*
3. *Reading of Reports and Presentation of Prizes*
4. *A Play : "Timothy Trot and the Birds"*
5. *Song by the School: "London Birds"*
6. *Folk Dances and a Sword Dance*
7. *Songs by the Junior Choir*
8. *The National Anthem.* [11]

In March 1939 Dorset County Council finally took over the remainder of the lease on the Killingham site and Bridport General School became a "Provided School", fully maintained by the County Council. Finally in 1941 an agreement was reached for the County Council to take over the school premises. This had actually been proposed as early as 1934, but was not implemented until seven years later. Thus ended nearly 100 years of voluntary or partially voluntary status.

1939 saw once more the outbreak of war. Once again the school had to contend with the disruption caused by evacuees. Mr Spenser reports their arrival in September 1939. Ethel Batchelor, who had been Head of the Junior School since 1936, reported on September 18th: *"School reopened this morning for morning sessions only as evacuee children will be using the building in the afternoon. The afternoons are being devoted to*

---

[11] Ibid

optional *Nature Study walks, and games."* [12] By November the evacuees had been transferred to the Wesleyan Sunday Schoolroom In South Street, and afternoon school could start again.

Like the other schools in the area, precautions were put in place, and trenches were dug as air-raid shelters in an area within the Killingham site on the King Street side, though they do not seem to have been used for anything other than practices. The disruption to the school particularly at the height of the German air raids, must have been considerable. An extract from the Senior School log for Sept/October 1940 gives some indication:

"Sept 6th: air-raid 12-10 - 1-30pm
Sept 25th: air-raid 11-15am - 12-30pm
Sept 27th: air-raids 11-10am - 12-15pm" and again *"1-35 - 2pm"*
Not much work must have been done that day.

Again: *"Sept 30th: air-raid 11-5am - 11-55am*
Oct 1st: air-raid 10-50am - 11-25am
Oct 7th: air raid 10-50am - 11-25am."
What is equally striking about this extract is the very regularity of the German raids.

Despite the existence of trenches, pupils at the time recall getting under their desks when the air-raid warning sounded, and when the bomb dropped on East Street on December 16th 1942 it was mercifully lunchtime, or loss of life among the pupils would have been inevitable.

There are two reports of this bombing from the perspectives of Miss Hounsell and Mr Spenser. Miss Hounsell, in the Infant Logbook, records with remarkable brevity: *"School bombed today - children took cover immediately on hearing siren. No casualties",* and then *"very few children present."* Mr Spenser, appropriately for someone who had seen service in the First World War, is more detailed: *"1-20pm air-raid warning. At 1-40 pm on a bearing 30 or 40 yards from the school. Much damage was caused to ceilings, roof and windows, so that it was found necessary to close the school until further notice."* [13] It did not reopen until Jan 18th 1943.

The school was within less than a hundred yards of this devastating explosion which totally demolished several houses just east of the King of Belgium Hotel (now The Lord Nelson). The force of the blast was away from the school building, otherwise it seems inconceivable that it could have escaped with only the relatively minor damage Mr Spenser records. The majority of children were away from the building when the bombs

---

[12] Ibid
[13] Ibid

185

dropped. Several reported seeing the planes fly over the town and hearing the explosions. One recalls debris falling as far south as Back Rivers.

In September 1945 Miss B. M. Hounsell left the Infants' School having served for seventeen years and was replaced by a Mrs Morris who only stayed for one term, and was in her turn replaced by Mrs Norman in January 1946. (Fig 31) Arthur Spenser retired in 1950, having been at the school through two world wars, and he was replaced by a Mr Hunsley, who saw the school through to closure in 1956 when he records in the last entry to the Senior School Logbook: *"25th July: All the pupils and staff, with the exception of the Headmaster will be transferred to the Colfox School in September."* He was leaving the school, but he had prepared for the transfer to the Alfred Colfox School by introducing a House System and Prefects to bring the Senior School into line with the Grammar School.

While the post-eleven pupils transferred to the newly built secondary school, the Infants and Juniors stayed put for a further couple of years, until they too moved to occupy the former Grammar School premises in St Andrew's Road. The headteachers at the time of the move were Mrs Lillie Briggs, in charge of the Infants School, and Miss Ethel Batchelor, Head of the Junior School. Along with its new premises the school got a new name. It was now to be called Bridport County Primary School.

The new **Bridport County Primary School** opened in September 1958 in the former Grammar School buildings. Ethel Batchelor became the first headteacher of the new school. On her retirement, Lillie Briggs, formerly in charge of the Infants' Department, succeeded her colleague and continued to build the reputation of the new school. It has been difficult to trace the archive for the Bridport County Primary, so the following information is necessarily brief and sadly incomplete. Lillie Briggs was followed as headteacher by Arthur Rees, who was in turn replaced by Mr Geoffrey Budd.

The accommodation was adapted to provide for the Infant classes in the buildings on the Coneygar Hill side of the school playground that had formerly housed the Grammar School's practical rooms. The main building and a number of temporary buildings housed the Juniors, and for a number of years the school continued to enjoy the use of the canteen built just after WWII, which served cooked midday meals. It also enjoyed the considerable luxury of the extensive playing fields on both sides of Coneygar Lane, and the large school hall. No other Bridport primary school at this period had such good facilities. The annual Sport's Day held on the school sport's field on the north side of Coneygar Lane was always well supported by parents, and the school boasted successful sports' teams. Their football, (Fig 32) athletics, cricket and netball teams were all successful in various competitions, such as the popular Kenway Cup football competition, the West Dorset six-a-side tournament and the West Dorset Primary Athletics Championships. Like the Grammar School before them, they used the school hall for a series of often quite ambitious school drama productions, such as A Christmas Carol and Toad of Toad Hall.

However good the playing-fields might have been, however, the old 1909 buildings were inadequate for the demands of a modern primary, and as numbers grew so more and more children were accommodated in temporary classrooms. In the 1990's the decision was finally taken to build a new school on the Coneygar Lane side of the site. The children moved into the new building in 1997, and the school was formally opened in 1998 by, appropriately enough, Sir John Colfox, whose family had had so much involvement with both the General Schools and the Bridport Grammar School. (Chapter XIII) A decision was taken at County level to drop the category of "County" school, and so the new school was renamed Bridport Primary School – rapidly shortened by its pupils to BPS. A more detailed history of this school remains to be written.

XII

ADULT EDUCATION IN THE NINETEENTH CENTURY

"If 'knowledge is power', ignorance is weakness, and the mother of wickedness. To our operatives we would say, 'Banish ignorance from your dwellings as a demon from the bottomless pit.' " Thus "The Working Man's Friend and Family Instructor" in the introduction to its first issue published on January 5th 1850. Education as a moral imperative seems a strange concept to us today, with our view of adult education as either strictly vocational, or part of the leisure industry, but in the nineteenth century it was a very powerful motive.

The nineteenth century was not simply a period of great progress in the education of the children of the working classes. It was also a period in which the desire of working men to be educated inspired a groundswell of activity which was a combination of self-help, and organisations dedicated to educating the working classes. This was a cause taken up particularly by the non-conformists, and by the left-wing political movements of the period. Indeed so identified with these two strands of political and religious life was adult education for the working classes, that it was viewed with deep suspicion, and often outright hostility by the establishment. It was seen as potentially, if not actually subversive.

However the need for working men to be educated in the scientific principles underlying their trades became more and more necessary as industrial development accelerated. The Mechanics' Institutes and the Society for the Diffusion of Useful Knowledge were set up to fulfil this need and unlike more radical organizations were actively sponsored by the middle classes. The first mechanics' institute, The London Mechanics' Institution, was established in London at 29 Southampton Buildings, Chancery Lane, in 1823. It was founded by Dr Birkbeck, the philanthropist, with the support of Lord Brougham, who was a leading parliamentary radical and an active supporter of Mechanics' Institutes. As well as his work for the Ragged Schools Union and the Society for the Diffusion of Useful Knowledge. Brougham, as MP for Winchelsea, was a champion of state-funded education and with remarkable persistence he introduced a series of education bills to parliament in 1820,1835,1837, 1838 and 1839, all of which were defeated. It is rather sad that he died in 1868 just two years before Forster's Education Act did succeed in beginning the long road to state-funded education in this country.

George Birkbeck, whose name is memorialised for posterity by the London University College than bears his name, was a Yorkshireman, born in 1776. In 1799 when he had become Professor of Natural Philosophy at Anderson's College in Glasgow, he began providing free classes for working-class men in mechanics and chemistry. By 1804 he had moved to London and become a physician, but he continued his work in education. He founded the London Mechanics' Institution in 1823 and became its first president. The aim of the Institution was enunciated as instructing its members *"in the principles of the Arts they practise, and in the various branches of science and useful Knowledge."* [1] It contained a library, reading rooms, class-rooms and a large lecture theatre for weekly lectures. It was to be the model for most of the Mechanics' Institutes set up around the country. In 1866 the Institution changed its name to Birkbeck Literary and Scientific Institution, and eventually after many further evolutions became Birkbeck College.

Mechanics' Institutes were deliberately non-religious and non-political and were viewed with some suspicion by those working men who were more interested in political ideas. These gravitated towards the Chartist Halls and Owenite Halls of Science. One of the problems the Mechanics' Institutes faced however was the very low level of education among the working classes at the beginning of the nineteenth century.

The Bridport Mechanics Institute

This establishment actually dates from 1834 but its precursor, an organisation under the name of The Association for Mutual Improvement, was set up in Bridport in 1830. [2] A contemporary newspaper report dated December 27th 1830 states: *"An Institution has been formed at Bridport which has for its object the mental and moral advantage of the inhabitants of the town and neighbourhood, but especially of the young men of the working classes by affording them the means of useful knowledge".* This Institution which was originally called The Association for Mutual Improvement was also intended to provide its members with *"interesting subjects of reflection and discussion and thereby establishing a wholesome moral restraint upon their amusements, keeping them from wasting their leisure time in vacancy of mind or unprofitable conversation, or sensual indulgence, in fact enabling them to become more thinking, and therefore more rational beings, and more useful and respectable members of Society."*

The meeting held on 14th December 1830 for the formation of this association received a cheque from Henry Warburton (MP for Bridport from 1826 – 1841) for £100, and about a hundred men enrolled as members. At

---

[1] A brief history of Birkbeck College: www.aim25.ac.uk
[2] Henry Nobbs Cox, the Ironmonger and son of the schoolmaster who ran Bridge House School in the late 1800's, collected a number of contemporary newspaper reports which he reproduced in his own papers. He reproduces a number of reports which relate to the setting up of the Mechanics' Institute.

the meeting a *"liberal subscription* (was) *entered into."* Among the Committee members were many familiar names: Joseph Gundry, Edwin Nicholettes, Dr Giles Roberts, Joseph Hounsell, and a number of other prominent citizens of the town. The first President was William Forster, the father of W. E. Forster MP and a prominent member of the Bridport Society of Friends.

The Association began its work straight away, and by January 5th 1831, a *"temporary habitation"* had been procured in *"Mr Hines shop and rooms in East Street."* This is now the side of the HSBC Bank. A contemporary newspaper report states that it was making *"rapid progress, aided by the assistance of many respectable inhabitants who meet every evening gratuitously for the purpose of instructing its members"* [3]. In addition to Hine's shop and rooms which were presumably used as a reading room and lecture room, *"Miss Hart's Schoolroom"* was hired for the sum of £5 per annum so classes in Grammar, Arithmetic and the Elements of Geometry, and Architectural Drawing could commence. These classes were conducted by various members of the Committee, the Rev Robert Cree, the Unitarian Minister, giving the Grammar lessons, Mr Samuel Taylor, the Mathematics, and Mr Sweeting the Architectural Drawing. The Reading Room was opened on January 28th 1831, and apparently already had a well-stocked library. This event was celebrated by an address delivered by the Rev. Robert Cree, the Unitarian Minister, in the Town Hall.

A copy of the text of his lecture survives in a leaflet published at the time.[4] The subject of the lecture was *"The advantages of cooperation in the pursuit of Knowledge, and the benefits resulting therefrom; together with some hints to the uninstructed, as to the Course of Reading they may advantageously pursue."* It is no surprise, bearing in mind the speaker, that the tone of the lecture is strongly moralistic. He exalts the function of education as the means to cultivate *"our higher powers";* thus fostering *"that divine spark of the intelligent life with which our Creator hath endowed us! The human mind, the candle, or the illumination of the Lord, within us, is especially, the subject of education,"* he asserts. Education is seen as saving men from the condition *"of the humbler creatures, which surround them. For what but wretched creatures must the men be, who should be guided, not by knowledge, but by prejudice – not by wisdom, but by passion – not by the maxims of prudence and the dictates of reason, but by the desires and the impulsions of sense and appetite."* The belief in the redeeming force of education was so strongly held that even as early as

---

[3] The Report of the Committee of the Bridport Literary and Scientific Institute dated October 10th 1864 sets out a history of the Mechanics Institute. This and various newpaper reports are quoted in H N Cox Papers: BMLHC

[4] Leaflet publishing the text of the Inaugural Lecture: DHC/ D/Col/ Q3

this first lecture, the numbers of subscribing members is 113, and by the time the lecture was published a month later it had grown to 145.

The Association did not delay in getting its educational programme started, and on the 4th February a course of twelve lectures given by Dr Giles Roberts commenced. This was the first of many series of lectures delivered by well-known figures, over the years that the organisation, under its various incarnations, was in existence.

On January 5th 1832 the Association held its First Anniversary Meeting in the Town Hall with the President of the Association, William Forster in the chair. The meeting heard a detailed report of what had been achieved to further education in the town in the past year. Then came the news that Mr Warburton intended to erect a *"large, commodious building"* for the Association's use. Perhaps it was the fact that the Associations patron was an MP that inspired Mr Williams, the secretary of the association to suggest that *"as Politics are a branch of human knowledge, highly important as affecting the comfort and happiness of every individual of the community, it was desirable that the Association should afford the means of acquiring political information"*. In consequence the committee agreed to make daily newspapers and periodicals and *"occasionally pamphlets on subjects of public interest"* available in the Reading Room, which meant an increase in the subscription to twenty-five shillings per annum for members and thirty-five shilling for non-members.

During the winter of 1833, just before the Association gained its own building in East Street, the Committee decided that in addition to the lectures some members of the Association would read papers on scientific and literary subjects *"got up in a popular manner so as to assume rather the unembarrassing freedom of a friendly address"*, as the 1864 Report puts it, such reading to give rise to discussion of the points raised. Once again the Rev Robert Cree and Dr Giles Roberts were among the members to deliver papers in this way.[5]

The foundation stone of this *"commodious"* building was laid in June 1832. A Newspaper report of the occasion states *"Mr Warburton arrived in Bridport to meet his constituents and lay the foundation stone of the building about to be erected in East Street for the use of the members of the Mutual Improvement Society of which Mr Warburton is the Patron. A large body of the Electors assembled at the Bull Inn and marched in procession to the eastern boundary of the Borough preceded by a band and a brilliant display of Banners. Shortly after 10, Mr Warburton arrived and was escorted by the party into the town amidst joyous acclamation. From the balcony of the Bull Inn he addressed the assembled multitude*

---

[5] Quoted in H N Cox Papers: BMLHC

upon the Reform Bill[6] amid cheers. After this Mr Warburton met the members of the Association for Mutual Improvement at the Town Hall and proceeded with them to the site of the intended building. The usual formalities of laying the foundation stone having been gone through, a lengthy address was given by Mr Williams, the Secretary in the absence of the President. At the close of Mr Warburton's address - Mr Williams was presented with a silver inkstand".[7]

By the end of 1833 the building was completed and on 25th January it was opened, once again Henry Warburton officiating, "on which occasion he delivered an admirable address on the origin and progress of the Arts and Sciences to a crowded and attentive audience."

By this time the name "The Bridport Mechanics Institute" was being used. The Newspaper report of this occasion goes on: "It deserves to be mentioned that Mr Warburton is a patron indeed, having solely at his own wish erected the building appropriated to the use of the Institution and express(ed) his intention of giving it for its perpetual use, by placing it in the hands of trustees for that purpose as soon as the Institution, now in its infant state, shall appear to be placed on a firm basis."

The report then goes on to describe the facilities: "The building is the most lofty in the town. The Institution has a Reading Room which is opened every day from 10 o'clock in the morning until 10 o'clock at night, and is regularly supplied with modern publications, Scientific and Literary periodicals, reviews......and daily and weekly newspapers. The Circulating ("Library" presumably - the word is missing) contains nearly 700 volumes consisting of popular and valuable works in History, Biography, Voyages, Travels and the Arts and Sciences, affording to the members an ample source of instruction and amusement, with the advantage of reading the books at their own homes. The Institution possesses a well arranged and spacious Lecture Room wherein lectures in Science and Literature will be delivered as frequently as circumstances will permit."[8]

In the October of the same years the resources available to the Institute were augmented by the gift from "His Majesty's Commissioners for the Public Records of the Kingdom" of fifty-two large folio volumes of their publications. To house these volumes suitably "the Corporation have liberally voted a grant of money to defray the expense of providing a proper bookcase..."

Henry Warburton's benevolence was long remembered in Bridport. A history of the nearby Unitarian Chapel refers to the Mechanics' Institute

---

[6] The "Great Reform Act" of 1832 increased the franchise to include a much greater number of propertied males: £10 householders in the boroughs and 40s freeholders in the counties. The total electorate was raised from 435,000 to 632,000.
[7] Quoted in H N Cox Papers: BMLHC
[8] Ibid

building as a *"handsome and commodious edifice, for which the inhabitants are indebted to the generosity of Henry Warburton, MP for Bridport."*[9], and a visitor in 1872 was told that the building had cost Warburton in excess of £16,000.

The Mechanics' Institute, which was one of the earliest in the country, post-dating the London Institute by only six or seven years, did not, unfortunately, have a very long life. There are various theories as to why it failed. One version suggests that it was because the members, instead of concentrating of self-improvement got involved in radical politics which did not find favour with those in power in a conservative region such as Dorset. They apparently made the mistake of petitioning parliament over the issue of whether or not education should be freed of church control. It appears they championed the secularisation of education. While this may well have been a popular view in "Dissenting" Bridport, in the view of the Dorset County Chronicle in 1838 secular schools were seen as *"the preparatory step to the Mechanics' Institutions"*. Both were clearly seen as radical and subversive in their aims.

A survey of 1839 indicates that the Bridport Institute was only one of nineteen such bodies in the country and was providing adult evening classes to a membership of 111, of whom only twenty were classed as "mechanics". Average attendance at lectures at that time was 150, and the library had over 1000 volumes.[10] An article by Joseph Maskell in "The History and Topography of Bridport, Dorset" written in 1855 notes, with a certain touch of hyperbole, that the setting up of the Mechanics Institute was *"the most remarkable event of the present century"* in Bridport. However he goes on to add that it was *"remarkable for its bright beginnings and its unhappy future"*. The 1864 Report[11] sheds no further light on the reasons for the decline, simply stating that the various activities described above were *"developed with considerable success till about 1840, when the minutes of the Association close and the earlier life of the Society began to ebb"*. That "ebb" continued until the Institute was closed in 1849. The report then goes on to say *"Its life however was not utterly extinct for in 1855 it was resuscitated and under a new Committee, the Literary and Scientific Institute was founded"*.

The Literary and Scientific Institute occupied the same building, no doubt given impetus by the Literary and Scientific Institutes Act of 1854. The Library which had been mortgaged was re-purchased for £20, and

---

[9]Jerome Murch: "A History of Presbyterian and General Baptist Churches in the West of England 1835", quoted in Proceedings of the DNHAS Vol 121 1999 p 136
[10] Proceedings of the DNHAS, Vol 100, 1978: p19
[11] The Report of the Committee of the Bridport Literary and Scientific Institute dated October 10th 1864 quoted in the H N Cox Papers: BMLHC. This report tells the story of the Mechanics' Institute very much from the perspective of the later organisation.

classes were again established in Writing, Arithmetic and Grammar, and draughts and chess were introduced. Once again lectures were given though the Report states *"of a widely different character from those delivered at the commencement of the Society"*.

The building in East Street had clearly fallen somewhat into disrepair, for before the formal opening in October 1864 repairs and refurbishments were necessary. The worn flight of steps (now replaced by a ramp) leading from the pavement to the main entrance to the building were repaired, the carved name that can be seen today was added to the façade, and inside the building, substantial alterations were made. The original staircase, described in a report in the Bridport News of 15th Oct 1864 as a *"long gracefully sweeping staircase leading to the Lecture Hall"*, though it was also described as being *"very steep and very dangerous"*, was taken down and replaced with two shorter flights at right angles to one another, doubtless the staircase that is still in the building today. The Lecture Hall was refurnished with benches *"with backs"*, and new lighting was installed.

The Reading Room was redecorated and adorned with busts of notable men of letters and base reliefs on allegorical subjects *"from the Gallery of Brucciani"*. Above the door was a base relief showing *"Minerva Uniting Art and Commerce"*, by Gibson. On the north side of the door was a bust of Sir Walter Scott, and on the south side one of John Flaxman, the sculptor. On the south wall were busts of Queen Victoria and Prince Albert. The west wall was presided over by William Shakespeare, Sir Francis Bacon, James Watt, and Sir Isaac Newton. There was also a bust of George Stephenson, and one of Alfred Lord Tennyson. The bust of Scott and the Minerva base relief were the gift of Mr William Colfox. The room was further adorned with a number of photographs. In addition to the Library, there was also a Museum housed in the building.[12]

The Literary and Scientific Institute seems to have flourished. Many visiting lecturers were drawn to the town, not least by the ease of travelling via the new railway link that had reached the town in 1857. A very popular visiting lecturer was the poet and schoolmaster, William Barnes, who visited the town quite frequently between 1858 and 1877. His lectures had titles such as "The Dorset Dialect", "The English Language" and "Notes on Dorsetshire", and he also included readings of his poetry, which was probably the most popular event. As one of the secretaries of the Institute, F. W. Matterface, put it in a letter in 1870, his poetry reading were something that *"no audience of Bridport folk ever tires of listening to"*. Barnes also lectured to the Working Men's Club; no doubt the one in South Street where John Beard also lectured from time to time. Also associated

---

[12] Bridport News: 15th October 1864

194

with the Institute was the classical actor W. C. Macreedy, who was made a life member in 1858 for his *"generous and valuable support"* to the Institute. Another note gives the tantalising information under the date Feb 1858: *"Mr Thackeray to be offered through Mr Macreedy to lecture for the sum of £20. £25 was voted later on but the lecture was never given".*[13] How sad!

In 1864 the "Electric Telegraph" was brought to the town from the railway station and a room in the Institute was let to them for a term of three years, renewed in 1867, but by 1870 the telegraph had been taken over by the GPO. In his speech at the opening ceremony of the refurbished premises in 1864, Benjamin Pearkes Gundry, the Mayor for that year, indicated the intention to establish a school of design at the Institute.

In 1865, the **Bridport School of Art** was established with Government assistance in funding, and for a number of years it and the Institute operated side by side in the same building. Though the Institute continued to flourish, the Art School ultimately became by far the more influential organisation to occupy the building. It operated as an evening school and came under the management of the Higher Education Committee. William Bush was the first art master. Yet even for such a respected organisation, funding was soon a problem. By 1885 the government grant seems to have ceased, for the expenses were being defrayed by subscription.

The Institute was no more immune to money-problems than the Art School. It too periodically ran short of money and as early as 1868 the subscriptions had to be raised. Further difficulties arose in 1873, when a Gentleman's Club was opened elsewhere in the town, and this resulted in a loss of membership, which the Annual Report of the Association states, *"is specially disheartening at a time when the general circumstances of the town are not promising for the acquisition of new members."*[14]

This decline in membership had no effect on the Art School which seems to have gone from strength to strength. Another art master was Faraday H Christie. Among those who benefited from the teaching at the school was the future Director of the Glasgow School of Art, Francis (Fra) Newberry (Appendix A). The art master who taught him in the early 1870's was a Mr Broadly, and it was a selection of Broadly's "studies" that Fra Newbery later presented to his former school, the Bridport Boys' General School.

In 1881 a number of meetings of the respective committees were held to discuss the possibility of amalgamating the School of Art with the Literary and Scientific Institute, and renovation of several rooms was

---

[13] H N Cox Papers BMLHC
[14] Ibid

undertaken, the new accommodation being opened in December 1885, for lectures, discussions and games. In 1899 the School of Art came under the supervision of the Bridport Borough Technical Committee,[15] and by the early years of the twentieth century was operating under the aegis of the Higher Education Committee.[16]

The Art School lasted well into the 20th century. It is mentioned by Arthur Champ in his Mates' Guide to Bridport of 1903, and by Kelly's Directory right through to 1939. Increasingly throughout this period the Literary and Scientific Institute is simply referred to as the School of Art, testimony to how important this educational establishment became over and above all the other activities for which the building was designed. In December 1904 the Institute celebrated its Jubilee, and a new subscription was opened to raise money for major improvements to the building including building a recreation room over the Library, but in the event not enough money was raised and in 1905, the committee had to content themselves with renovating the Reading Room, hall and staircase and painting the outside of the building.[17] From 1922 until the Second World War, in addition to the School of Art, the building was providing accommodation for a Men's Club.

Like so many other educational organisations, neither the Institute or the Art School seem to have survived the Second World War. During the War the building was temporarily used by the American troops stationed in Bridport before the Normandy landings. The Medical Detachment of the 2nd Battalion of the 16th Infantry were based there, and the reading room was used as a Red Cross Club for the American soldiers and officers.[18] A contemporary photograph shows the men relaxing over tea and cakes while one of their number entertains them from a piano in the corner of the room.

After the war, continuity with its past use was reasserted when the lease was taken over by the County Council and in 1952 the old Reading Room became the Bridport Public Library. The building also continued to be used for adult education, as the Workers Education Association, among other organisations, used the building for lectures and courses. For a while after the Library had moved to its present site in South Street, another continuity was established, as artists engaged in a range of projects, briefly took over the old rooms, but now, once again, as in the late 1840's, this notable building in its prominent position in Bridport's streetscape is looking for a new identity and use.

---

[15] HN Cox Papers: BMLHC
[16] Mates Guide to Bridport, 1903
[17] HN Cox Papers: BMLHC
[18] "Seven Months to D-Day - An American Regiment in Dorset" by Robin Pearce, pub. Dovecote Press pp 38, 40. Copies of photographs (BMLHC)

It would appear however, that while the Mechanics' Institute closed, technical education continued in the town In one form or another, and at one point a **Working Men's Institute or Club**, both names are used, was operating in the "Old Castle" in South Street, now the home of Bridport Museum. A fire at these premises in 1876 necessitated their removal to premises in East Street, and after its refurbishment the building was used as a Conservative Club. In 1888, funding for adult technical education was improved when the Local Government Act authorized the new local authorities to spend the proceeds of a penny rate on technical and manual instruction. Precisely what effect this had on Bridport is not clear.

What is also not at present clear is to where, precisely, in East Street the Working Men's Club relocated, though a record in the Bridport Borough Survey shows that a property in Downes Street, now numbers 13 and 15, and in the lease described as a *"former warehouse and stables"*, was leased to Bridport Working Men's Club for 99 years. Possibly this was the same club that had operated first in South Street and later in East Street, but more research is needed to be certain.

In 1903 an establishment known as the **Bridport Technical Instruction Institute** was operating in Chancery Lane. According to Arthur Champ writing in his Mates Directory in 1903: *"For a number of years the Town Council have had the principal control, subject to grants from the County Council, of the technical and scientific instruction given in the borough. Classes in many subjects have been conducted at the School of Art (East Street), and at the Technical Instruction Institute (Chancery Lane). Excellent courses of Oxford Extension Lectures have also been given at the Town Hall."* He adds that this branch of education is now to come under the newly formed LEA.

Where precisely in Chancery Lane this Technical Institute was I have not been able to ascertain. Nor have I been able, so far, to find any more information about it. It is also mentioned in Kelly's Directory of Dorsetshire of 1903, but again no detail is given. One building that seems a possible venue is the building still called Bartholomew Hall, but so much of Chancery Lane has been altered or rebuilt, that it is not easy to identify a likely candidate. A further conundrum is the name "Chancery Lane". In the Ordnance Survey of the town conducted in 1887, this narrow alleyway running south and connecting East Street to Folly Mill Lane was called "Bakehouse Barton". When and why it was changed to Chancery Lane is just another a tantalising question, particularly bearing in mind the fact that the first Mechanics' Institute in London was located in the more famous Chancery Lane!

Yet another kind of adult education was set up by the Quakers in their Meeting House in South Street in the 1890's. This establishment was known as the **Bridport Adult School** and its purpose seems to have been as much religious and social as educational. It was part of a movement started by Quakers in Birmingham, and seems to have been designed to combat the social evils prevalent in the overcrowded conditions of working-class homes, and bring men to a better understanding of their responsibilities. The classes met at 9am each Sunday Morning in the Bridport Friends Meeting House. The session which lasted about an hour started with hymn singing. Then the men *"took out copy books and wrote scripture texts"*. On Monday and Tuesday evenings the members of the school could meet and take books from the lending library, and play games. The commendable aim of the School was to give each member *"an opportunity of helping others and trying to bring more members in, and they must all learn how to live in their homes and control their tempers."*[19]

The Bridport News Dec 4th 1896 reporting on the Annual Meeting of the Adult School in the Town Hall, quotes one of the speakers, the pharmacist, Mr James Beach, as saying *"when men begin to educate themselves they* (have) *a greater sense of the importance of the work than, perhaps, boys going to school would have."*

The Adult School was still in operation into the early years of the twentieth century for Mr Alfred Humphries of Delapre House, interviewed for The Journal Series, Feb 8th 1963 in the Bridport News recalls it being led by Mr E. S. Reynolds. He also recalls that speakers were invited to give half-hour talks on subjects of local interest, such as the history of the town, to the students, who were mostly *"old and middle-aged people.... who were unable to read and write."* He described how *"those being taught to write had their hand guided as they shaped simple words"*, and how after their Bible study sessions *"these illiterate men would discuss with energy and authority, their views on commerce, theology or politics."* The inclusion of game-playing seems to have been a common feature of these adult education establishments, for the report of the fire in the Old Castle records that the "bagatelle" board was rescued from the fire and was only a little damaged.

Provision for those who wished to study vocational skills beyond the school-leaving age was not well-catered for in Bridport. The School of Art in its heyday had provided for those who wished to study art, but that was effectively an evening institute. There was of course the usual range of apprenticeships, but initiatives such as the Industrial Branch of the Girls' General School, and the various evening schools tended to be either short lived, or limited in scope, and the only other form of tertiary education was through the various private colleges in the nineteenth century and the Secondary, later Grammar School in the twentieth. Throughout the early twentieth century Bridport had a number of small secretarial "schools"

---

[19] Bridport News: Dec 4th 1896

dotted around the town but the arrival of St James's College from London was to offer to local girls the chance of secretarial training on a par with that available in London.

St James's Secretarial College, Bradpole.

St James's College was the Dorset branch of a highly prestigious London secretarial college founded in 1912 at 34-35 Grosvenor Place, overlooking the back of Buckingham Palace and the Palace gardens.[20] The students came to Bradpole at the beginning of the war, probably evacuated, and the College was set up in the former Rectory, a rambling building set in extensive grounds on the opposite side of the road to the church. There was another branch of the college at Cheddington Court in Cheddington, possibly also a result of evacuation from the London blitz. The reason for choosing Bradpole seems to have been because Mr Spenser Munt, Principal of the College, and his wife already knew the area from holidaying there in the 1930's.

The College was a boarding establishment and throughout its time in Dorset drew girls from a wide geographical area as well as offering advanced secretarial education to local girls who qualified for a place. Girls progressed to St James's only on the successful completion of School Certificate, later GCE O Levels. The College specialized in Languages, teaching French, German, Spanish, Portuguese, Italian and Russian, Commercial German and French and German and French shorthand. In addition to the General Secretarial Course it also offered Advanced Book-keeping and Accountancy.

A number of students progressed to work in government offices notably the Foreign Office. The College closed in the 1980's, though the London establishment still exists and has recently, in 2002 amalgamated with the Lucy Clayton College to form the St James's and Lucy Clayton College based in Wetherby Gardens in London. The Bradpole College buildings have since converted to a nursing home, while retirement accommodation has been built in the grounds. Its closure saw the end of an era as it was the last boarding college to offer places to local girls. As such it marked the end of a line running back through St Hilda's and the Grove School to all those many boarding high schools, colleges and seminaries that preceded them.[21]

---

[20] "About St James's College" on the college website: www.stjamescollege.co.uk
[21] I am indebted to Mrs Pam Puley, a former student in the 1940's for much of the information about St James's College

XIII

SECONDARY EDUCATION 1902 - 1956

The new century began with another radical Education Act. The 1902 Act effectively laid down the basic principles on which education is still organised and funded today. It abolished the School Boards, which were often only managing one or two schools in country areas, and made education the responsibility of the County and Municipal Councils. Each Council was required to establish a Local Education Committee to oversee education in their locality, and it established for the first time the principle of paying for education through the rates.

One of the areas of concern to the authorities at the time was the extent to which elementary schools had been developing Higher Classes for those children who were not able to gain scholarship places to the few Grammar Schools but who still wished to take their education beyond the basic elementary stage. This ad hoc secondary provision obviously needed to be given some structure, though it was not given real structure until the Butler Act of 1944.

Though not making Secondary Education compulsory at this time, the 1902 Act made it possible for Secondary Schools to be set up to oversee education across the country. It is no coincidence therefore that it was after the implementation of this Act in 1903 that Bridport Town Council began to look at the possibility of establishing a secondary school in the town. The recommendation of the Forster Act was education to 13 or fourteen, but it was only a guide. The 1918 Education Act raised the School Leaving Age to 14, but Grammar and Private schools were already educating children to 16, and beyond if they wished to go to University. There was a pressing need for the mass of the population to have access to similar opportunities.

Bridport Secondary School: 1909 – 1927

Throughout the nineteenth century anyone with an ambition to become a teacher was trained "on the job". Starting often as a monitor, they would then become a pupil teacher, and only after passing the period of training in their own school be eligible to teach. In the second half of the nineteenth century, as training colleges were set up, notably St Mark's College in Chelsea, the Borough Road College, already mentioned in connection with John Beard, and the two diocesan training colleges: one for women at Salisbury and for men at Winchester, the successful pupil teacher would have the opportunity to go on to further study. The much prized "certificated" teacher was the recipient of the "Certificate of Merit"

200

awarded on successful completion of their training, but teachers without the certificate, but with a proven track record of service could continue to teach, and were regarded as qualified teachers, though their pay was less.

This "apprenticeship" system, which often saw teachers trained in very small elementary schools, was discontinued by the 1902 Education Act, and the newly formed Education Department required that all prospective teachers should be taught in special pupil teacher centres or secondary schools. As Bridport had neither, impetus was given to finding a site or a building for a secondary school. The Town Council Higher Education Committee in consultation with the County Education Committee first started considering the problem in about 1903, and, as the matter was pressing, they decided that, until a suitable building could be erected they would establish a centre for training teachers in temporary quarters. The Unitarian schoolroom in Rax Lane was offered by the Trustees of the Unitarian Chapel as a pupil teacher centre. It was here that the Secondary School began in what Walter Ferris Hill described as *"rather depressing"* and *"quite unsuitable rooms".*[1]

While Walter Ferris Hill (Fig 34) is always credited with being the first headmaster of the Secondary, later Grammar School, in fact the first headmaster was Mr A.C. Badcoe BSc who led the school for two years, thereafter becoming an Assistant County Education Officer. Walter Ferris Hill took over as Headmaster in 1906. At that time the school had only sixty-seven pupils, and a staff of two assistant mistresses to help in running the embryo school. On his appointment he was promised that a new school would be built and ready in six months. In fact it was three years and six months before the school had its proper premises. The lead up to the creation of the Secondary School is described in the Bridport News.

"At the same time (as the creation of the pupil teacher centre) *it was felt there was need of a good secondary school, particularly for boys, in the town which could be worked with the pupil teacher centre. After discussing the ways and means and possibilities of the thing the suggestion was placed before the Town Council and the matter was seriously discussed. One difficulty was the securing of a suitable building for this purpose, and the Higher Education Committee visited several premises, but after consulting with various inspectors, they found that none of these were* (sic) *suitable. It was at this juncture that Col. And Mrs Colfox generously offered the present site on St Andrews Road for new buildings.*

There was a divided opinion as to the wisdom of erecting new buildings and incurring a heavy outlay and several discussions took place in the Town Council Chamber. Eventually in March 1905 a resolution was

---

[1] Bridport Grammar School Old Grammarian's Magazine, July 1937: "Happy memories" by Walter Ferris Hill (BMLHC)

carried that a secondary school and pupil teachers' centre be established under the auspices of the town council"[2]. Plans went ahead and building started in December 1907. The foundation stone laying "being gracefully performed by Mrs Colfox".

The land for the school, which borders St Andrew's Road and runs down from Coneygar Hill and the grounds of Lt Col Colfox's home in Coneygar House, was donated by him and his wife Constance. Though we have already met Thomas Alfred briefly in relation to the Boys' General School, it is now time to introduce him more fully. Thomas Alfred was the eldest son of William and Anna Colfox, who were, by now, wealthy landowners in the town. In 1886 Alfred as he was generally known married Constance Nettleford, youngest daughter of Lord Nettleford, head of the Birmingham-based family of wealthy industrialists. On their marriage, as a wedding present, William bought Alfred and Constance Coneygar House, a small villa on Coneygar Hill, just to the north of the town. The original house was built in the 1840's, but Alfred proceeded to enlarge it, building a substantial north-eastern wing in 1904. It was the acquisition of this house, and the land that went with it, that enabled Alfred to donate the land for the new school.

The building in St Andrew's Road was completed in 1909. It cost £5,227. To help with the immediate costs the Town Council received a loan of £3000 from the County Council, which had to be repaid out of the rates. At the time of opening £427 was still outstanding and Lt Col Colfox took the opportunity in his speech at the opening ceremony to appeal for more funds. His commitment to the school was not simply confined to raising money. Alfred Colfox was to become the first and longest serving Chairman of Governors of the new Secondary School. E. S. Reynolds was his Vice-Chairman.

As previously mentioned the cost of building the school weighed quite heavily on the rates, the Mayor, Councillor William Saunders Edwards, in his speech at the opening refers to the difficulty of having to levy a 2d or 3d rate. It was clear from the Mayor's speech at the opening ceremony that the matter of the cost of the school was still of concern to the Town Council and we can get a flavour of the rancour that must have existed when, even as late as the actual opening of the building, he refers to "bury(ing) the hatchet"[3] and confesses that he opposed the building in the beginning. He spends some time in his speech urging economy. The school governors must "keep a sharp eye on things" and make sure, if possible, that income exceeded expenditure. The estimated cost of educating a student at the school was a great increase on the £5 per-

---

[2] Bridport News: August 6th 1909
[3] Ibid

202

annum cost for each elementary school pupil. Secondary pupils would cost from between £12 to £15.

The day-to-day funding of the school was via fees, though a quarter of the places under the education authority scheme were free and the school offered a number of bursaries and scholarships some funded by the County, some from the Daniel Taylor Charity and other charities in the area, so that, in the words of Colonel Colfox, *"practically every child who wished to avail himself or herself of the advantages of this school, sufficiently bright and intelligent to benefit by the instruction, would be able to come".* [4]

The school building was formerly opened on the last Friday in July 1909 by the Earl of Shaftesbury. As a ceremonial gesture, Lord Shaftesbury was presented with a silver key by the Mayor with which to open the school doors. Also present among the guests at the opening of the school were Katherine Bussell, Principal of The High School, Thorneloe House and Mr Badcoe, the Secondary School's first headmaster. The report in the Bridport News on 6th August gives a very detailed account of the opening ceremony and merits quoting from at some length:

It begins in enthusiastic terms: *"At last Bridport, as one of the chief boroughs of Dorset has taken her proper place as a prominent educational centre in the county."* The account pays tribute to Mr Edward Seaman Reynolds to whose *"unflagging energy, ability and expert knowledge"* can be attributed the fact *"that the town now possesses the very latest ideas in the equipment of a modern secondary school".* The building was designed by architects Messres F Cooper and Sons, was built of Bothenhampton stone with Ham Stone dressings for plinths, doors and windows and had a Brosely tiled roof.

The description of the building in the Bridport News report will be familiar to anyone who attended the school either as a grammar school pupil or later as a pupil of Bridport County Primary, and even now the main features of the old building are clearly visible in its new incarnation as the Adult Education Centre and the St Andrew's Pre-school. The report states: *"The main features of the new building are the four large classrooms, capable of accommodating 110 pupils. These rooms are divided by movable partitions, so that any of them may be thrown together, or the whole made into one large school hall. The one at the end will be set apart for art work..... On the other side of the corridor is a large and well-fitted chemical and physics laboratory.... There is a comfortable study for the headmaster at one end of the corridor and for the assistant staff at the other end. At the end of the playgrounds there are covered sheds for both boys and girls, and adjoining these is a room for teaching cookery and*

---

[4] Ibid

other domestic subjects for the girls and a manual instruction room for the boys."

From the outset the school was to be co-educational, at that time a controversial decision, as, certainly at secondary level, most schools were still segregated, and elementary schools had just begun to de-segregate their senior departments. Just how controversial can be gleaned from the remarks on the subject made by Canon Goodden at the opening ceremony.

He *"knew when they* (co-educational schools) *were started there sprang up here and there fears and doubts with regard to the wisdom of educating boys and girls together."* But he added that, once experience of such a system was gained these fears *"melted into thin air and dissolved into vapour".* However it was only partial coeducation. The boys and girls were taught most subjects together in class, but the playgrounds were strictly segregated by a stone wall, and boys and girls had separate entrances to the school, separate cloakrooms and the masters and mistresses had separate staffrooms.

The first board of governors was Thomas Alfred Colfox (Chairman), Mr E S Reymolds (Vice Chairman), Mrs Allden, Mrs Constance and Miss Alice Colfox, Mr John Suttill, Mr W A Alexander, Councillor W G Cornick, Rev J Dempsey, Rev H R W Farrar, Mr F W Matterface and Alderman Randall. Mr F W Hallett was Clerk.

The staff at the opening were Walter Ferris Hill, Headmaster, Arthur E Champ, formerly Principal of Coniston School who was appointed as art master, and was also to take manual instruction with the boys. He also taught mathematics later on. Miss E Witham L.L.A, Senior Mistress (not to be confused with Beatrice Witham who joined the staff later), and Miss Margaret Field BSc, who would teach science. The number of students at the outset was clearly too small for the school to be financially viable, for Colonel Colfox, in his speech, placed emphasis on the need to recruit many more students if the school was to succeed, and meet its costs. In fact the school started with a roll of eighty-one. It is also clear that the school was to take boarders. Arthur Champ's former school, Coniston, at 69 Victoria Grove, became the official boarding house for the boys of the Secondary School, and the girl boarders were housed in Walter Ferris Hill's own house, at 77 East Street. Later in the school's life a boarding house, often known as "the Hostel" was established in East Street.

There need have been no fears, for the numbers in the school quickly grew, and in 1918 Alfred and Constance Colfox gave the school a further grant of land on the other side of Coneygar Lane for playing fields. These provided the boys with a football field, while land adjoining the school was later laid down to tennis courts for the girls. Indeed so successful was the school that before the end of the 1914-1918 War it had outgrown the original premises and the Bridport Secondary School

Magazine of 1918 records a roll of 148 students, and that they are using *"the new classroom"* and also *"St Andrew's schoolroom"*. This was the schoolroom attached to St Andrew's Church further down St Andrew's Road that was also used by St Ronan's School for a time. Indeed, in 1917/18 alone, the roll had increase by forty-eight, an unprecedented rise, possibly reflecting the presence of evacuees. The years that followed up to the Second World War saw a series of enlargements of the school until, as Walter Ferris Hill put it on his retirement in 1937 *"they are now at maximum capacity on the present site."* [5]

The Secondary School very quickly became an integral and vital part of the town. Drama seems to have been a strong feature of the school almost from the beginning, and in 1912, as part of the town's fund-raising activities for the new Cottage Hospital Building Scheme, the school put on an evening of drama and music in the Rifle Drill Hall in St Michael's Lane. As well as performing part of an operetta "The Fairy Chain", they presented an extract from "The School for Scandal" by Sheridan, and a series of "Historic Dances" completed the programme.

School Sports' Days were well established by 1914, the first being held in 1912 (Fig 35) and it is interesting to compare the events with a similar occasion today. There were the usual athletic events: sprints over 100 yards and 220 yards, a quarter-mile race, but there were also many fun events such as a *"three-legged race"*, a *"bicycle slow race,"* and tugs of war between former and present pupils.[6]

The outbreak of war in August 1914 affected the Secondary School, as it did all the other schools in Bridport. Walter Ferris Hill was on holiday in London when, a couple of weeks into the summer holidays, he was notified that the school had been commandeered by the Red Cross and converted into a hospital. *"All furniture, pictures, books, in fact everything moveable was taken out of the School, piled roof high under the two Playing Sheds, and covered with tarpaulins borrowed from the Great Western Railway. I was told that the interior of the school looked 'perfectly sweet' as a hospital, and I shall always regret that no one thought of taking a snap-shot for future generations"*. However before any casualties arrived the scheme was abandoned and the school returned to its former function. Walter Ferris Hill recalls *"having broken my holiday, I was able, with the help of a few willing friends, to restore the School to pristine beauty, before the beginning the term."*[7]

---

[5] Bridport Grammar School Old Grammarian's Magazine, July 1937: "Happy memories" by Walter Ferris Hill (BMLHC)
[6] Bridport Secondary School Magazine 1914 (BMLHC)
[7] Bridport Grammar School Old Grammarian's Magazine, July 1937: "Happy memories" by Walter Ferris Hill (BMLHC)

Meanwhile the school's Chairman of Governors, Lt Col Thomas Alfred Colfox, was also involved in the war effort. As a young man he had joined the Queen's Own Dorset Yeomanry. (Fig 39) He achieved the rank of Lieutenant Colonel, and was given a year's extension when his period of command came to an end in 1913, but on the outbreak of war, despite his eagerness to serve, he was considered too old to volunteer for the front, so he threw his energies into recruiting for the 5th and 6th Battalions of the Dorset Regiment, and in 1914 was asked by the War Office to raise a second Regiment of Yeomanry, which he commanded in various deployments on the Home Front until 1917. Meanwhile his two sons, William Philip and Thomas David, both joined artillery regiments and were sent to the front.

As we have already seen, the First World War brought considerable hardship to Bridport. The Secondary School Magazine for 1918 refers to *"unemployment and social distress."* The school had established gardens in the field above the building and had been growing vegetables as part of the war effort, though the 1918 crop of potatoes *"were not as good as last year because a great number of potatoes were diseased."* The pupils collected waste paper also as part of the war effort, and were continuing the School War Savings Association, which had amassed a total of £450 18s 6d. The Magazine comments: *"We are saving more earnestly for peace than we did for War."*

A school prospectus for 1926 gives an indication of the curriculum offered at the school. It is effectively a standard grammar school curriculum with the exception of Latin. There was Religious Instruction *("In accordance with the principles of the Christian Faith but not containing any instruction distinctive of any particular denomination")*; Mathematics, comprising Arithmetic, Algebra, Geometry and Trigonometry; English Language and Literature; Geography and map work; English and European History; French; Science comprising Physics, Chemistry and Nature Study, Drawing; Class Singing (Old Notation and Tonic Solfa), Needlework, Cookery, Manual Instruction and Physical Exercise.

Students were admitted on the successful completion of an entrance exam which was held on the day prior to the beginning the term, and if successful were required to remain at the school until they were at least sixteen. The school catered for students from eleven to eighteen, and prepared students for the London Matriculation and Oxford School Certificate examinations. Uniform was minimal to begin with: girls had to wear a hat with the school badge and boys a cap and badge, though later the grammar school would have a much more prescribed uniform. By this time Arthur Champ was no longer providing boarding facilities and boarders were accommodated at the hostel in East Street.

Bridport Grammar School: 1928 – 1956

In 1927, quite possibly as a result of Thomas Maxwell Telford joining the staff to teach Latin, a decision was made to change the school name to Bridport Grammar School. I had hoped that the Governors' Minute Book[8] might shed some light on this decision but while it records the change of name between the meetings of 2nd December 1927 and that of 10th February 1928, there is nothing in the minutes to indicate any discussion of the matter. Other than the name, and the appearance of Latin in the curriculum, very little else seemed to change, even the school crest remained the same, just changing the wording from Bridport Secondary School to Bridport Grammar School, but becoming a Grammar School obviously increased the school's prestige.

Until the 1930's the school was still dependant on fees and charitable donations. In 1926, for example, it was charging fees ranging from £15 a term for full boarders over twelve, down to £10 for weekly boarders under twelve-years-old. Daily fees, which covered stationery and games, were £4 per term, and text books were loaned to students for a fee of 6s-8d per term. They were still in receipt of funds from the Daniel Taylor Charity, but money was still tight and in 1930 to celebrate the schools 21st anniversary, Walter Ferris Hill set up the "Coming of Age" Fund to provide an endowment fund for the school. As part of the fund-raising effort the school performed a comic opera called "Aladdin and Out". However, in 1932 the school passed into the ownership of the Local Education Authority, and from that point on became a state-funded school.

By 1937 many of the regular events of the school year were established. In addition to the annual Sports Day there was the annual Cross-Country race which took place over a course which ran up the Beaminster Road to Gore Cross and back to the school via, Pymore and Coneygar Hill. The school was playing regular matches against neighbouring schools. The School Choir, started in 1936 was being run by Mrs Tighe, Tommy Telford was running the Debating Society.

Walter Ferris Hill continued as Headmaster until 1937 when he was succeeded by Mr Frederick J. Jordan who was headteacher through the difficult war years. Alfred Colfox finally retired as Chairman of Governors after serving for more than thirty years. Walter Ferris Hill refers to the general regret felt that, owing to poor health, Lt Col Colfox was not able to preside over his, Mr Ferris Hill's, last Speech Day in July 1937.[9] Alderman

---

[8] DHC/ S319/½: Bridport Secondary/Grammar School Minute Book 1926-1941.
[9] Bridport Grammar School Old Grammarian's Magazine, July 1937(BMLHC)

E. S. Reynolds took over as Chair of Governors and served throughout the 1940's. In 1947 he was joined by a new headmaster, Mr F. G. Morris, who took over on the retirement of Mr Jordan. He came to Bridport from the City of Bath School. Throughout much of this period continuity at the school was also guaranteed by the long-serving Senior Mistress, Miss Edith Bickford. She transferred to The Alfred Colfox School in 1956 and became its first Senior Mistress, before retiring in the early 1960's. (Fig 34)

She was one of a number of remarkable teachers that Bridport has been blessed with over the years. She was born in India, the daughter of Brigadier General Edward Bickford. Her subject was mathematics and she had gained her degree at Royal Holloway College outside London. She was a county hockey player, and used her expertise in the game as a referee for school matches. She was also a JP. She lived to the ripe old age of 96, dying in 1992. Her name is remembered in the academic prize for senior mathematics established in her memory, and awarded to pupils at the Sir John Colfox School until very recently.

Also remembered in the same way was Francis Tighe, who taught Art and Music at the school for twenty-two years until his sudden death in 1951. The Bridport News' reports of his death and funeral give a picture of his career. Like Arthur Champ before him he was a gifted artist in his own right, painting watercolours and producing wood and lino cuts in a most distinctive style. He was a member of the Mapperton Art Society and exhibited at their annual exhibitions. Some of his paintings are now in the collection of the Bridport Museum, and his distinctive illustrations for the Bridport Borough Guide brought his work to a wide audience. He was also a gifted musician, a violinist. He encouraged a large number of pupils at the Grammar School to take up the violin, (Fig 36), and became greatly involved with the Bridport Amateur Operatic and Dramatic Society from 1929 to 1937. For the productions of "Merrie England" and "The Pirates of Penzance" in 1934 and 1935 he was Musical Director, and for other productions he either played first violin in the orchestra or took part on stage. With a group of like-minded enthusiasts he was involved in setting up the Bridport and District Music Club.

Like so many other teachers, his time at the Grammar School was forcibly interrupted when he was called up for the duration of the Second World War. His wife, also a gifted musician, took his place on the staff. To endow a school prize in his memory was the idea of the Headmaster, Major Urwin Thornburn, and proposed at the first school speech day after Francis Tighe's death.

The Second World War was, if anything, even more difficult than the First for all the inhabitants of Bridport, as this time the town was bombed several times, with significant loss of life. In addition there were evacuees to be accommodated, rationing to contend with, as well as troops billeted in and around the town, and latterly a proposed prisoner of war camp (never built) nearby in the fields bordering the River Asker.

On the outbreak of war, trenches were dug at the upper perimeter of the Grammar School field bordering Coneygar. A former pupil at the school during the War recalls that Mr Jordan initially organised the boys to dig the trenches, but when the job proved rather too much for them he negotiated a deal with some of the local troops. The soldiers completed the trench-digging in return for the use of the boys' football field. While this relieved the boys of much hard labour, it also had a down-side, for the troops often left the field so churned up that the boys had little but a sea of mud in which to play football.

Many teachers who were not called up nevertheless did war service on the Home Front. In addition to his responsibilities as Headmaster, Frederick Jordan was a sergeant in the Home Guard, and Commanding Officer of the ATC (Air Training Corps), which used the school premises as a base. He was also Captain in the Army Cadet Force. Mr Richard Inkpen Headmaster of Allington School, served as an officer in both the ATC and the Army Cadets, while Grammar School Senior Mistress, Edith Bickford, assisted by Dolly Abbott of the General School ran the Girls' Training Corps. Tommy Telford also helped with the ATC and Mr Alston, Senior Grammar School Science Master, did duty as a sergeant in the Special Constabulary. In Michael Norman's words: *"The school staff set an example"*. Mr Jordan was awarded the British Empire Medal for his service on the Home Front. [10]

Also setting an example and helping to train the Cadets and the Air Cadets was Alfred Colfox's eldest son, the former MP for West Dorset, Sir Philip Colfox. (Fig 40) He had been a gunnery officer in the First World War, being invalided home in 1917 after a serious injury made further involvement at the front impossible. On his return and while he was convalescent in 1918, he had briefly returned to his old school, Eton College, as an under-master, teaching mathematics. He went into parliament in 1918 and represented West Dorset from 1922. He was awarded a baronetcy for his parliamentary services. He joined his father as a governor of the Grammar School in 1934. Having resigned his seat 1941, he devoted his energies to the war effort, running a detachment of the Home Guard, from his home at Symondsbury Manor which was now the Colfox family home. The Manor stables housed the Home Guard transport

---

[10] This information comes from a taped Interview with Michael Norman recorded as part of the Dorset Schooldays Project (BMLHC/ BMS/SCH/05), and WWII archive material BMLHC. My thanks to Pam Jordan for confirming the information about her father's BEM.

in the form of several BSA motorbikes for riding dispatches, although his eldest son, John, then aged sixteen, enjoyed riding round the countryside on one of the bikes much to his father's displeasure. Sir Philip's work with the young cadets was particularly to teach them the mathematics they would need once they were called up for a career in the armed forces.

In 1941, in response to rationing and food shortages, the school looked into the possibility of offering students a cooked midday meal, despite the fact that they had no canteen. From the Easter term 1942 the Cookery Room at the School was converted into a canteen to provide hot meals for the surrounding rural schools as well as the grammar school. Despite the improvised facilities, they managed to produce over 300 meals a day. The purpose-built school canteen was not erected until 1949. Cookery lesson did continue, but had to move down to the Unitarian schoolrooms in Rax Lane.

Denys Tamblyn, who taught geography and history and Francis Tighe were called up for war service, and had to exchange the *"sober black of an academic gown"* for *"Air Force blue and khaki"* as the School Magazine of 1944 puts it. To add to the strain, pupil numbers, swelled by evacuees, increased substantially, reaching 237, putting yet more pressure on accommodation at the school. There were nine classes and only six classrooms, a library and an art room to house them. The Sixth Form often found themselves being taught in the corridor outside the Science Room. It was in response to this overcrowding that the school once more acquired the use of the schoolroom at St Andrew's Church. They also used the church for morning assemblies, and from 1943 trekked down to St Michael's Lane for PT (Physical Training), where a *"well-fitted Gymnasium and Shower baths"* had been installed at the Drill Hall.[11] Mr Jordan supervised the boys' PT in this building, and put on PT Displays. Much of the school's usual activities had to cease during the war, but Mrs Tighe kept the school choir going and the upper school enjoyed *"Mrs Lesters Dancing Class".*[12] There was no swimming at West Bay for the duration of the war, but the occasional use of a private swimming pool at West Milton was offered by the public-spirited owner so some of the boys could still enjoy swimming from time-to-time.

The start of the Second World War saw a huge influx of evacuees, particularly from London. Their arrival at Bridport Station is recalled by a former pupil who as a member of the scout troop was sent to help the volunteer reception party. He recalls being shocked by the state of some of the city children who *"really were in rags".*[13] It was his job to escort them to Allington and East Road where they were to be billeted. Many of these

---

[11] Bridport Grammar School Magazine 1944(BMLHC)
[12] Ibid
[13] Taped Interview: Michael Norman: Dorset Schooldays Project (BMLHC/BMS/SCH/05)

210

children only stayed in Bridport for a short time, the phoney war of the first months making their families question the need to have them out of London. Many went back into the bombing, and some were re-evacuated once the Blitz started.

As a schoolboy during the war, Michael Norman, recalled many episodes that probably made wartime life for a young boy quite exciting, despite the dangers. He clearly knew all about one of the Home Guard ammunition huts which was sited *"on the hill above St Andrew's Road"*. It stored the ammunition for the Home Guard, who took their rifles home with them but not the ammunition. He remembers that the key to the hut was hidden at the bottom of the door! He also recalls how one of the fields between the railway and the River Asker was marked out with a double bank of barbed wire and ear-marked for a prisoner-of-war camp. One night bombs fell in the fields and the river near the back of his house in East Road. The blast blew the doors off his rabbit hutches and all the rabbits escaped and had to be rounded up the following day.

When the bombs fell on East Street in December 1942, the Grammar School pupils were outside the school buildings as it was the lunch-break and were able to watch the approach of the planes and actually see the bombs dropping. For Michael Norman this event must have been particularly traumatic as his grandmother, Mrs Elizabeth Jane Norman, who lived in No 97 East Street, was killed in the attack. In the latter years of the war, the students were drafted into various jobs during the holidays, including helping with the post over Christmas (senior pupils only), and flax-pulling in the summer to help the local trade. During the Easter and October break, they were employed planting and lifting potatoes.[14]

Thomas Alfred Colfox, the School's long-serving Chairman of Governors, died on April 18th 1945, only months before peace in Europe. He was in his 88th year. His son, Sir Philip was already a governor of the school. He is first reported as presiding at the Grammar School Speech day in 1948, when the then Chairman, Alderman Edward S Reynolds was unable to attend due to illness. Not long after that Sir Philip took over as Chairman.

Gradually, after the war, the school got back to normal, though the use of St Andrew's Church went on throughout the 1940's and 50's. 1948 saw the first Sports Day after the war, and Beatrice Witham who had taught Domestic Science at the school since the First World War, died. A fund of £108 was raised in her memory to endow a prize and to plant flower-beds round the school; an appropriate memorial considering her passion for flowers and plants, particularly wild flowers, which was given expression at

---

[14] Bridport Grammar School Magazine 1944 (BMLHC)

211

the school through the Natural History Club which she ran. She also coached tennis and hockey and had been one of the first members of Bridport Hockey Club when it was restarted in 1919 after the First World War. (Fig 34)

Major Urwin "Ned" Thornburn took over the Grammar School Headship in 1951. He came to Bridport from Wrekin College in Shropshire where he had been senior history master and a housemaster. He had also seen distinguished war service with the 4th Battalion of the Kings Shropshire Light Infantry. He led D company from the landings in Normandy through a series of major battles including those to liberate Caen and Antwerp. He won the Military Cross for the latter action, and is commemorated in the village of Aubusson by the singular honour of having the village square named after him: "Place Major Ned Thornburn MC". His Company liberated the village in July/August 1944, and after the war he was made a Freeman (Citoyen d'Honneur) of the Commune of Aubusson. His reputation on the other side of the Channel, was, and is still, not widely known in Bridport. No doubt his military background gave him an immediate rapport with his new Chairman of Governors, Sir Philip Colfox.[15]

The Grammar School building that Major Thornburn came to in 1951 was remarkably little changed from the day it was built in 1909. The dominant feature of the school was still the Hall. It was used less and less for assemblies each morning, so the dividing screens that created four self-contained classrooms, each with their own door into the corridor, stayed in place. These classrooms were designated alphabetically A-D, though, by the 1950's, D had become the Library. A long corridor ran the length of the building from the main door in the northern façade down to the mistress's staffroom at the southern extremity of the building. On the opposite side of the corridor to the Hall were respectively Miss Bickford's Room (Senior Mistress), the men's staffroom, a storeroom and the boys' cloakroom adjoining the boys entrance. The girls' entrance was in the southern wing opening onto their playground at the back of the building, and just inside the door were toilets and a cloakroom. The playground was still divided into girls' and boys' areas by the stone wall. The area now occupied by the new Bridport Primary School was largely grass and hard tennis courts and the field on the opposite side of Coneygar Lane, still used by the school for sports, was the boys' football pitch that proved so popular with the troops during the War.

For a total of twelve years before the school's closure in 1956, St Andrew's Church was used daily for assemblies, and pupils were

---

[15] Major "Ned" Thornburn's three part history of the 4th Battalion KSLI's Normandy Campaign, compiled after he retired, is published by the 4th Battalion News KSLI Museum Trust, The Castle, Shrewsbury.

crocodiled down the road each morning before lesson began. It became seen, in the eyes of Major Thornburn at least, as acting as the *"school chapel"*.[16] The Grammar School uniform in the 1930's consisted of royal blue dresses with coffee-coloured cuffs and collar, a dropped waist and box-pleated skirt. There was also the more usual uniform of black gym slips, white blouses and a dark-blue and gold-striped tie. War-time austerity changed the dresses once again to a simple blue cotton pinafore dress. Boys wore jackets, the school tie and a navy cap with concentric gold hoops.[17]

It fell to Major Thornburn to oversee the massive transformation of post-war secondary education in Bridport. In 1956 he became the first headmaster of the Alfred Colfox (Bilateral) School, and in 1957 the Grammar School building was finally closed only to reopen a year later on September 10th 1958 to accommodate the General Junior and Infants Schools, relocated from King Street and renamed Bridport County Primary School.

---

[16] Bridport News: July 6th 1956
[17] I am indebted to Mrs Pam Puley for the information in this section. She walked round the present building with me pointing out the various rooms, and their uses.

XIV

TO THE END OF THE CENTURY

Reorganisation of Schools: 1934-1956

It is necessary to backtrack a little at the beginning of this chapter, in order to set the scene more fully for the major developments that were to take place over second half of the twentieth century. Back in fact to the 1930's, because the reorganisation of the post-war period in Bridport had its roots in the pre-war decade. Reports of the proceedings of the Education Committee through the interwar years, show that the problems posed by the increasingly inadequate facilities for education in Bridport were coming up regularly for discussion. Shortcomings in the provision for handicraft teaching led in 1926 to the Education Committee leasing a building in Chancery Lane to provide a Handicraft Centre for the town. The Secondary/Grammar School supplied the benches and tools, in return for free use of the facility three half-days a week.[1]

In 1934 came the first proposal for a new Central School for Bridport to be built to accommodate all the pupils currently being educated by Bradpole School, Bridport General Schools, Bridport C.E. School and Allington School. The Committee further considered that if the village schools of Bradpole, Pymore, Symondsbury, Loders, Salway Ash, Askerswell, Chideock, Burton Bradstock, Shipton Gorge and Powerstock were also to be included, any central school built would have to provide 600 places.

This proposal to set up a single primary school to take both children from the General Schools and St Mary's C.E. School was fiercely opposed by both those who wanted to see a continuation of a Church of England school and those who championed non-denominational education. There was much lobbying by the managers of St Mary's for full provision for Infants and Juniors, while the managers of the General School wanted a County Junior and Infants School. This document also considers the Visitation Convent Primary school which had at that time twenty-seven junior pupils and seventy-two Infants. The development plan envisaged taking in the nineteen pupils from Chideock R.C. School and building, on a two-and-a-half acre site, a building sufficient for five classes. In embryo, the above is, in fact, what eventually came about with some modifications. The cost and problems of finding a suitable site meant that the plan was abandoned quite quickly, and in its place was the much less ambitious reorganisation of the Bridport schools using the existing accommodation

---

[1] Bridport Secondary/Grammar School Minute Book 1926-1941(DHC/ S319/1/2)

that has already been described. The various village schools were not included in this exercise.

In 1936 the Committee was again discussing Bridport in their meeting of 4th March. This time it was the increasingly inadequate Grammar School buildings that were of concern and the proposal was made to build a new Grammar School on land at the corner of Coneygar Lane and Pymore Road; probably that now occupied by St Catherine's Primary School. The 1909 Grammar School premises would then be used as a Senior Elementary School for Bridport and the surrounding villages. The Governors of the Grammar School were apparently in agreement, but again nothing came of the plans.[2]

Once the partial reorganisation of the mid-1930's, which resulted in Allington becoming a Senior School, and the General Schools providing a Senior Department, was accomplished, no further plans seem to have been made. But, towards the end of the war, and particularly after the Butler Education Act of 1944, there was renewed discussion, particularly focusing on the provision of primary schooling.

The Butler Education Act, enacted in the closing years of the Second World War, was far and away the most radical reorganisation of education that the country had ever seen. It set up the post-war tripartite system of education and for the first time secondary education for all was made compulsory, either in grammar, secondary modern or technical schools. The school-leaving age was raised to 15. Instead of the various scholarship exams which had been the route into grammar schools for bright elementary pupils before 1944, the universal 11+ exam was introduced. This exam sorted children into three categories: those who were highly academic and would benefit from a grammar school education; those who were able but more technically minded, who would go to the technical schools, and those whose ability was not deemed such that they would benefit from either academic or technical education, who would go to secondary modern schools.

The failure of the Butler Act was that in many areas technical schools were never established, and grammar school provision was not enlarged enough to cope with the numbers likely to qualify, so the education system that actually emerged in the forties and fifties was hugely divisive and ultimately very unpopular, as most children found themselves in secondary modern schools. As students were expected to leave these schools at the statutory leaving age of fifteen and therefore before sitting the General Certificate of Education Ordinary Level exams, most therefore

---

[2] Information taken from DHC/ S117/12/15: Reorganisation of Schools (Bridport District) covering the period 1934 - 1956

left school with no qualifications at all, until the introduction of the CSE (Certificate of Secondary Education).

By the late 1960's the country was pushing for a new shape for education, and change came in the form of the introduction of the comprehensive system. The comprehensive movement which began in the late 1950's and 60's notably in London under ILEA, the Inner London Education Authority, saw the building of large comprehensive schools which would cater for all abilities. In a sense Bridport was once again in the vanguard of these developments, as the new secondary school, the Alfred Colfox School, built in 1956 for all the secondary age children of the town and surrounding area, was in embryo comprehensive, even though it was at first described as a "Bilateral School", that is one comprising a grammar and a secondary modern stream under one roof.

Also as a result of the Butler Act, a new settlement was reached with the still large number of voluntary church schools in the country. This set up two categories of Voluntary Schools, Voluntary Controlled where the Church's input was restricted to the religious teaching, worship and ethos of the school but in all other respects the schools were LEA owned and run, and Voluntary Aided where the schools remained the property of the Local Parish under the supervision of the Diocese, and had much more control over their own affairs. St Mary's Primary School, previously a National School became Voluntary Controlled under the new Act.

But to return to the 1940's, Dorset LEA, faced with the demands of the Butler Act, was still wrestling with the problem of how to implement the requirement of the Act without spending money they did not have. Once again the issue of new building versus the adaptation of existing buildings was at the core of much of the argument. In 1947, as already described in detail earlier, there was much opposition to the proposal to make the Gundry Lane site the main Infant School. In 1949 the Committee were still talking about a Bridport Junior School, but the only proposal was that it should be two-form entry. In the same year the Committee envisaged the provision of a nursery school *"if there was local demand"*. There was a proposal, never acted upon, to provide a nursery school for sixty pupils to be built in the year 1959/60.

To some extent, the rather ad hoc pre-war reorganisation enabled them to delay the provision of the 1944 Act at secondary level. Bridport already had a Grammar School, albeit bursting at the seams. There was also the Allington site which became the Secondary Modern School, and Secondary provision also at the King Street site, while the Unitarian Grammar School was also making a contribution, but it was not a situation that could continue indefinitely. The option to provide full tripartite secondary education must have looked prohibitively expensive, and so the preferred option was much what had originally been proposed for elementary education in the town – one school for all.

In 1950 the plans to build a new Bilateral Secondary/Grammar School to take all 11+ pupils were finally mooted. This meant that the future of Bridport General School as a County school in the old Grammar School buildings could be foreseen, but this still left the Church of England, St Mary's School in very poor accommodation. There was yet another proposal to build a new Voluntary Junior and Infants' School, and the date proposed for the transfer was 1959/60. Even at this late date concerns were expressed about the old Grammar School site for an Infant School, and a proposal to use the Allington school site or Bridport General School King Street site for the Primary Infants was made but never acted upon.[3] In the event the schools were largely reorganised using the existing buildings, and the only new school built was the Alfred Colfox School, and even that was left incomplete.

The Alfred Colfox School

In 1955-56 the building of the new secondary school began on land to the north of Bridport close to Gore Cross in the parish of Bradpole, and in 1956 it opened. The recommendation that the school should carry the Colfox name was made at a meeting of the Secondary Education Sub-Committee of the County Council in January 1956[4]. The aim was to recognise the huge contribution of Thomas Alfred Colfox to the original Grammar School. In case there was any confusion, Sir Philip, who was by that time both a member of the Education Committee and Chairman designate of the new school's governing body, insisted that the school be called not simply "Colfox School" but the "Alfred Colfox School".

The intention was to maintain as much continuity as possible between the Grammar School and the new school. As Major Thornburn told the assembled pupils and their parents at the final Grammar School Speech Day held on 5th July 1956 in the Palace Cinema, *"A very great responsibility is going to rest on you boys and girls - and on all your parents - next term. You will be custodians of the Grammar School heritage, of*

---

[3] Ibid
[4] Bridport News: 20th Jan 1956

217

those Grammar School standards of which I have just spoken - a standard of scholarship, a standard of conduct, a standard of citizenship and a standard of Christian devotion."[5]

The Bridport News of September 14th 1956 heralded the opening of the Alfred Colfox School with the headline *"Light, Law and Liberty for the First Bilateral School in Dorset."* This made reference to the new school motto: "Lux, Lex, Libertas", which is the motto on the Colfox family crest which the school adopted as its badge. The account of the opening goes on to describe the new building in some detail, though the second phase of building had not, at that point, been completed. Ronald Coatsworth a member of staff of the new school, recalled the opening: *"It was beautiful weather. All the children came and were assembled in the front of the school and allotted their various classes. They were then escorted by the prefects to their new rooms. Everything was so new and bright and shiny (including their faces) and the whole process was conducted in almost absolute silence. The silence did not last very long – within two days they had learned their limits and were as noisy as any other group of young children."*

Designed by the County Architects, and built by the LEA, the school cost what now seems the ludicrously small sum of £160,000. The paper follows this fact with the comment: *"This is well below the Ministry of Education's permissible* (upper presumably*) limit in both cost and floor area per child."* Was this something to be proud of? One of the economies that kept the costs down was to leave out the corridor on the first floor, which should have linked the two staircases. This was to cause endless inconvenience to staff and pupils for the next forty-three years.

When the school opened, only Phase One of the building had been completed and this was the main three-storey classroom block with the Assembly Hall and administrative offices. Only 400 of the projected 600 students could be accommodated in the new building until Phase Two was built, so only the senior classes went up to the Bradpole site in that first year, while the two junior years stayed in the old Grammar School building in St Andrew's Road. As the science and domestic science rooms were also in Phase Two, the Grammar School was still used for these subjects too, so, for a year, both pupils and staff had to travel up and down St Andrew's Road, shunting between the two sites, and no doubt adding to the complications of getting the new school established. The second phase of the building consisted of the Gym, and a two-storey wing to house science and craft rooms.

However, even with two phases of the building completed, the school was still not large enough for all the pupils who now qualified for

---

[5] Bridport News: July 6th 1956

218

secondary education. With the former Grammar School building now needed for the new County Primary School, there was an urgent need to find alternative accommodation for the junior classes who could not be fitted into the new school. The only option was to use some of the rooms in King Street recently vacated by the General School Juniors and Infants who were now occupying the old Grammar School. It must have seemed like a complicated game of musical chairs.

A plan of the King Street School buildings, produced by the County Architects in 1957 shows, coloured in red, the rooms allocated to "Alfred Colfox School" and in blue the rooms available to St Mary's.[6] In effect Colfox had most of the two-storey former Girls' School for the four First Year (Year 7) classes that were based there. They occupied two classrooms on the first floor and three on the ground floor, plus cloakrooms, leaving the former Boys' School to St Mary's. The junior special needs class (then called the Remedial Class) was also located at King Street under the aegis of Mr Ian Macmillan. The other teachers based at King Street were Doreen Gale, Brian Pursey, Pat Green and Betty Starkey. Staff on both sites had to commute back and forth from King Street to the main Gore Cross site for four years from 1958 to 1962. Possibly to facilitate timetabling across two sites, the school experimented with a seven-day timetable at this time, though one cannot help feeling this must have added to, rather than eased, the complications faced by staff, as each week the timetable started on a different day.

Both Brian Pursey and Doreen Gale taught PE, and were therefore needed regularly at the main school. Betty Starkey recalls commuting up to the main building to teach English, RE and some history.[7] Both Brian and Doreen later took up middle management positions within the school, Brian taking charge of the Fifth Year after the raising of the school-leaving age in 1971/2, and Doreen becoming Head of York House and devoting much of her later career to working with pupils with special educational needs. She finally retired in 1993 after thirty-four years' service.

Despite the fanfares which heralded its opening, the new Gore Cross building was never large enough. In calculating projected numbers, the County planners had apparently not taken into account St Ronans private primary school, nor, perhaps more understandably, the "bulge" in the post-war birth-rate, which, by this time, was feeding an increasing number of children into the secondary school system. There was only one solution, which Colfox would be forced use many times throughout the lifetime of the 1956 building: temporary classrooms. By 1962 the first of these "huts", each housing two classrooms, appeared on the new site. Only

---

[6] Copy of map BMLHC
[7] I am indebted to Betty Starkey for the information about the King Street "Annex".

219

then could the four King Street classes be accommodated, and at last, six years after the school was opened, all its pupils and staff were in one place.

As I have already mentioned, the Alfred Colfox School was built as a "bilateral school". The bilateral strategy was set even before the new school was built. To prepare for this move, the Grammar School had created a Secondary Modern stream about six years before closure. The Allington Secondary Modern School and the Senior Department of the General School at King Street, as well as a Grammar School adjoining the Unitarian Church, all closed when Colfox School was opened, and all the students were transferred. The term "bilateral" fell quickly out of favour. In his speech at the first Speech Day in 1957, Major Thornburn made plain his dislike of the word: *"This school is, in literal terms, a Comprehensive or Universal school, and as such is an act of faith on the part of the Dorset Education Committee."* It was he asserted *" the first, and at present the only, school in Dorset which caters for all the boys and girls of secondary school age in the district."* As his view was shared by Sir Theodore Tasker, Chairman of the County Education Committee, who was also the guest speaker at the Speech Day in 1957, the term "bilateral" was swiftly dropped.[8] However, there was no intention to mix children academically, and in the early years the school was rigidly streamed. There was in addition to the Modern and Grammar School streams a "Tech" stream in the Fourth and Fifth Forms (Years 10 and 11) in the early years of the school. The innovation was to have all the children from one area under one roof, but the education under that roof reflected the tripartite system introduced nationally in 1944.

Continuity from the Grammar School to the new "Universal" school was created in many ways, not least by the fact that the Headmaster and Senior staff, Major Thornburn, Edith Bickford and Tommy Telford continued to lead the new school. Among the staff who transferred were Mrs Tighe, who taught English, Frank Newing who became Head of Physics, Denys Tamblyn who taught geography and ultimately became Deputy Head of the new school, and Wilfred "Andy" Chapman-Andrews, Head of English. Staff were also drawn from the other former schools: Mr Richard Inkpen, and Mr James "Jimmy" Holmes coming from Allington Secondary School, and William Bayne-Cole from Bradpole School. The gold and navy Grammar School uniform tie and cap were retained, though the rest of the uniform at the new school was resolutely grey: grey jackets to which the new badge could be sewn, grey trousers, grey skirts, grey pinafore dresses, and white shirts and blouses.

---

[8] Bridport News 19th July 1957

220

Drama at the new school was a straightforward continuation of the Grammar School. The Eveleigh Cup Inter-form Drama Festival which started at the Grammar School continued into the lifetime of Colfox School, initially under Andy Chapman-Andrews, then under his successor as Head of English, Bruce Critchinson. Having produced the first of his annual school plays, a production of "A Midsummer Night's Dream", at the Grammar School in 1949, Andy went on to exploit the much better facilities of the new school hall, with it's permanent stage, lighting, and good acoustics. The seamlessness of the transition is nowhere better illustrated than by looking at the back page of any of the play programmes for productions at Colfox through to the 1980's. The list of past productions always begins with the "Dream" of 1949.

The Debating Society was revived in 1963 by Bruce Critchinson, who had joined the staff in 1961. The Society's highest achievement came in 1978, when they won the Observer Mace Debating Competition, taking on and beating teams from the best schools in the country. The two students who represented the school at the London final were Judith Chant and Anthony Vaughan, and the curiously topical motion they successfully opposed was: "This House is in favour of Devolution". Taking over as Head of English from Andy Chapman-Andrews, in 1972, Bruce Critchinson built on the school's tradition for drama, by staging a number of outstanding productions. Still remembered are his productions of "The Insect Play" by Czech writers, the Brothers Capek in 1974, "Alice in Wonderland" in 1975, and the 1977 production of "A Midsummer Night's Dream", which was made into a film, completed in 1978, and premiered at the Palace Cinema on 18th May of that year. He left the school in 1979 to become Deputy Head of the Archway School, Stroud in Gloucestershire.

The focus on music that characterised the Grammar School under Frances Tighe was also a feature of the new school. When Rex Trevett joined classically-trained Head of Music, Frank Clarke, in the Music Department in 1973, he added to the already strong classical tradition fostered by Frank, an entirely new repertoire of popular music, jazz and above all the big band sound. A year after Rex joined the staff, he created the Colfox Big Band. By 1976 there were thirty-seven musicians in the band including some staff members, and from that point on the Band simply went from strength to strength, gaining a reputation well beyond the confines of the school. The Music Department under Frank Clarke had always supported the various drama productions, and Rex arranged and composed music for a series of school productions, including the 1977 "Midsummer Night's Dream", for which he wrote the incidental music. After Frank Clarke's retirement, Rex took over as Head of Music. The 1970's saw the introduction of the school Music Festival as a complement to the

Drama Festival. The aim of both events was to get all the children in the school involved in performance of one kind or another.

The continuity, desired by Major Thornburn between his two schools also extended to a range of endowed prizes, presented to senior students, until quite recently, at the annual prizegiving. Many of those prizes commemorated Grammar School staff such as Francis Tighe, (Senior Art), Beatrice Witham (Domestic Science), Edith Bickford (Mathematics), Andy Chapman Andrews (English Verse) and Tommy Telford in the Maxwell Telford Prize for Languages. Frank Newing, Head of Physics, was remembered in the Newing Prize, and the Maggs Prize for History commemorated K E Maggs, another ex-Grammar School teacher.

"What's in a name?" Though the school was officially called the "Alfred Colfox School", locally the name was generally shortened to "Colfox School" and by 1972 the governors, who, by this time included Sir John Colfox as Vice Chairman, had taken the decision to make the simpler name official. Times had changed; Sir Philip was dead and his personal desire to avoid confusion over the dedication of the school no longer seemed an issue. He had died barely four months after his resignation as Chairman of Governors in July 1966. His eldest son, now Sir John, had already been a governor of the new school for ten years when his father died. He recalls joining the governing body in 1956 as the representative of the Bridport Rural District Council. When Sir Philip retired from the governing body due to ill health, Mr Campbell W Edwards took over as Chairman, and Sir John was appointed Vice-Chairman. Finally, on October 22nd 1977, Sir John took over as Chairman of Governors, and went on to serve the school as Vice Chairman and Chairman for a total of twenty-eight years.

One of the reasons why Colfox School never had enough space was that parts of the original plan were never built. Phase Three which should have seen the replacement of the concrete sectional buildings *"built by the Ministry in 1951"* for *"handicrafts"* [9] seems to have dropped off the drawing board as early as the opening in 1956 as the Bridport News report makes no mention of it. Ronnie Coatsworth, who saw the original plans for the Technical Block which should have completed the north side of the quadrangle, told me what a lovely design it was; *"complete with clock tower".* The old 1951 prefabricated buildings that housed metalwork and woodwork, were destined never to be replaced. Arthur Goldsmith and after him Chris Thorne had to go on running the Design and Technology Department in cold, cramped conditions right up to the final demolition of the school.

---

[9] Bridport News: Sept 14th 1956

In 1971 the government decided to raise the school-leaving age to sixteen, and this change was implemented from September 1972. The effect of this was to increase the school population considerably, as all those students who had previously left at the end of the Fourth Year (Year 10) now stayed on for a further year. As this was more than half the year-group, a new two-storey building was constructed in the central quadrangle to accommodate the new enlarged Fifth Year (Year 11). It housed extra classrooms, and a dining room and kitchens on the ground floor. Upstairs were more classrooms, and an office for Brian Pursey, now in charge of the new Fifth Year. This building, despite many efforts to change its name, went on being known as "The RoSLA Block" long after people had forgotten what RoSLA stood for.[10] Even when Peter Brown's reorganisation made it the Sixth Form base, it was some time before the new name stuck.

Much of the peripheral landscaping of the school was done by the first cohort of pupils, in 1955/6: laying paths and digging the original swimming pool; some of the work being done even before the pupils had moved onto the site. At the final Grammar School Speech Day, already quoted, Major Thornburn paid tribute to *"Mr Jolliffe and Mr Morrison..... who with some assistance from the older boys .... had quietly built a learners' swimming pool in the new school grounds."*[11] Later in March 1958 Ronnie Coatsworth, Head of Rural Studies, with the assistance of eight of the boys planted the windbreak of conifers that protected the school site to the north. 2,500 trees were planted in ten days. In all, Ronnie and his students added 3,500 trees to the site.

At the north-western corner of the site completely hedged by the same double row of conifers was a large sheltered garden area, where students were taught to grow vegetables, under the Ronnie Coatsworth's watchful eye. (Fig 43) There were also large greenhouses in a sunny corner of the central quadrangle, which with the rest of the farm building were also erected by the boys. As befitted a rural school, there was a small school farm, also the responsibility of Ronnie Coatsworth, which included two pig-sties where pigs were reared; a flock of sheep that grazed different areas of the site not used as playing fields, and a very small chicken battery-unit which occupied a wooden building next to the pig-sties and was the subject of at least one student protest when issues around humane farming methods became current. The flock of sheep grew to be so much a feature of the school that visitors would often refer to it as *"the school with the sheep".* The sheep even featured on photographs of the school in the school prospectus. The proceeds from the sale of produce from the school

---

[10] RoSLA stands for "Raising of the School Leaving Age".
[11] Bridport News: July 6th 1956

223

"farm" helped finance it. However the increasing difficulty of financing the farm meant that was gradually dismantled with much of the livestock being sold even before Ronnie Coatsworth's retirement. Finally the sheep were sold, and a distinctive feature of the school was lost.

Another area where Colfox School excelled right from the outset was in the field of sport. Under a succession of Heads of PE, including, Vince Evans and Neil Blair, the reputation of the school, particularly in athletics, cross-country running and rugby grew, until the distinctive canary-yellow sports shirts of Colfox athletes were both well-known and feared, as their wearers so often "ran away" literally with the prizes. The school did well in a range of competitions, both at local, county, and national level. Neil Blair was particularly influential in boosting the performance in athletics and distance running, (Fig 44) particularly cross-country. In the early 1980's, when marathon running became popular, he was the driving force behind the Bridport Mini-marathon. This quite major event started in the centre of Bridport, and was run across a course between Bridport and Beaminster, until the difficulty of policing the event on busy roads put an end to the venture after only a few years.

An admitted advantage to the Girls' and Boys' PE Departments was the big flat open area of playing fields, adjoining the school, which enabled Colfox to host full-scale athletics meetings as well as providing training facilities for the young athletes, boys and girls, who represented the school at district, county and national level across all sports. The field accommodated two rugby or football pitches depending on the term. In the autumn term rugby was taught and played; in the spring term football was the boys' main sport. There were also two hockey pitches for the girls. Cricket took over the centre of the field in summer, while the running track circled the outfield and the cricket nets were shielded by a small copse of beech trees on the north-western perimeter of the site. A range of sand-pits for long-jump and triple-jump bordered the pitches on the north-eastern perimeter, and a number of tennis courts were ranged on the opposite side of the field alongside Dodhams Lane. The hard courts doubled as netball courts in the winter. Once the large heated swimming pool, built with money raised by the Parents' Association, was completed in 1974, the school had outdoor sports facilities of a high order.

Indoor facilities however were a different matter. The old gym, built in 1957, was soon outgrown, and despite efforts to lobby for a sports hall, even at one point supporting a proposal for a facility to be shared with the town, the school had to wait until the new building in 1999 for a purpose-built sports hall, and at that point it also gained an all-weather Astroturf pitch. The school Year Book for 1984/5 underlines the problems. It praises the games staff for the wide range of sports available, which included in

224

addition to the outdoor sports, basketball, volleyball, gymnastics, trampolining, badminton and circuit training, all of which need indoor facilities. But goes on to complain about the *"poor facilities available to the school"*. In fact, by this time, in addition to the gym, the school hall was in regular use for PE.

For anyone who took part, either as a competitor or a member of staff helping to run the events, two contrasting sporting events of this period remain as compelling memories. The first is the annual School Cross Country, run in December, over a course that took in the fields and hills around Dodhams Lane and usually involved at least one runner having to be rescued from muddy field gates. The other is the annual school Sports Day. Held in July, usually in glorious weather, this event was a full-scale athletics meeting in which tutor groups within each year group competed against one another to take the Year prize. Starting after an early Morning Break it took the rest of the day. The organisation, which hardly varied from year to year, had a momentum all its own, as staff who largely judged or stewarded the same events each year had little need of briefing.

Major Thornburn served the school as Headmaster until 1979 (Fig 42), when he was succeeded on his retirement by Mr Peter Brown. Peter Brown was already an experienced headmaster when he came to Bridport. He had been head of Wyndham School in Cumbria for some years before making Colfox his final post before retirement. It was during Peter Brown's time as Headteacher that the Combined Beaminster-Colfox Sixth Form was set up to amalgamate post-sixteen teaching across the two schools. At a time when small sixth forms were coming under increasing pressure from a government eager to push the role of Tertiary and Sixth Form Colleges, this allowed both schools to retain their sixth forms while widening the curriculum and sharing the teaching. With transport provided by the County Education Department, students and sometimes staff travelled, and still travel, the six miles between the two schools by shuttle-bus. A joint management team had to be set up to coordinate the often very complicated arrangements necessary, and the first Coordinator of the Beaminster/Colfox Sixth Form was John Labrom. (Fig 45)

Peter Brown also revived the house system which had pretty much faded out of existence during the preceding twenty years. The early Colfox School Houses had commemorated notable Dorset worthies: Reynolds, named after the former Mayor and Grammar School Chair of Governors, Barnes and Hardy of literary fame, and Forster after William Forster MP author of the 1870 Education Act. In this they had built on the tradition of the Grammar School Houses which all commemorated educational benefactors of Bridport: Colfox, Reynolds and Taylor.

In a break with the past and in consultation with the staff, Peter Brown decided to create four houses (later reduced to three) based on

British royal dynasties so Windsor, Stuart, York and Tudor Houses were created, and the school was radically reorganised along house lines with Heads of House taking responsibility for much of the day-to-day supervision of the students progress and welfare. Chemistry teacher, Brian Bowles headed Windsor House, Doreen Gale took charge of York House, Chris Thorne was Head of Tudor House, and Elizabeth Truscott who also taught Domestic Science, was Head of Stuart House. Each house was designated by a different colour, and students wore navy-blue school sweatshirts displaying the house badge stitched in the house colour.

It was in Peter Brown's time as headteacher that the only other new building to improve the school's facilities was completed. In 1984 a new fully-equipped science wing was built, providing a complete suite of science laboratories, prep-rooms etc, on two floors and making, for a while at least, science provision at the school the envy of neighbouring schools, and giving a great boost to the Science Department, which at that time was led by Colin Wood. The science wing was named the John Fowler Building after Professor John Fowler, Head of the Gray Cancer Research Laboratory at Mount Vernon Hospital, in Northwood, and Director of the Cancer Research Campaign. A former Bridport Grammar School pupil, he was invited to open the new wing in November 1984.

The Year Book for 1984/5, gives a fascinating glimpse of the school in that year. It was the brain-child of Bob Wolfson, who had joined Freda King and Robin Middleton as a third Deputy a few years earlier. In the diary section the entry for September 1984 reads: *"Another year, and a delayed start as the builders haven't finished, ...when we do get in, the building has actually been painted, but the Science Wing hasn't been finished. Too many customers, not enough buses."* In July 1985, Peter Brown retired. The Year Book contains an interview with him, and again the parlous state of the buildings and facilities is mentioned. When asked what he will miss when he leaves, he lists the Big Band, the *"stylish"* debates, cross country races and the marathon, the students commitment to community service, as well as the *"rich drama that is in the school's culture"*. But he goes on with clear irony: *"I'll certainly miss the cramped geography of corridors and stairs, and the tired huts and older classrooms! ... the rain and the mud – and Colfox kids who make so little fuss about being muddied and drenched."* [12] 1984/5 was also the tenth anniversary of the founding of the Big Band and the year Humphrey Dibdin, Head of History, became Mayor of Bridport.

Peter Brown was succeeded in 1985 by Mr Christopher Mason, who came to the school from Ferndown Upper School. He became only the

---

[12] "84 And More – The 1984-85 Colfox School Year-Book" published by Colfox School and printed by CJ Creed.

226

school's third headteacher. He assumed the headship twenty-nine years after the school had opened, by which time the problem of the school's decaying and inadequate buildings was becoming ever more acute. The "huts" by this time had burgeoned into a small village of mobile classrooms on the edge of the school field, generally referred to as "Hutland". Running the gauntlet of south-westerly gales and rain was a regular winter hazard; hence Peter Brown's reference to pupils being *"muddied and drenched"*. As a temporary measure a two-storey pre-fabricated block was erected on the site of the original learners' swimming pool, to replace the mobiles. This tiny pool was so small that it was difficult to imagine anyone swimming in it. Three good strides would have got an adult from one end of the pool to the other! It had been re-designated a wild-life pond, when the new swimming pool opened in 1974. As the pond contained quite a collection of crested newts, building over it was not a simple matter, as the newts had to be relocated carefully before building could start.

At last, after much political manoeuvring and with the support of the County Council, plans to build a new school, so often mooted in the past and so often shelved for lack of money, finally came to fruition. It was decided, as the Local Authority could not raise the funds to build a new school, the only way forward was to use private money, and a partnership was set up with Jarvis plc to build a new school. It was the first school in the country to be built via a PFI (Private Finance Initiative). The PFI agreement between the County Council and Jarvis plc was signed in November 1997, Bournemouth architects, Terence O'Rourke, were appointed to draw up the design, and building started shortly after on the area to the north of the existing school that had housed the school gardens, the long-jump pits and the rugby pitches.

It fell to Chris Mason to oversee the building of the new school. At about the same time the government had introduced the idea of specialist schools and Colfox applied successfully to become a Language College. There followed a couple of years of inevitable discomfort, as half the site turned into a building site and the outdoor facilities for games were greatly curtailed. The old Colfox building had its official farewell party on Saturday July 17th 1999, with, appropriately, the Big Band performing at the dance in the evening. A few days later, on July 25th the now empty building was handed over to fire-fighters from a number of fire brigades including Bridport's, to deliver the coup de grace. A massive exercise was organised which involved setting parts of the old buildings on fire in order to test equipment and provide training for young fire-fighters, among whom were one or two former pupils. "Operation Colsmoke", as it was called was

227

described as *"Colfox's final contribution to the town .... a valuable lesson in how to save lives."*[13]

In September 1999, the school moved into its new architect-designed premises, and what was left of the old school was demolished, crushed and buried under newly-contoured playing fields. On December 14th, 1999, Princess Anne, the Princess Royal, landed by helicopter at Gore Cross and travelled the short distance to the school to conduct the official opening. The new school was given a new name. This time, in honour of Alfred Colfox's grandson, Sir John, who had served the school variously as governor, Vice Chair and Chair of Governors over a total of forty-five years, the school was named the Sir John Colfox School. It was an appropriate gesture, not just because of his own contributions to the school, but also in recognition of his family's long commitment to education in the town. Sir John finally retired from the school governing body in 2000 when he was awarded the unique honour of being named "Governor Emeritus" in recognition of his desire to maintain a connection with the school.

The last post-war school to be established in Bridport by the Dorset Education Committee was **Mountjoy School,** which was built expressly to cater for children with *"severe, complex or profound and multiple learning difficulties"*[14]. If Alice Lee Colfox had been alive to see it, the founding of such a school in Bridport would have delighted her, as she worked tirelessly for children with just such learning difficulties, in the early years of the century. It was built on a small site adjoining West Bay Road to the south of the former town boundary, interestingly enough opposite the house that was formerly occupied by Southayes School, and it is that small site which, as I write, is creating huge problems for the school, for it too has run out of space. It too has had to resort to temporary classrooms, which in this case have all but swallowed up the available playground space for the children. As I write the lobbying goes on to find a site and provide a new school for these children.

And so the long story of schools in Bridport closes, though of course such a story actually has no end. In some ways it is curiously circular, with the past informing the present and the present recalling the past. When Princess Anne opened the new Sir John Colfox School, many of the speakers expressed the same sentiments as Lord Shaftesbury, ninety years earlier, when he opened the Bridport Secondary School. After congratulating the Mayor and Councillors on building such *"beautiful*

---

[13] Bridport News: 16th July 1999
[14] Mountjoy School Prospectus: 2004

228

premises", he added that *"they represent the very latest ideas in modern design of schools.....admirably fitted for the purpose for which they have been built......A school which will be second to none in the county".* It is perhaps a small irony that while the first school was built on private benefaction, public subscription, and a penny rate, the second was only made possible by bringing in private money once again. Nothing much, it would seem, ever changes.

Appendix A

Francis (Fra) Henry Newbery (1855-1946)

Walk into Bridport Town Hall and the eye is immediately drawn to the allegorical figure of Bridport presiding with her distaff of flax over the Mayor's Chair. She is flanked by murals depicting the staple trade: home-workers braid nets, and men make ropes. Behind her a view of ships and the sea, reminds the onlooker of the town's shipbuilding trade. On the walls are a series of huge canvases showing notable events in the town's history. The man who left this valuable legacy to the town was a shoemaker's son, who came to Bridport in the middle of the nineteenth century, and from such unlikely beginnings, became an artist of international reputation.

Francis Henry Newbery[1] (Fra Newbery as he liked to be called, though at the General School he was known as Frank) was born in Membury in Devon, on the 15th May 1855. The family moved to Bridport, his mother's home town, when he was three. He went to school at Bridport General Infants' School and moved into the Boys' School probably at the age of six or seven, where he came under the guidance of John Beard the school's charismatic and influential headmaster. It was John Beard who spotted the young boy's artistic talent and fostered it. Though Francis came from a reasonably large family: he had three brothers and two sisters, he seems to have been the only one to show artistic talent.

In 1870, Francis, no doubt with the encouragement of John Beard, became a pupil teacher at the General School, and began to attend the Bridport School of Art evening classes held at the Literary and Scientific Institute in East Street, under a Mr Broadly. He completed his three-year apprenticeship under Mr Beard at the Boys' General School on March 31st 1874. He must also have been teaching at the School of Art for in the Bridport News Dec 15th 1876 it is announced that *"Mr F H Newbery, late Assistant Art Master in the Bridport School of Art has received the appointment of Art Master to the large middle-class schools recently erected at Hackney by the Grocers' Company"*. This followed his move to London in 1975 and an initial teaching post at the Cowper Street Corporation Schools in the City Road. The 1881 census records him at the age of 25 boarding with the family of a widow, Ann Kennett, at 89 Greenwood Road in Hackney, London. He is described in the census return as a "Teacher of Art". By 1877 he had joined the National Art Training School at South Kensington where he was taught by Edward Poynter and other contemporary artists, and once qualified, he went on to teach for several years at the South Kensington School of Art.

In 1885, at the age of thirty, came the appointment which was to make him famous. He was appointed Director of the Glasgow School of Art. In 1889 Francis

---

[1] In addition to references in the text further information in this appendix is drawn from: "Francis Newbery and The Glasgow Style" by Isobel Spenser. Information on the epona..lib.ed website and on the website of the Plymouth Diocese describing The Church of the Holy Spirit and St Edward in Swanage, and the Logbooks of the Boys General School: DHC/MIC/R/893,894

married a former student, later a teacher at the College, Jessie Wylie Nowat. She was a skilled designer in her own right specialising in needlework, book decoration, mosaic and enamelling. They had two daughters, Elsie and Marie, born in 1890 and 1892 respectively.

The Glasgow School of Art was made famous by the work of artists and designers such as Margaret and Frances Macdonald, Herbert McNair and Jessie King, but above all by the work of Charles Rennie Mackintosh, whom Fra Newbery chose to design the new building for the School of Art which opened in 1897. Mackintosh also designed the rooms for the display of work sent by the College to the Turin Exhibition of Decorative Art of 1902, which further enhanced both the College's reputation and that of Newbery himself. In recognition of his success in Turin, he was awarded an Italian knighthood: the Cavaliere Ufficiale dell'Ordine Della Corona D'Italia.

While at Glasgow, Newbery associated with some of the major painters and designers of the day. He exhibited with the Glasgow Boys and had close ties to John Lavery, James Guthrie, and EA Walton. Jean Delville, a notable figure in the Symbolist movement was drawn to the College by it's reputation and from 1901 to 1905 he supervised the painting schools. Francis Newbery continued to teach and paint in addition to his administrative duties. Throughout his career he exhibited world-wide, and built up an international reputation. As well as Turin, he also exhibited at two Paris Salons, the Royal Scottish Academy, the Royal Academy and the Royal Society of Portrait Painters. Works of his are in the permanent collections of galleries abroad: Turin, Venice, Munich; as well as British galleries: in Newcastle in the North of England, and in Paisley and Glasgow in Scotland. Locally his work can be seen in Exeter, and in Dorchester Museum.

His friendship with Rennie Mackintosh lasted beyond their association over the design of the School and the Turin exhibition. It may have been the reason for a visit to Bridport that Mackintosh made in 1895 in the course of a sketching tour of the West Country. While in Bridport, Mackintosh sketched several buildings in the town, including the Chantry, and made drawings of architectural details from St Mary's Church. Copies of these can be seen in the local history collection of Bridport Museum. In the summer of 1914 Mackintosh joined the Newberys in Walberswick near Southwold in East Anglia. It was here, probably under the influence of Fra Newbery that Mackintosh started painting landscape watercolours.

During the academic session of 1916/17 Francis fell ill with the first of a series of nervous illnesses brought on by the strains of running the Glasgow School. He was finally granted early retirement on medical grounds in 1918. He returned to Dorset, settling at Corfe. At first he and Jessie lived at the Greyhound Hotel, before finally purchasing their house, Eastgate, which was to be their final home. Here he was able to concentrate on his painting. From the 1920's a stream of work comes from his brush: portraits of friends and associates such as David Brynley, the musician, and Charles Prideaux, a former curator of Dorchester Museum, both works now in the private collection of that Museum, as well as Bridport Town Hall.

He never forgot his roots. Before his retirement he had instituted a series of prizes for art at his old school, Bridport General School, making several visits to give out prizes in person. He further marked his gratitude to the town by painting the series of pictures which he gave to the town, and which hang in the Town Hall. In

231

March 1923, he gave "The Romance of Bridport", an allegorical painting, for which he was made a Freeman of the Borough at a civic ceremony in Bridport Town Hall. This ceremony is described in detail in the Bridport News of 16th March 1923. This gift was followed by three others: "A Civil War Incident", "Joan of Navarre Entering the Town", and a painting of Dorset country folk in a twilight setting. In 1925 the Council Chamber was redecorated to Newbery's design and his final gift to the town was a set of murals showing "The Shipyard at Bridport Harbour", "The Weaving Shop", "The Spinning Walk", "The Yarn Barton" and "Net Braiding", all flanking the allegorical female figure of Bridport, spinning flax, distaff in hand.

In 1924 his portrait of Charles Prideaux was exhibited at the Society of Portrait Painters Exhibition at the Royal Academy. C S Prideaux was a Dorchester dentist and amateur archaeologist, who took on the role of Curator of Dorchester Museum from 1932 until his death in 1934. Another major work undertaken in 1926 was the design of the new Sanctuary for the Catholic Priory Church of The Holy Spirit and St Edward in Swanage. In addition to designing the Sanctuary, he painted a triptych altarpiece, the central panel of which represents Edward the Martyr who was murdered at Corfe Castle. The painting of St Edward is flanked by panels representing St Aldhem, first Bishop of Sherborne and St Elgiva, first Abbess of Shaftesbury. To complete the work, Francis and Jessie designed the altar, altar rails and stained glass.

Throughout his later years he suffered recurring bouts of severe depression, through which he was nursed by his wife. He died in Corfe on 18th December 1946 at the age of ninety-one, and is buried there.

232

Appendix B

William Edward Forster MP (1818 - 1889)

Walk past the post office in the village of Bradpole and turn left into a narrow lane now called Forster's Lane. A substantial farmhouse that once housed the local abattoir gives way to a more modest dwelling on the walker's right hand. This, now called Forster Farm, is the birthplace on William Edward Forster MP, who was author of the 1870 Elementary Education Act. Forster lived his early years in Bradpole and gained some of his education in Bridport. His parents, both Quakers, were prominent members of the Bridport Quaker Meeting, and his father was the first President of the Bridport Mechanics' Institute.

Francis Newbery's mother apparently remembered Forster as a *"long-legged lanky lad"* who used to travel from Bradpole to attend a school in Bridport riding a small pony. Some accounts refer to a donkey, but the pony was actually his mother's mount, which she used to ride to the Meeting in Bridport. The animal was apparently so small that Forster could stand up with his feet on the ground and allow the pony to walk away from under him. This "party-piece" apparently caused great amusement to passers-by and it is recalled by more than one person writing about his life in Dorset. Fra Newbery, describes him as attending a "private establishment for day and term boarders" in East Street, which is likely to have been George Moatt's Academy in East Street.[1] In fact he only attended the school for occasional French lessons. Until he went away to school in Bristol at the age of thirteen, Forster's education was largely informal, starting at home, where his mother and his nurse Maria were his teachers, and graduating at the age of ten to be tutored on a fairly irregular basis by the Rev. Thomas Taylor.

His parents, William and Anna Forster were active missionaries in the Quaker cause. Anna Buxton came from a very well-to-do Essex family. Her brother Thomas Fowell Buxton, later Sir Thomas, was a philanthropist and MP, and was a role-model for the young William Edward as he was growing up. On at least one occasion he visited the House of Commons to hear his Uncle speak in debate. Anna converted to the Quaker faith as a young woman, and took up philanthropic work, which was how she met her future husband. After their marriage the two continued to preach and visit other Friends on missionary work. Indeed Anna even visited Ireland on such work while she was pregnant with William Edward, and William senior went on an extended visit to America 1820, when his son was only two years old. This visit arose as part of his mission to work for the abolition of slavery. This visit, much agonised over, was intended to last only till 1823, but was extended when William decided to include a visit to see at first hand the practice of slavery in the West Indies. He did not return to Dorset until 1825.

The Forsters knew or were related to other Quaker reformers. Anna was related by marriage to Elizabeth Fry, the great prison reformer. Although she was not in fact his aunt, William Edward referred to her in a letter home as *"my Aunt Fry"*. Fra Newbery refers to William senior as "Dr" Forster, but it seems most likely this was merely a courtesy title probably used locally by the people of Bridport and Bradpole.

---

[1] "Reminiscences" by Fra H Newbery: Dorset Year Book 1928

William and Anna were married in Shaftesbury in 1816 and set up house in the cottage in Bradpole. They lived there until 1837 when they moved to Norfolk. William Edward was born in Bradpole on 11th July 1818. In a letter to a friend just after his marriage, William senior describes the cottage and its surroundings *"Our cottage is a plain-built stone house, thatched roof, and casement windows; one end comes to the footpath alongside the road. In front we have a neat forecourt; at the back a small orchard, and at the other end I hope to make a good garden. There are two parlours; one of them a neat snug room, not very large; the other, I think, may be improved and made very habitable. There is a small light room for a store closet, and a comfortable kitchen. There are four lodging rooms on the second floor - I think of converting one of them into a sitting-room - we have also good garrets."*[2]

For William and Anna the only drawback of living in Bradpole was the mile and a half journey to the Meeting in Bridport. The Forsters lived very frugally, and, shocked by what they saw of the poverty of their village neighbours, did their best to help the local people. In a letter to a school friend who had been invited to stay in Bradpole, William Edward wrote: *"thou know'st what a humble poor way we live in, but I know thee too well to fear thy minding that"*[3] The Quaker form of speech is very evident in this short extract. As already mentioned, William senior was much involved in the anti-slavery movement, which had been started by members of the Society of Friends and then taken up by political philanthropists such as William Wilberforce. It was while engaged on an anti-slavery mission in Tennessee in the USA that he fell suddenly ill, and died after just a few days illness, in March 1854.

At the age of thirteen, in 1831, William Edward's life in Bridport came to an end when he was sent away to a school which was run by another member of the Society of Friends, Joel Lean, at Fishponds House, Bristol. William stayed at this school just over a year. In October 1832, he moved to a school at Grove House in Tottenham run by a Mr Binns. This school was very close to the home, of his father's family, of whom he saw much more once he was living in London. In 1837 the family's connection with Bradpole finally came to an end when William and Anna moved to Norwich. Once his formal education was at an end, William Edward joined them there, and from that point on his only connection with Bridport was in the occasional visits he made.

From being a young boy he had cherished an ambition to enter Parliament, and had intended to study law as a means to that end, but his father vetoed that choice and after much deliberation decided that his son should follow a career in business. His first job was in the employ of a Mr Robberds in Norwich. This job only lasted a short time, and as his health was not very good at the time, his parents decided he should travel to Darlington to visit some friends in that town. Out of this visit came the job that was to set his course for much of his future life. In 1838 he started work in a woollen mill owned by the Pease family who were also Quakers.

At twenty-three he moved to Bradford and joined the firm of T.S.Fisons. Within twelve months of his arrival in Bradford in 1841 he had joined forces with William Fison and together they acquired a disused cotton mill, and set up a wool business in Bradford. About this time he met and got to know Robert Owen, of New

---

[2] "Life of the Right Honourable William Edward Forster" by T Wemyss Reid 1888
[3] Ibid

Lanark, Thomas Cooper, the chartist, and Thomas Carlyle, the historian. In the autumn of 1845 the failure of the potato crop in Ireland precipitated the famine and in 1847 William joined his father in a mission to that country to distribute what food, clothing and money they could. They went to Connemara and William was deeply shocked by the conditions there, used as he was to the deprivations of the poor in England.

In 1850, three years after his return from Ireland he married Jane Arnold, sister to Matthew Arnold and eldest daughter of Dr Arnold, the great headmaster of Rugby School. His marriage to Jane Arnold under Anglican rites forced the Society of Friends to disown him, but though he had already given up Quaker dress by this stage in his life, he continued to use the familiar Quaker forms of speech he had grown up with and was used to using to those closest to him. He always addressed his wife, Jane as "thou". The split with the Quakers was not acrimonious and indeed he was congratulated on his choice of a wife. His connection with the Arnolds was not his first brush with education as an adult, for in Norwich, while working for Robberds he had become a Sunday School teacher, but the Arnolds now brought him squarely into the world of education. Matthew Arnold, in addition to his work as a writer and poet was also a school inspector.

Forster became Liberal MP for Bradford in February 1861, the year the American Civil War broke out. He became Under Secretary for the Colonies in 1865. In 1868 Gladstone was once more Prime Minister and Forster became Vice President of the Privy Council. Up to this time education had come under the aegis of a committee of the Privy Council and it was they who had administered the system of grants to schools. As Vice President, Forster was given the task of shaping *"a national system of education"*. It was estimated at the time that one and a half million children did not go to any school. Many children were working ten or eleven hours a day in the burgeoning factories that were driving the nations prosperity at huge human cost.

Ranged against Forster in his attempt to introduce state education were the Church of England that feared encroachment on their church schools, the National Education Union that wanted simply an extension of the voluntary principle, and the Education League that represented the dissenting religions. In addition there were the conservative elements in society who simply saw compulsory education of the labouring classes as a dangerously radical idea. On the other hand Forster's own Liberal party felt that education should be compulsory, secular and free. Forster compromised. The Act did not make elementary education compulsory; that did not come until 1880, when it was considered that there was enough provision nationally to make education up to 10-years-of-age compulsory. It also did not encroach on the independence of the voluntary schools, but the setting up of the school boards was very influential locally in improving educational provision, and went a long way to providing elementary education for many more children.

The school boards were elected by the ratepayers in their district and the country was divided into about 2500 school districts. The boards were granted a modicum of freedom of operation and could make their own bye-laws which enabled them to charge fees if they wanted to, or let children attend school free. Even more radical was the fact that the Act allowed women to vote for the school boards, and they were also allowed to stand as candidates to serve on the boards, though few chose to avail themselves of this. Ironically, given William Forster's connections with Bridport and Bradpole, there was strong resistance locally to the school boards, most schools jealously guarding their independence, and where a school board was involved with a local school, as in Bothenhampton, the Chairman was the vicar of the parish.

Forster's connection with Bridport may have become somewhat tenuous by this period of his life, but it seems he did not forget his old home and from time to time came back to visit. Francis Newbery was still at the Bridport General School when Forster was *"in the thick"* of his Education Bill, and he recalls a visit Forster made to the Boys' General School at that time to consult with John Beard *"on some point"*. Newbery remembers him as being *"very tall and thin. His face with its keen blue eyes... well coloured, something like a Dorset russet apple, and he had a reddish hair and beard, the latter cut fairly short"* [4] This is probably the same visit recalled by a member of the Reynolds family, Fanny, who, in a letter to her mother dated June 2nd 1871, describes a visit Forster paid to the Quaker Meeting House in Bridport. She was sitting out in the court while her children played when her husband, Arthur, conducted some visitors into the Meeting: *"a great tall gentleman first, a lady and two girls, so of course ... I went in to see and who do you think this was but W.E. Forster himself."* Forster asked to be remembered to Fanny's mother Eleanor Clark. Fanny Reynolds goes on: *"We offered of course to show them the graveyard, the stones have just been put up - and then went round with them to the boys' school but could not get them to stay to see the girls."* [5]

Some years later in 1879, Forster was again in Dorset. This time his visit was recorded in the Logbook of Bradpole School: *"15th April: The School was visited by the Rt.Hon.W.E.Forster and Mrs Forster. During the visit the children sang songs and on their departure the right honourable gentleman expressed himself pleased with the school."*

In 1880, with Gladstone once again Prime Minister, Forster was sent to Ireland as Chief Secretary, and became embroiled in Irish politics, not a situation he relished, particularly when called on to steer through parliament proceeding to authorise the suppression of the Land League. Oddly enough he was against Home Rule, and prepared to take a hard line with those fighting for that cause. As a former Quaker he abhorred violence but was prepared to authorise its use it if absolutely unavoidable. Parnell and the leaders of the revolt were imprisoned but when the majority of Gladstone's cabinet voted in 1882 to release the Irish leaders from prison, Forster disagreed with the policy and feeling his position undermined, he resigned.

Just how dangerous the role of Chief Secretary to Ireland was, became apparent when his successor Lord Frederick Cavendish was murdered in Phoenix Park by gunmen. It became clear at the subsequent trial of the gunmen, that Forster's own life had also been in danger for many months before his resignation. It was ironic that early in his career he had enunciated his political aims as being, *"to give relief, lasting relief to poor Ireland; and to get the children of the working classes out of the gutter by educating them"*. [6] In at least one of these aims he was

---

[4] "Reminiscences" by Fra H Newbery: Dorset Year Book 1928
[5] BMLHC
[6] This quotation and much of the information in this section comes from the "Life of the Right Honourable William Edward Forster" by T Wemyss Reid 1888

236

successful. Between 1870 and his death in 1886 the number of schools in England and Wales increased from 8,281 to 19,133 and provided places for over five million children. Forster died on 5th April 1886 and is buried at Burley-in-Wharfdale in Yorkshire, the county that had became his home for most of his adult life.

Though he did not live long in Bradpole, the village remembered him and three years after his death in 1889 a Memorial Hall was constructed for the benefit of the people of the parish. The deed transferring the land for the "William Forster Institute" describes the building as being *"for the purpose of* (providing) *a library and reading room, with the general object of promoting the moral, social and intellectual and the rational recreation of the inhabitants of Bradpole and their friends"*. It provided evening classes for men and women on different evenings. A Savings Bank was set up for sixpenny deposits, paying out 10% on the first £25 and 5% thereafter. In addition the Hall was used for festive suppers.

The William Forster Institute was built under the Literary and Scientific Institutes Act of 1854. The architect was Frederick Cooper of Bridport who gave his services free. The Vicar of Bradpole, Canon Broadley, gave the site free, and the cost of building the Hall was £400. The money was raised by subscription and among the original subscribers were William Hounsell, the Earl of Ilchester, Thomas Alfred Colfox, Sir F.A. Weld, General Pitt-Rivers, and, such was William Forster's national reputation, the Lord Mayor of London. It remained an educational as well as a social resource for the village, until 1948 when its social function took precedence and it became the village hall for Bradpole. A framed photograph of William Forster can still be seen in the hall, as can a list of the names of all the founders of the Institute. Both were renovated by John Sales, then curator of Bridport Museum, in 1978.[7]

---

[7] Information on the Forster Memorial Hall in Bradpole drawn from various material held in the William Edward Forster File, Bridport Museum Local History Collection.

Appendix C

The Revised Code 1862 - 1890

The 1862 Code was extremely prescriptive. It specified a syllabus consisting of Reading, Writing and Arithmetic. The syllabus set out what would be expected of scholars in each of the six standards. For example a child in Standard 1 would need to be able to read a narrative written in monosyllabic words, while by Standard 6 he or she should be able to read a short paragraph in a newspaper, or other "modern" narrative. Writing ranged from forming letters on a slate, to writing down a paragraph dictated from a newspaper or "modern" book, and in Arithmetic the Standard 1 child should be able to form the figures up to twenty on a slate, while by Standard Five he or she should be able accurately to compute a sum using compound rules (long division and multiplication) using weights and measures. Standard 4 required the ability to do the same kind of calculations related to money.

The code stated that grants could only be earned on pupils under twelve years of age, effectively discouraging the education of older children. The grant was dependent on a certain number of attendances being made by the children and was subject to the results of an individual examination, by the government inspector, of each child in the three specified subjects. The schools had to be adequately housed and staffed, but the scale of staffing was less in proportion to the number of scholars than before. At the same time a lower class of certificates was instituted in order to make grants available to schools taught by teachers of lower educational attainment.

The grant was limited to twelve shillings per child, four shillings earned if the child achieved average attendance and eight shillings based on the result of the examination. If the child failed any one of the "Three R's" examined, then for each failure one third of the grant was withheld. Children under six years-of-age were exempt from examination, and there were no second chances. A child could not be presented for examination a second time in the same grade. Half-timers were eligible for the same grants as those attending full time. The six standards were compulsory. Also a requirement of the Code was that a Logbook should also be kept as a daily record of the school.

The result of the Revised Code was that children were kept grinding at the three 'R's' in an endeavour to ensure success in the examination, but to make the grant more certain they were put into as low a grade as possible. For example in 1863/4 of all elementary schools examined in England 41% of the number of scholars in average attendance were individually examined; and 86% of those over 10 years were examined in too low a grade. In 1881 with 70% examined 48% were in grades too low for their age. This system, because of the pressure it exerted in schools that were often short of money, tended to discourage the teaching of unexamined subjects, such as geography, grammar and history.

As a result the Code was further modified in 1867. An additional grant was offered to encourage more rapid promotion of the scholars through the Standards; to encourage staffing with better qualified teachers, and to provide for the introduction of at least one specific subject so as to remove the reproach that all teaching was reduced to the bare elements of the standard examination. At the same time schools were encouraged by special bonuses to train pupil teachers.

238

After the 1870 Education Act, a new Code was drawn up: the compulsory reading of the scriptures in school was withdrawn and the standards were altered. Standard 1 was abolished and Standard 2 became Standard 1 and so on. A new Standard 6 was added. Then in 1882 a Standard 7 was introduced. The grants were reduced to ten shillings per head, six shillings for attendances and four shillings for each pass in the "Three R's". However a further three shillings was paid for a pass in two further subjects which could include algebra, geometry, natural philosophy, physical geography, the natural sciences, political economy, English literature, or the elements of Latin, French or German, as well as history, geography and grammar. These subjects were studied by children in the three upper standards. To earn the attendance grant a child had to achieve a minimum of 150 attendances a year, and the total grant could not exceed the total local income obtained from the school fees, subscriptions or rates (match-funding in other words). The accommodation of the school had to provide a minimum of eight square feet per child, and attention had to be given to lighting and ventilation. Two years later provision for warming schools was made an essential requirement of the grant. Schools had to be in the charge of certificated teachers but in order to fill the gap made by this regulation, certificates might be granted to efficient acting-teachers who had ten years experience and were over the age of thirty-five.

There were further amendments to the Code up to 1890 all aimed at widening the curriculum. In 1874 a sum for singing was included, then in 1875 the teachers in the Lower Standards were specifically to choose two subjects, as "class subjects" for the examination, from history, geography and grammar. The Grammar Syllabus required the scholars in Standard 2 to point out the nouns in the passages read or written; in Standard 3 they must be able to point out nouns, verbs and adjectives, while by Standard 6 full parsing with analysis of a complex sentence was required. In geography, Standard 2 should understand the points of the compass; the form and motion of the earth, and the meaning of a map. While Standard 3 should know the outlines of the geography of England, with special knowledge of their own county. Standard 4 added Ireland and the Colonies, while by Standard 5 the geography of Europe, physical and political had to be covered. Standard 6 had to know the outlines of the geography of the world. In history the children needed to cover the outlines of the narrative of English history from the Norman Conquest (Standard 3) to the death of George III in 1820 (Standard 6).

In 1877 the Code ruled that no more than three pupil teachers were allowed for each certificated teacher, and for larger schools, where the average attendance exceeded 220, an additional assistant was required. In 1882, to prevent hardship, the Code allowed grants to be paid on the average attendance of the whole school, and all children who had been on the books for twenty-two weeks, whether or not they had completed 150 attendances, were examined. Merit grants of one shilling, two shillings and three shillings were introduced. In 1890, drawing was made compulsory for boys, and science, physical exercises and manual work were encouraged.[1]

---

[1] Information taken from "History of Elementary Education" by Birchenough [1932]

239

Henry Saloway's Roll of Honour

Alone of all the Headteachers who had the unenviable task of guiding their schools through the 1914-18 War, Henry Saloway kept a record in the school Logbook of all the old boys who achieved commissions, and all those who were killed in the war. This is in the form of handwritten notes at the back of the St Mary's Boys' School Logbook: 1906 - 1921. These pages are reproduced here.
Page 1

240

25 Edgar Hallett : killed in Belgium
&26 F Mingio killed in France
27 Alfred Wadham. *Roll of Honour* Killed by fall from train (Australian)
23 Arthur Ward . killed in France 27 Arthur Gale
Joseph 27 – Arthur G Gale 28 killed in Mesop.
John Jeans – Killed in Flanders

2 John Eveleigh (Ullery) "   "
3 William Newman Drowned at Portsmouth.
4 William Abbott " in N Sea Battle
5 Ernest Turner " " HMS Hampshire
6 Reg. Geo Symes Killed in France
7 Charles H Stone "   "   "
8 Capt H E Kitcher "
9 Lieut. T H Rowson "
10 Pt Edgar Samways   Lewis Fry
11 R. I Foord
12 Geo Oxenbury
13 Wm Travers Drowned in destroyer
14 Joe Bartlett – Killed in France
15 Saddr S & J Rowe "   "
16 H Wheadon killed.   Fry.
17 A " drowned –
18 Hilary Gilbert – Killed in France
19 Albert Marsh "   "
20 W Butcher "   "
21 Harry C Hallett died in India

At top of Page 1: Fred Swaffield
          Fred Bartlett
          (27) Lewis Fry (Crossed out: though his name appears again
          further down page 2 without any detail attached)
          Albert Marsh: -   DCM
          Joseph Fowler: -   DCM

241

```
Wm Legg:           -      MM
F Brooks:          -      MM
```

```
Major:        R Major              Lieut –Col now Jamaica
Captain:      H Kitcher            Killed - Tablet in St Mary's
Lieutenant:   T Rowson             Killed
  "           G Hart               RAF Now San Paulo Brazil
  "           H E Hounsell         RAF now LCC
  "           M Turner             Capt  now BN
  "           S Pitman             RNVR now Lieut Com
  "           J Sprackling         RAF
  "           S Stone              now Bank of South America
  "           C Major              RAF   Eastleigh
  "           V?S B Northover      RAF now ?
  "           H Strawbridge        Ind Army  now USA
  "           A Collins            dead
  "           S Pester             RAF now TA Engineer Capt
```
(RAF should probably read RFA: Royal Field Artillery. What is BN?)

Page 2
(This page is not in numerical order. I have tried to sort it our for ease of reading.)

1. Joseph Jeans   -   killed in Flanders
2. John Ellery   -   killed in Flanders
3. William Newman   -   drowned at Portsmouth
4. William Abbott   -   drowned in sea battle. (Went down in the Black
                           Prince during the North Sea Engagement according
                           to Logbook entry July 12th 1916)
5. Ernest Turner   -   drowned in HMS Hampshire (The ship was mined
                           off the Orkney's. Lord Kitchener on board - Logbook)
6. Reg. Geo. Symes   -   killed in France
7. Charles H Stone   -   killed in France
8. Capt. H E Kitcher -   killed in France
9. Lieut. T (Thomas)H Rowson - killed in France (At Ginchy - Logbook)
10. Pt Edgar Samways -   killed in France
11. Pt F (Fred) Ford -   killed in France
12. Geo. Oxenbury   -   killed in France
13. Wm Travers   -   drowned in destroyer (In the Channel - Logbook)
14. Jos. Bartlett   -   killed in France
15. Saddler Sgt. J Rowe   killed in France
16. H Wheadon (probably W H Weadon) - killed in France
17. A Wheadon   -   drowned
18. Hilary Gilbert   -   killed in France (While on patrol - Logbook)
19. Albert Marsh DCM -   killed in France
20. W Butcher   -   killed in France
21. Harry Marsh   -   killed in France
22. Sgt B G Hallett   -   died in India (Of heatstroke - Logbook)
23. Arthur Ward   -   killed in France
24. Alfred Wadham   -   killed by falling from a train
                           (In Australia - Logbook)
```

242
```

25. Edgar Hallett   -   killed in Belgium
26. F Ninnis(?)   -   killed in France
27. Arthur Gale   -   killed in Mesopotamia
(There is also an A Hallett recorded on the page, but not assigned a number in the list.)[1]

As you can see from the reproduced pages, some of the above names are difficult to read, and some of the places of death conflict with the contemporary entries in the Logbook, for example in the Logbook Henry Saloway records John Ellery of the 5th Dragoon Guards as having been killed in "the Persian Gulf Operation".

The numbered names make up the roll he read out in the Armistice services held by the Boys' School every November 11th. Some of the names are not exactly as they appear on the Bridport War Memorial, and the name F Ninnis does not appear at all on that Memorial. As it is also difficult to read the precise spelling in Henry Saloway's Roll, and the name Ninnis does not appear in the Logbook record, it is difficult to know who this was, or what was his connection with Bridport.

---

[1] The pages from the Logbook are reproduced by kind permission of the Governors of St Mary's School. The Log Books are now in the keeping of the Dorset History Centre: DHC/S.329

243

BIBLIOGRAPHY

UNPUBLISHED SOURCES
Dorset History Centre

Allington National School Logbook: 1870-1900 (DHC/MIC/R/890)
Allington National School Logbook: 1900-1956 (DHC/MIC/R/891)

Bradpole Primary School admissions register 1944-59 (DHC/S74/3/3)
Bradpole Vestry Meeting Minutes 1848-50 (DHC/MIC/R/327)

Bridport National Girls' School Logbooks: 1870-1902: 1902-1906: 1906-1925; 1925-1930;1930-1933 (DHC/S.329)
Bridport National Boys' School Logbook: 1906-1931; 1921-1933 (DHC/S.329)
Bridport St Mary's Mixed School Logbook: 1933-1977 (DHC/S.329)
Bridport National Infants' School Logbook 1918-1935 (DHC/S.329)
Bridport Secondary/Grammar School Governors' Minute Book: 1926-1941 (DHC/S319/1/2)
Bridport General Boys' School Superintending Committee Minutes: 1844-1864 (DHC/S117/1/1/1)
Bridport General Boys' School Lease of the Killingham site (DHC/S117/12/8)
Bridport General Girls' and Infants' School Management Committee Reports: 1868-1895 (DHC/S117/12/2)
Bridport General Boys' School Logbook 1862–1909 (DHC/MIC/R/893)
Bridport General Boys' School Logbook 1910-1956(DHC/MIC/R/894)
Bridport General Girls' School Logbook 1862- 1885; 1885-1914 (DHC/MIC/R/894)
Bridport General Infants' School Logbook 1914-1941 (DHC/MIC/R/894)
Dorset County Education Committee: Report on Reorganisation of Schools (Bridport District) 1934-56: DHC/S117/12/15)
Dorset County Council Public Assistance Committee Minutes 1945-1948 (DHC/DC/A/17/1/4)
Inaugural Lecture of the Bridport Association for Mutual Improvement 1831 (DHC/D/Col/Q3)
Letters relating to Elizabeth Channon Lee (DHC/D/Col/C49)
Map of Bridport (18th Century before 1786) (DHC/BTB/R2)
"Rules of the Industrial Branch of the Bridport Girls' and Infants' General Schools" printed by T Male, Bridport (DHC/S117/12/1)

Church of England Record Centre

Miscellaneous correspondence including plan of the proposed school in the Churchyard: Allington National School File
Miscellaneous correspondence: Bradpole National School File
Miscellaneous correspondence: Bridport National School File
St Mary's Church Bridport: Annual Report 1897: Bridport National School File

244

Bridport Museum Local History Collection

Austen Whetham: Deed of transfer of Thorneloe School Day School Connection: 1913.
Jennifer Ackerman: Notes on the Day School of the Sisters of the Visitation Convent.
Bridport Municipal Charities: Historical Survey May 1954
Bridport Secondary and Grammar School and Old Grammarians Magazines: 1914–1950.
Census returns: Bridport, Allington and Bradpole: 1841-1891.
The Colfox Paper.
The Henry Nobbs Cox Papers.
Jennifer Jennings: Notes on The Grove School (handwritten).
"John Beard – A Brief Biography" published by the John Beard Memorial Committee 1911.
William Forster and Bradpole: miscellaneous items relating to Forster and the Forster Memorial Hall.
Survey: "Property in Bridport owned by West Dorset District Council".
Ordinance Survey Map of Dorset including street map of Bridport: 1888
Prospectus: Coniston School (BRPMG55)
Prospectus: Grove School 1940
Southayes School: Miscellaneous notes.
Basil Short: "Unitarian Matters" : unpublished lecture notes.
Basil Short: "Bridport – some Historical Sites and Buildings": typed notes.
Sally Trevett: Notes on St Hilda's School (handwritten).
Sound Tapes : Dorset Schooldays: Oral History Project:
  Interview with Mildred Larcombe (BMS/Sch/06/07)
  Interview with Michael Norman (BMS/Sch/05)
  Interview with Elizabeth Wild (BMS/Sch/01)

Bridport Reference Library

Prospectus: St Ronan's School: 1983
Basil Short: "Bridport: History and Topography": text of a series of lectures delivered in 1980 under the aegis of the University of Bristol Department of Extra-Mural Studies.
John Stephens: "The Correspondence between the Bridport Churchwardens and the Charity Commissioners of England and Wales and the Trustees of the Daniel Taylor Charity 1897" published by W C Frost, Bridport

Miscellaneous

"Bridport Unitarian – The Chapel in the Garden": Leaflet produced by the Unitarian Chapel with notes by Alfred Munden.
"84 and More – The 1984-85 Colfox School Year Book" (Colfox School 1985)
Prospectus: Mountjoy School 2004
Worcester Census:1881

PUBLISHED SOURCES

The Bridport News: 1855-1967
(The Bridport News has had a series of titles over time. It started in 1855 as "The Illustrated Bridport News". It then became for most of the nineteenth century "The Bridport News and Dorsetshire,Devonshire and Somersetshire Advertiser", then the name was shortened to "The Bridport News and Dorset, Devon and Somerset Advertiser", In the 1960's it was "The Bridport News and Devon and Dorset Reporter", then it became "The Bridport News and Dorset County Journal", and finally today the front page simply reads: "The Bridport News". For ease of reference I have simply referred to the paper at whatever period as the Bridport News.)

Barry J Briggs: "The Wesleys and the early Dorset Methodists" (Windsorrel Publications 1987)
Edward Cree: "The Cree Journals – The Voyages of Edward Cree as related in his Private Journals 1837 – 1856": Ed Michael Levein (Webb & Bower 1981)
Arthur Champ (Ed): "Mates Illustrated Bridport 1903".
Alan T P Cooper: "Bell v Lancaster – Contribution to Elementary Education of the Rev Andrew Bell, Rector of Swanage": Dorset Year Book 1971/2
"Richard Head" : entry: Dictionary of National Biography (1917)
Directories:
- Kelly's Directory of Dorsetshire: 1848-1939
- G Harrod & Co Postal and Commercial Directory of Dorset and Wiltshire: 1865
- Pigot and Co's Dorsetshire Directory: 1823/1842
- Universal British Directory of Trade, Commerce and Manufacture: (c)1792
- Dorsetshire Towns Directory: 1874/5

Jo Draper: "Bridport Literary and Scientific Institute": Proceedings of the Dorset Natural History and Archaeological Society: Vol 121, p136.
Suzanne Finch: " 'A Fine Meeting There was there'. 300 Years of Bridport's Quaker History": (Bridport Quaker Meeting, Friends Meeting House: 2000)
H J Hutchins: "The History and Antiquities of the County of Dorset" Vol 2: (1774 and 1863 editions)
Richard Hindson: "Bridport Burgh and Borough 878AD-1974AD: A Short History" (Hindson 1999)
Cyril Kay: "Bothenhampton and its Churches" (Bothenhampton District Church Council:1982)
Patrick Keane: "Prophet in the Widerness – Rev William Barnes as an Adult Educator": Proceedings of the Dorset Natural History and Archaeological Society: Vol. 100 p19.
Fulbrook Lane: "Bridport in the Nineteenth Seventies and Eighties" (Fulbrook Lane: 1934)
John Lawson and Harold Silver: "A Social History of Education in England" (Methuen & Co Ltd: 1973)
Jerome Murch: "A History of Presbyterian and General Baptist Churches in the West of England" (1835)
Francis H Newbery: "Reminiscences" : Dorset Year Book: 1928
Aimee R Natal: "Charlotte Mason" : www.infed.org

Miss O'Farrell: "The Work and Aims of the Parents' Union School": The Parents' Review: Nov 1922.
Robin Pearce: "Seven Months to D-Day – An American regiment in Dorset" (Dovecot Press)
A W Penrose: "T E Walker": Dorset Year Book 1958
J W Rowson: "Bridport and the Great War" (Wyman & Sons Ltd: 1923)
T Wemyss Reid: "Life of the Right Honourable William Edward Forster" (1888)
Frances M Reynolds: "Daniel Taylor of Bridport 1642-1714 and The Trusts He Founded" (Reynolds 1980)
Basil Short and John Sales: "The Book of Bridport" (Barracuda Books: 1973)
Basil Short: "A Respectable Society 1593-1835" (Moonraker: 1976)

Abbreviations

DHC: Dorset History Centre, Dorchester, formerly the Dorset Record Office.
BMLHC : Bridport Museum Local History Collection held at The Coach House, Gundry Lane, Bridport.

INDEX

249

Hounsell, H E 119, 120, 242
Hounsell, Miss BM 181, 185-186
Hounsell, Dr John 34, 36
Hounsell, Joseph 20, 76, 78, 81, 146, 153, 156-157, 190
Hounsell, Mrs Henry 168
Hounsell, William 61, 103, 109, 237
Howe, Miss 66
Hughes, Ann R (Ladies' Academy) 24
Hull, John, William & Thomas 36
Humphries, Alfred 198
Hunsley, Mr (General School) 186
Hussey, Anna 21
Hyall, John MA (Rector St Mary's 1468-1481) 11

Infant School Society 84, 88
Inkpen, Richard A 146, 209, 220
Inspections, HMI 100, 101, 104, 123, 135, 141, 142, 143-144, 168, 176, 179, 182

James, Elizabeth (Chapel House School) 29, 39 (Grosvenor House School) 29-31
James, Lucy 103
James, Miss Annie 55
James, Selina & Bessie 99
James, W & Co (Line and Twine Manufacturers) 31
James, William 30-31
Jeanes, Joseph 118, 242
Jefford, Ellen 22
Jeffries, Mr 154, 157
Jennings, Jennifer 65-66
John Fowler Science Wing (Colfox School) 226
Johnson, Mark Edwin 136-137
Jolliffe, Bernard 181, 223
Jones, Elizabeth A 22
Jones, Emily 142
Jordan, Frederick J 207-209
Jules Biacq, Canon 149

Keddle, Rev SS 143
Keech, Mr (Caretaker) 111
Kenny, Rev Edward 149
King, Freda 226
Kingman, Miss 123-125, 145
King-Smith, Dick (Writer) 132
Kitcher, Capt HE 119, 242
Knight, George 85

Kupp, Mrs (formerly Miss Mingis) 66, 68

Labrom, John 225
Lacey, Miss 70
Ladies' College, West Street (See also Diplock, Elizabeth & Druscilla) 39-42, 85
Lancaster, Joseph 84, 89, 153, 160
Lane, Fulbrook (writer) 37, 41, 104, 139, 142-143
Lawrey, Millie Austin 114, 124
le Conteur, Marie 53
Lee, Elizabeth Channon (See also Elizabeth Colfox) 86, 154-155, 170-171, 172
Lee, John Channon 155
Lee, Rev Melville 94-96, 98-99, 101
Legg, William 121, 242
Lenthall, Lola 30
Linstead, Ethel May 54-56
Literary and Scientific Institute 26, 193-196
Local Education Authority (See also DCC Education Committee) 123, 152, 176, 197, 207, 216, 218, 227
Locke, Susan 22
Long, Lawrence 37
Lord, Frederick & Charles 24
Lorton, Miss Muriel 65-68
Loveridge, Selina, Charles & Blanche 98

Maclellan, Rev REB 78, 153
Macmillan, Ian 219
Macreedy, WC 195
Maggs, KE 222
Major, Cecil 119, 242
Malthouse and Brewhouse Charity 14-15
Manson, Alice 21
Marsh, Albert 121, 241
Marsh, Harry 119, 242
Marston, Miss 47
Mason, Charlotte 63-65
Mason, Christopher 226-227
Matterface, FW 194, 204
Matthews, J 146
Matthews, Sergeant 169
Maund, Miss LM 47, 49
May, Rev Edward 142
Mechanics' Institute, Bridport (See also Literary and Scientific Institute) 189-193, 233
Mechanics' Institutes 188 – 189
Merric, Berthe 42
Middleton, Robin 226

252

Wakeford, Elizabeth 23
Waldron, Robert 36
Walker, Rosa 114, 124 146
Walker, Theodore 123, 145-146
Wall, Rev Henry (Young Gentlemen's School) 31-32
Wallace, Rev J 153
Wansey, Anna (See Colfox, Anna)
Wansey, Louisa (See Colfox, Louisa)
Warburton, Henry MP 189, 191-193
Ward, Percy (Arthur?) 121, 242
Warr, H 117
Warren, Elizabeth 165
Watts, Sergeant 40
Webb, Mr (Bridport National Boys' School Master) 104
Weld family 148, 152
Weld, Christina 152
Weld, Lt-Col 152
Wesleyan Methodist Chapel Sunday Schoolroom 83
West Mead House 55, 155, 156
Westlands, Crock Lane (See also St Ronan's School) 69
Wheadon, William H 120, 242
Whetham, Austen 54
Whetham, Esther 54
Whetham, William Townley 103, 168
Whethan, Stephen 51, 103, 157
White, Anna 48
Whittle, Louisa 37
Wicker, GF 38
Wild, Elizabeth 56-57
Williams, Ernest 37
Williams, James 153, 157
Williams, Mr (See probably Williams, James) 191-192
Williams, Rev David 92
Williams, Rev Herbert 140
Williams, William (Gentlemen's Day School) 26
Wills, Rev John P 60
Willson, Mary 107
Wilmshurst, Mary & Sarah (School) 23
Winter School, The (See also Bridport General Girls' School) 82
Witham, Beatrice 204, 211-212, 222
Witham, Miss E 204
Witherell, Richard H 21
Wolfson, Robert (Bob) 226
Wood, Rev Samuel 75-81
Woodhead, Miss A 138
Working Men's Club 194, 197
Working Men's Institute 163

World War One: 117-122, 178-180, 205-206; egg collection 118, 180; garment-making 117-118; hay-making 118-119; blackout 120; shortages 120-121, 179, 206; blackberry-picking 180; chestniut collection 120; acorn collection 120; flax-pulling 121; evacuees 120, 179; refugees 118, 122.
World War Two: 126-128, 184-186, 208-211; evacuees 83, 127, 137, 184-185, 209, 210-211; trenches 127, 185, 209; air-raids 127-128, 185-186, 211; air-raid shelters 127-128; garment-making 150; fund-raising 150; troops 196, 209; cadets 209-210; home-guard 209-210, 211; flax-pulling 211; rationing 210.
Worthington, Rev T 37
Wyld, Rev J 157

Young, Robert 37

256